MONROE *and* CONECUH COUNTY ALABAMA MARRIAGES

1833-1880

By:

Dr. Lucy Wiggins Colson, P.D.

Member Hunts Spring Chapter, NSDAR

&

Dr. Robert Ellis Colson, P.D.

SOUTHERN HISTORICAL PRESS INC.

Please direct all correspondence and orders to:

www.southernhistoricalpress.com
or
SOUTHERN HISTORICAL PRESS, Inc.
PO BOX 1267
375 West Broad Street
Greenville, SC   29601
southernhistoricalpress@gmail.com

ISBN #0-89308-335-6

Printed in the United States of America

INTRODUCTION

When the state of Alabama was formed at its Constitutional Convention of 1819, the county of Monroe had already been in existance for four years having been formed from the Mississippi Territory on June 29, 1815. The first county seat was established at Claiborne on the Alabama River. At that time Monroe County had one of the largest populations and largest land size of any county in the state. This remained true until Conecuh, Wilcox, and Clarke counties were formed from Monroe County. The county seat was moved to Monroeville in 1832, where it has remained since that time. In 1835 there was a courthouse fire that destroyed all of Monroe County's records except the Orphan Court Minutes (1816-1821), which are in the state archives in Montgomery.

Early settlers and adventurers traveling south and west from the Carolinas and Georgia all had only one route from the Georgia State line westward. They traveled the Old Federal Road through Indian lands and the Mississippi territory crossing into Monroe County near Old Texas and passing near Midway, Pine Orchard, and Burnt Corn. Many found a new home in Monroe County.

The marriage records in this volume are among the earliest records on file in Monroe County. They are transcribed just as they were recorded in Book A (1833-1880). Though tempting, there has been no effort made to correct any spelling (s) from the original text. For this reason it will be necessary for the researcher to check all possible spellings for any names sought. The original book of marriages has not been kept in good condition by those who have been entrusted with it in years past. There are pages torn out or parts of pages missing. It is hoped that the effort set forth here will ensure the preservation of the valuable historical information contained in the original recordings. Since this project has been undertaken the book has been rebound and each page laminated. For this act of preservation we commend the staff of the Probate Judge's office.

The index to Book A was added later and is badly incomplete lacking about one third of all entries. Adding to the problem is illegible handwriting in the original recording. Often times an S,L,T, and J all look the same.

As in any book of this nature there is a great probability of errors. This volume is without doubt no exception. However, accuracy has been our principle concern throughout, and great care has been taken to ensure its integrity. Many additional hours have been spent prior to publication checking and rechecking the information contained herein. We, hereby, apologize to anyone who finds mistakes in their family entries, and would like to hear from anyone who has corrections and/or additions.

There are about 4,000 marriages and approximately 13,000 names of individuals including those who proveded a security bond and those who performed the marriage.

In both the Monroe County section and the Conecuh County section an asterick following either the name of the bride or the groom indicates that the marriage was performed by consent or by written affidavit of a parent or guardian. A marriage by consent means that one or both parties was not of legal age. This information may prove to be of use to the researcher in approximating ages.

The date of marriage used was the date that the ceremony was actually performed. The date of recording was often different from the date the marriage was performed by several days to several weeks.

We would like to thank Mr. Art Anderson and the Huntsville Church of Jesus Christ of Latter Day Saints for their help and patience in the research and writing of this book.

Monroe County

1. GROOM 2. BRIDE	DATE	SECURITY BY SERVICE BY
ABANT, Henry C. Frances Pitts	03-12-1843	John M. Foster Elias Brown
ABBEY, John S.E. Fanny Stringer	07-01-1838	H. McMillan T. Bryan, JP
ABBOTT, C.H. Tina Weaver	10-16-1873 (Return not executed)	_____ _____
ABERNATHY, T.G. Mrs. L.J. Foster	04-19-1876 (At Mrs. Leslie Johnsons)	J.L. Skipper, MG
ABNEY, John Amanda Curry	04-24-1875 (At Pineville)	William Graham L.M. Riley, Jr. JP
ABNEY, William H. Elizabeth E. Sanders	11-20-1851	Daniel McColl W.M. Longmire, JP
ABNEY, William H. Sarah Ann Sanders	07-16-1846	J. DeLoach Joseph Mitchell, MG
ADAMS, B.B. Mrs. M.D. Henry	11-13-1858	John A. Simmons _____
ADAMS, Edwin B. Catherine Oliver *	12-12-1835	Thomas Roach John J. Roach, JP
ADAMS, Robert A. Keziah Carter	12-05-1869 (At Mrs. Eden Carters)	T.J. Carter A.J. Lambert, MG
ADCOCK, William Anna Lambert *	12-08-1849	Andrew Lambert T. Burpe
ADDAMS, Riley Matilda Collins	07-03-1864	J.J. Simpkins J.J. Simpkins, JP
ADDCOCK, John Elizabeth Pitman	05-10-1839	James H. Boyle T. Burrps
ADKINSON, Thomas J. Sarah B. Broughton	02-10-1859 (At N.N. Broughtons)	Green K. Fountain R.D. Thompson
AGEE, James Martha W.A. Marshall	04-24-1834	William R. Agee J.H. Stroebel, MG
AGEE, James W. C.W. Sylvester *	02-28-1847	T. Burps
AGEE, Joseph Sarah J. Thompson *	01-2801845	J. Dumas T. Burps
AGEE, N.A. N.L. Robertson	02-28-1867	W.R. Agee W. W. Spence, MG
AGEE, William P. Caroline A.E. Thompson	02-2801843	Joseph Agee _____
AGEE, William R., Jr. L.M. Robertson *	04-18-1867	J.F. McCorver W.W. Spence, MG
AILSTOCK, Alex Josephine Kimbel	11-28-1880 (At William Middletons)	William Middleton Elder Thomas Bolton
ALDRIDGE, A.J.B. Mary Roberts	12-16-1847	W.N. Aldridge R.O. Connel, JP

```
ALDRIDGE, A.J.B.                12-16-1847              W.N. Aldridge
  Mary Roberts                                          R.O. Connel, JP

ALDRIDGE, Jonathan              02-09-1836              Joel Rawles
  Mary Ann Curry *                                      James Andress, JP

ALDRIDGE, Pinchney O.           08-02-1837              Robert C. Connell
  Fenby Wood                                            Asa Parker

ALDRIDGE, W.H.                  07-19-1844              Daniel McColl
  Julia Hendrix                                         J.G. Wallace

ALDRIDGE, W.W.                  12-09-1847              John L. Roberts
  Caroline Cato *                                       J.G. Wallace

ALFORD, John P.                 05-04-1865              T.H. Coker
  Martha A. Soloman *   (At William Robinsons)          William Robinson

ALFORD, William B.              11-10-1840              Stephen Wright
  Sarah Ann Thames                                      W. Holloway, JP

ALLDRIDGE, A.G.                 12-23-1851              C.R. Broughton
  Sarah McColl                                          H.A. Smith, MG

ALLEN, James G.                 12-27-1840              John W. Foster
  Nancy Boon                                            Alger Newman, JP

ALLEN, Warren                   02-10-1841              S.N. Reed
  Elizabeth Booker *                                    T. Bryan, JP

ALLISON, James A.               05-02-1867              James W. Johnson
  Sarah Salter        (At home of Mrs. Salter)          P. McGlenn, JP

AMMERMAN, W.H.                  02-22-1866              S.C. Richardson
  Mary McKinney       (At Monroe Co. Cthouse)           M. McCorvey, Judge

ANDERSON, A.N.                  12-28-1876              John W. Morgan
  M.E. Jones          (At home of J.W. Morgan)          Joel Hardee, NP

ANDERSON, Andrew M.             10-24-1859              Matthew Anderson
  Ada Middleton *                                       T.E. Feagin, JP

ANDERSON, C.R.                  09-19-1866              M.W. Middleton
  Matilda A. Falkenberry * (At Colden Falkenberys)      William G. Curry

ANDERSON, Edmond                10-17-1872              S.J. Cummings
  Celia A. Salter     (At Monroeville)                  J. Mentor Crane, LM

ANDERSON, James A.              09-03-1857              John DeLoach
  Louisa Brown                                          A.C. Ramsey, MG

ANDERSON, J.B.                  09-22-1880              Rufus Byrd
  Susan Byrd          (At Mrs. Mary Byrd's)             Joel Hardee, NP

ANDERSON, J.H.                  04-16-1867              A.J. Pinkerton
  Tabatha Ann Ikner   (At Willis Middleton's)           Jesse Hayes, JP

ANDERSON, Joel                  08-01-1838              William Holloway
  Jane Middleton                                        William Holloway, JP

ANDERSON, John W.               10-02-1856              James McColl
  Rosalie J. Witter *                                   W.C. Smith, MG

ANDERSON, Willis                10-06-1876              Richard Wiggins
  Mary A.J. Jones *   (At Stephen Jones')               Joel Hardee, NP

ANDRESS, Evant                  01-26-1877
  Harriett Whisenhent (At H.L. Whisenhent's)            J.T. Bayles, MG
```

ANDRESS, Evant S.   01-23-1856   R.N. Fore
  Amanda A. McClure   (At Samuel McClure's)   John McClure, MG

ANDRESS, F.E.   12-20-1876   S.J. Andress
  C.E. Bayles   (At William Bayles')   L.W. Duke

ANDRESS, Isaac F.   10-12-1848   W.A. Whisenhent
  Charlotte Whisenhent *   Elias Brown, MG

ANDRESS, James W.   11-07-1867   Isaac Andress
  S.M. Sowell   (At home of Mrs. Sowell)   John McWilliams, MG

ANDRESS, James   05-28-1843   O.A. Stevens
  Molly East *   ‾‾‾‾‾‾

ANDRESS, James N.   04-01-1841   Elkunah Stucky
  Elizabeth Owens *   M.D. Dixon, JP

ANDRESS, John   01-30-1849   E. Craig
  Lucy A. Womack *   D.C. Fowles

ANDRESS, Joseph   06-18-1873   John Childress
  Georgia Anna Middleton *   T.M. Riley, Jr.

ANDRESS, Redden N.   08-27-1857   H.M. Riley
  Elizabeth P. Riley   ‾‾‾‾‾‾

ANDRESS, S.J.   02-20-1873   A.N. Bayles
  Bettie J. Burgess   (At Mrs. Ann Burgess')   D.T. McCants

ANDRESS, Stephen   12-18-1855   W. Pate
  Mary J. Riley *   (At home of Eliphas Riley) Joel Hardee, JP

ANDRESS, Stephen D.   09-15-1853   L.G. Cumming
  Sarah A. McMillan   H.A. Smith, MG

ANDRESS, Stephen D.   01-03-1848   Willis Rogers
  Martha Nettles *   J. McWilliams, MG

ANDRESS, William   10-17-1854   G.W. Stacie
  Mrs. Elizabeth Bertrand   Joel Hardie, JP

ANDRESS, William   11-06-1851   Adam Wiggins
  Mary Ann Holly   T.E. Feagan, JP

ANDRESS, William F.   11-01-1866   Isaac Andress
  Dianna J. Wiggins (At home of Cooper Wiggins) M.M. Graham

ANDREWS, A.P.   10-31-1875
  Francis Brantley *   (At home of John Owens)   ‾Joel Hardee, JP

ANDREWS, James   11-14-1869   J.J. Snowden
  M.A. Collins *   (At home of G.W. Collins)   T.E. Feagin, JP

ANDREWS, John   12-13-1866   T.E. Feagin
  Mary Gillis   J.F. Burson, MG

ANGUIR, Dr. Samuel T.   06-28-1842   William F. Howell
  Miss Kendall   Thomas Burps, MG

ANTHONY, John C.   06-13-1860   Jacob C. Johns
  Mary M. Gibson   John Hardee, JP

ANTHONY, W.A.   12-22-1879   Dr. Griffin
  Allis McClammy (At the home of her father) John Hardee, JP

ANUNSON, Washington   11-27-1839   W.B. Greens
  Sarah Leo *   W.W. Bruton, JP

                              3

```
ARCHIE, James O.                01-21-1869              H.M. Graham
  Frances Rosco              (At J.W. Broughton's)      W.W. Simmons, Notary

ARLEDGE, Martin                 12-12-1835              John Chisholm
  Sarah Curry *                                         _____

ARLEDGE, W.M.                   08-02-1865              H.M. Andress
  Martha M. Rogers                                      W.W. Spence

ARMFIELD, J.M.                  12-06-1867              J.G. Bradley
  M.D. Bradley              (At home of T.A. Nettles)   C.W. Hare

ARMSTRONG, John B.              04-17-1867
  Mary A. Norris                                        _____
                                                        A.S. McMillan, JP

ARMSTRONG, Robert A.            02-26-1873              L.S. Watts
  Bettie J. Crosbery       (At Dennis Crosby's)         C.W. Hare, MG

ARNOLD, Mark                    11-10-1856              William Jones
  Tabitha A.E. Grooms                                   _____

ARNOLD, William                 05-04-1846              A.B. Ward
  Dicey Morgan                                          J.G. Wallace, JP

ARRINGTON, Alfred               05-24-1855              J.A. Hightower
  Mrs. Mary Pace                                        _____

ARRINGTON, James M.             12-26-1878              D.J. Quarles
  Amanda Holder                                         J.D. Weatherford, NP

ARTHUR, Adam B.                 01-21-1845              Neal McCorvey
  Cinia A. Robinson                                     John McWilliams

ASBERRY, Henry H.               11-18-1855              John Honeycutt
  Celia A. Taylor          (At home of Mrs. Taylor)     J.J. Eubanks, JP

ATKINSON, E.H.                  10-22-1874              H.W. Fountain
  S.J. Spurlin                                          H.H. Hybert

ATKINSON, John N.               01-31-1864              B. Crawford
  Elizabeth A. Giddings                                 J.R. Watson, JP

ATKINSON, John Nelson           12-21-1842              William Dampier
  Frances Morris                                        Hickman Fowler

ATKINSON, Samuel                11-11-1869              F.B. Clausell
  Emily Giddins            (At Abram Gi-dings')         Emanuel Cline, MC

ATKINSON, Thomas                03-03-1834              James G. Butler
  Sarah English                                         _____

AUTREY, Alexander A.            05-14-1846              McDuffie Mann
  Martha E. Crook *                                     A. Pearse

AUTRY, J.J.                     12-16-1858              B.E. Crook
  Ann E. Crook        (At home of Major Wm. Crook)      M. McCorvey

AVANT, Henry C.                 03-12-1840              Elias Brown
  Frances Kidd                                          John W. Foster

AVANT, William D.               11-20-1852              L.M. Singuefield
  Mrs. Amy Ann Strickland                               T.L. Densler, MG

AVERY, A.H.                     02-29-1858              F.M. Jones
  M.E. Gordon *                                         Henry Urquhart, MG

AVERY, C.B.                     04-22-1862              W.H. Parker
  Mary A. Parker                                        _____
```

AVERY, John   02-23-1854   G.R. Longmire
    Sarah E. Sawyer *   John McWilliams, MG

AVERY, Joshua   09-12-1843   Nathan Sanson
    Emily Sanson   Daniel P. Wright, JP

BAILEY, James H.   07-12-1848   James Dunnam
    Sarah Ann Dunnam *   (At Elm P. Church)   James Jenkens

BAILEY, John B.   03-07-1861   James M. Smith
    Ann Elizabeth Robinson   J.J. Simpkins, JP

BAILLEY, R.J.   05-08-1862   J. Rall
    Rebecca E. Bailley * (At home of Mrs. Robinson)   T.E. Feagin, JP

BAIRD, John C.   03-18-1869   E.A. Henderson
    Bettie Justice *   W.W. Spence

BALDWIN, Dr. Aaron   04-11-1847   L.A. Kidd
    Caroline Morrisette   Nathan G. Phillips

BALDWIN, B.F.   06-25-1866   B.C. Davison
    Eunice Desmond   _____

BALL, Amos   05-17-1838   Daniel McColl
    Rachel Bass   Thomas Wilson, JP

BALLARD, John L.   05-13-1875   T.S. Goodloe
    Mary A. Goodloe *   (At home of J.W. Rothwell)   J.W. Rothwell

BALLARD, Robert   01-22-1835   William H. Arthur
    A.T. Smith *   Thomas S. Witherspoon

BARBOR, Bartholomew   12-28-1854   Isaac Williams
    Catherine Whissenhent (At Zachariah Whissenhent's) J.M. Powell, JP

BARDEN, Henry E.   01-29-1880   H. Peese
    Mary Sellers   _____

BARDEN, James W.   05-18-1865   James M. Loftin
    Delila Loftin   (At home of Mr T.E. Loftin)   N.B. Phillips, MG

BAREFIELD, Stephen   08-12-1869   H.C. Middleton
    Frances Jones   (At H.C. Middleton's)   Joel Hardee, JP

BARLOW, Jesse   09-07-1861   Mason Barlow
    Francis Ward *   J.J. Simpkins, JP

BARLOW, Julius   05-30-1873   F.A. Seymore
    Mrs. Sarah V. Brewer (At Claiborne)   John Thames, JP

BARLOW, Levi   06-02-1853   William Barlow
    Nancy J. Johnson *   Joel Hardee, JP

BARLOW, William   01-13-1876   _____
    Pamelia Gosphin   (At home of bride's father)   John Hardee

BARNES, James W.   07-26-1866   John T. Faulk
    Mrs. Nancy Coleman   C. Shannfield, JP

BARNES, John   01-08-1846   R.C. Torry
    Margaret Amelia Alan   H.A. Smith

BARNES, John Y.   08-15-1844   W.P. Leslie
    Mrs. E.M. Bates   Thomas D. Sow

BARNES, Nathaniel S.   01-05-1845   W.S. Wiggins
    Elizabeth Bayles   J.G. Bradley, JP

5

BARNES, Thomas H. Nancy D. Jenkins	08-03-1837	C.D. Tobin J.H. Schroebel
BARNES, T.J. Laura Williams	01-03-1868 (At home of Mrs. Williams)	J.J. Fry John T. Bayles, MG
BARNETT, James H. Mary A. Bird *	07-16-1865	John DeLoach A.G. Duke, JP
BARNETT, W.H. Mary E. Smith	02-28-1877	T.F. Lewis James S. Rencher
BARR, William Mrs. Nancy Pricket *	02-02-1862 (At home of James Daniel)	J.W. Posey A.J. Lambert, MG
BARTLETT, Samuel D. Rebecca A. Henson	08-13-1865 (At Mrs. Emiline Henson's)	Neil McMillan Emanuel Cline, MG
BARTLETT, A.B. Mrs. Lucinda J. Straughn	07-08-1869	N. McMillan E. Cline, MG
BARTON, Charles Mrs. Louisa Bozeman	05-24-1860	Beil Salter W.W. Simmons, JP
BARTON, Willoughby B. Margaret Lambert *	12-24-1857 (At Mrs. Lambert's)	W.J. McArthur R.O'Connell, JP
BARTRAM, James Elizabeth Stacey *	04-16-1849	Joel Hardee, JP
BASDIN, Andrew Mary E. Davis	11-25-1859 (At home of Edmund Davis)	William Davis Robert D. Thompson
BATEMAN, Bryan Ann Eliza Reaves *	02-03-1842	Richard Reaves T.J. Foster, MG
BATES, Seymour Elizabeth Sullivan	10-09-1839	Henry Sullivan James T. Wilson, JP
BATES, Seymour Martha A. Sharp	07-25-1835	Joseph Boney
BAXLEY, Anderson Mrs. N.M. Lucas	11-11-1869 (At Jesse Baxley's)	Jesse Baxley Joel Hardee, JP
BAXLEY, Jesse Sarah Singuefield *	12-18-1855	M. McMillan John McWilliams, MG
BAXLEY, Joshua Margaret Blackwell	12-30-1857	Jesse Baxley William C. Faulk, JP
BAYLES, J.H. M.J. Wiggins	03-22-1874 (At home of W.S. Wiggins)	W.R. Chunn D. McCants, JP
BAYLES, John E. Susan F. Thompson	09-05-1855 (At S.R. Thompson's)	W.J. Bayles John S. Bayles
BAYLES, Michael Margaret J. Hestle *	08-24-1854 (At Dixon Hestle's)	J.D. Hestle J.M. Boyles
BAYLES, P.N. Martha J. Simms *	03-01-1860 (At home of Mrs. Noah Agee on Thursday evening)	Noah Agee R.D. Thompson, JP
BAYLES, William Dorcus Holley *	09-20-1855 (At home of John Holley)	W.P. Hestle John S. Bayles, MG
BEARD, Alexander Martha Wiggins *	01-28-1856	Neal McCorvey C. Thames

BEARD, Johnathan Julian Cahall	10-21-1837	David McColl Asa Parker, JP
BEARD, Martin Sarah Ann Owens	08-14-1849	William Young Joel Hardee, JP
BEDINE, Jacob Mrs. Elizabeth Loftin	01-22-1842 ("License returned, declined to be married")	Daniel McColl J.M. McColl
BELBERRY, Nathaniel Tockie Bazzille	12-14-1879 (At Mrs. Burkette)	J.H. Rumley J.A. Mason, JP
BELL, Burros Martha Hinson	09-07-1869	W.H. Bell E. Cline, MG
BELL, David Sophronia McMillon	02-15-1834	Nathan Bell ———
BELL, Hezekiah M.A. Hinson	12-11-1872 (At home of Emer Hinson)	W.H. Bell E. Cline, MG
BELL, Jackson Rebecca Nowlin	02-03-1842	Neil McMillan J.G. Wallace JP
BELL, John C.L. Hinson	02-26-1873 (At home of Emmie Hinson)	Carey Watson E. Cline, MG
BELL, Nathan Mary E. Hestle	09-19-1837	Lemuel Craps ———
BELL, William Matilda Galuspy	06-14-1834	J.J. Staples ———
BELL, William B. Mary J. Threat *	01-17-1839	L.P. Spykes John C. Kaldwin
BELL, W.H. N.J. Hinson	09-20-1872 (At home of Emer Hinson)	L. Watson Emanuel Cline, MG
BERWIN, Ernest Caroline Block	10-22-1848	Daniel McColl G.D. Foster, JP
BETHEIA, J.H. Catherine Sart *	05-03-1845	W.W. McColl ———
BETHEN, Evander J. Sarah Ann Sowell	11-02-1847	Neil Salter William R. Agee
BETTS, Edward Cannon Eliza C. Salter	01-17-1835	James M. Betts ———
BETTS, Issac H. Amanda T. Anderson	12-22-1840	Samuel L. Smith H.B. Fursh, LLW
BETTS, Jacob F. Ann B. Clark	10-11-1848	J.B. Malden H.J. Hunter, OM
BETTS, James M. Cynthia Mariah Kreighton	01-19-1835	Cannon Betts ———
BETTS, W.H. Virginia Mosely	12-01-1869 (At home of Mrs. E. Mosely)	Sam Nash W.G. Curry, MG
BIGGER, George I. Maggie E. McCants	10-16-1873	Joe Snell
BIGGS, G.M. Laura Latham	12-28-1879 (At home of Mrs. Latham)	J.M. Biggs W.A. Lock, MG

BIGGS, John W.   12-27-1876   George M. Biggs
  Emma Gouldsby   (At home of Mrs. Gouldsby) L.W. Duke

BIGGS, J.T.   11-18-1874   W.F. Biggs
  E.A.V. Salter   (At brides father's)   L.W. Duke

BIGGS, Miles   12-24-1848   Winfrey Biggs
  Rebecca E. McClure   William W. Simmons JP

BIGGS, Randolph   05-25-1846   Mitchell McDaniel
  Phebe Partin *   Elisha Mosley, JP

BIGGS, T.J.   08-30-1866   T.L. Downs
  Mary C. Smith   (At brides father's)   O. Shannfield, JP

BIGGS, W.F.   08-04-1873   J.T. Biggs
  Elizabeth Daniel   (At brides uncle's)   L.W. Duke

BIGGS, William J.   12-28-1871   Basal Miler
  Josephine Stanton   (A- Peter Rickard's)   W.J. Curry, MG

BIRT, Thomas *   12-21-1876   James M. Watson
  Martha McMillan   (At J.J. McMillan's)   B.B. Green, JP

BISS, John D.   07-07-1869   N. McMillan
  Martha Morris   E. Cline, MG

BIVIN, DeCall   08-15-1850   Dempsey Bonner
  Rachel E.G. Bonner *   Elias Brown

BIVIN, John   12-02-1844   Samuel Hixon
  Rebecca J. Creighton *   John McWilliams

BIVIN, John   09-12-1855   A. Hixon
  Eveline Torrey   ————

BIVIN, Nathaniel   11-04-1847   William Bivin
  Winney M. Bonner *   E.L.E. Brown

BIVINS, Jacob   09-22-1835   Benjamin Coleman
  Leouisa A. McCorkle   Asa Parker, JP

BIVINS, Robert   12-02-1852   F.R. Robbins
  Eliza Robbins *   G. Longmire, MG

BLACK, John   03-04-1841   Tully Biggs
  Mary Ann Falkenberry   A.S. McMillan, JP

BLACK, John C.   02-27-2838   Samuel McCants
  Isabellaa Black   Thomas Wilson

BLACK, Neil   01-07-1849   Joseph Nettles
  Sarah Ivey *   John McWilliam, MG

BLACK, William R.   09-07-1854   Wilson S. Wiggins
  Catherine T. Wiggins   (At Wilson S. Wiggins)   J.W. Leslie

BLACK, William R.   11-13-1872   Isah Talberz
  C.J. Wiggins   (At Thomson Wiggins')   John W. Leslie, Judge

BLACKBURN, David L.   07-25-1853   James J. Sessions
  Emeline A. Lindsey *   ————

BLACKMAN, James   12-31-1875
  Sarah E. Robinson   (At J.W. Robinson's)   J.L. Eddins, MG

BLACKMAN, Leamar   03-25-1847   John J. Deason
  Mary Deason *   W.C. Ross, JP

BLACKWELL, Edward Harriet Ward *	02-02-1835	Francis Ward
BLACKWELL, Gabriel Nancy Boatwright *	02-03-1863	H. McKenzie T.E. Feagin, JP
BLACKWELL, John Elizabeth Owens	01-27-1870 (At home of Phillip Owens)	G. Blackwell Joel Hardee, JP
BLACKWELL, John Mary J. Harrison	07-14-1880 (At Richard Harrison's)	Emanuel Cline, MG
BLACKWELL, Nicholas Margaret Lampey *	06-09-1853	L. Moyer Uriah Atkinson
BLACKWELL, Nicholas Louisa C. Hendrix *	02-21-1861	A.B. Tucker W.W. Simmons, JP
BLACKWELL, Stephen Cornelia J. Galloway	02-23-1862	John DeLoach W.W. Simmons, JP
BLACKWELL, Stephen J.A. Downs	09-12-1878	G.W. Salter, JP
BLACKWELL, Thomas E. Eliza Holden	02-10-1876	W.G. Middleton, JP
BLACKWELL, William Mrs. Sarah Knowles	08-30-1855 (At home of Mrs Sarah Knowles)	M. Patrick Uriah Atkinson
BLAKELY, G.W. Sallie Chapman *	12-26-1869 (At J.E. Crenshaw's)	J.E. Crenshaw Joel Hardee, JP
BLANKENSHIP, John Eliza Carter	08-20-1833 ("Burned")	T.J. Watts Thomas Trowell
BLANTON, F.M. Margaret Watts	08-20-1863 (At Robert D. Thompson's) on Thursday morning)	T.J. Watts Robert D. Thompson, JP
BLANTON, James Catherine Mathews *	02-21-1867	John Roley E. Andress, JP
BLANTON, M.H. Lanorah E. Rawls	10-11-1871 (At home of Noah Rawls')	J.M. Wood, MG
BLANTON, Sidney Rebecca Ward *	03-21-1878 (At Mr. Thomas Ward's)	Burney Sawyer, MG
BLANTON, W. Mary Ward	08-10-1869	Burrell Norris N. Triebleman, JP
BLOACK, Dane W. Jeanetta Kahn	02-21-1854 (At Claiborne, Ala.)	Moses Rankin James J. Barclay, JP
BOATWRIGHT, Patrick Nancy Wright *	02-21-1865	Thomas J. Duke J.W. Feagin, JP
BOATWRIGHT, W. Cyntha Gann	02-26-1867	R. Boatwright William Robinson, JP
BOATWRIGHT, William Happy Rikard *	01-12-1836	James Boatwright Asa Parker

BOATWRIGHT, Y.A. Nancy Andrews	04-18-1880 (At Y.A. Boatwright's)	D.R. Griffin John E. Parrett, JP
BODDIE, John Annie H. Perryman *	07-09-1879 (At Mrs M.D. Perryman's)	J.S. Waters Ed E. Cowan
BODIFORD, Jabe Z. Demeris Sawyer	11-11-1869 (At home of D. Sawyer)	D. Sawyer John W. Leslie, Judge
BODIFORD, G.W. Sarah J. Lowery	03-18-1880 (At Mrs Betsey Lowery's)	A.J. Holt Burney Sawyer, MG
BOGDON, Joseph Angeline Wilson	10-13-1839	James M. Burke John C. Baldwin, VDM
BOGGAN, John H. Molly A. Young *	12-20-1859	William.W. Dailey ————
BOGGAN, Thomas M. Ann E. Dailey *	12-22-1859	William W. Dailey T.E. Feagin
BOHANNON, David Lucinda McKinley	02-13-1842	———— Elias Brown
BOHA_NON, David H. Mary McKinley	04-22-1838	Jacob Strock C. Thames
BOHANON, A. E.B. Morris	12-14-1870 (At David Bohanon's)	A.J. Morris Francis Walker
BOLTZ, Michael Emily Daily	01-09-1858	William Hawkins L.W. Lindsey
BOND, John A. Mary A. Anderson *	07-14-1869	John W. Morgan John Hardee, JP
BOND, Shadrick Amanda Linum	04-15-1880 (At home of Joel Hardee)	———— Joel Hardee, NP
BONDURANT, F.S. Fannie S. Stiggins	12-15-1880 (At James Stiggins')	J.B. Stiggins Elder C.E. James
BONNER, Dempsey A. Hannah Forehand *	07-11-1839	Allen T. Goody Elias Brown, MG
BONNER, George Mary Jane McGill *	02-12-1844	Jordan Bonner William R. Agee
BONOFORD, Andrew J. Nancy Qualls *	04-07-1843	Dixon Hestle ————
BOOKER, Garrett N. Martha P. Lett *	10-25-1853	W.L. Raines W. Longmire
BOOKER, Gaston G. Parmelia Brooks	11-14-1875 (At home of brides' father)	William J. Booker
BOOKER, James M. Martha Snowden	11-11-1859	W.H. Loveless John Hardee, JP
BOOKER, John Sarah McClammy *	06-16-1842	James Brown William Holloway, JP
BOOKER, John Rebecca Patrick *	03-09-1865	P.H. Davis F.A. Mason
BOOKER, John L. Harriette Loveless *	10-31-1877 (At John Booker's)	William Booker W.J. Booker

BOOKER, J.W.   11-21-1878   A.M. Ingram
  E.C. Ingram   (At home of A.M. Ingram)   Joel Hardee, NP

BOOKER, M.H.   03-29-1866   J.F. McCorvey
  Frances Brown *   William A. Litz, MG

BOOKER, Monroe   01-01-1871   John DeLoach
  M.M. Brown *   (At home of brides' father) G.R. Scroggins, MG

BOOKER, Nolen G.   10-08-1876
  Nancy J. Stuckey   T.M. Riley, Jr., JP

BOOKER, N.S.   12-06-1867   T.H. Raines
  Mary Faulkenberry * (At Mrs Faulkenberry's)   W.G. Curry, MG

BOOKER, R.B.   12-24-1879   W.F. Booker
  Mattie Salter   (At minister's residence)   John Booker, MG

BOOKER, W.B., Jr.   10-31-1877   John L. Booker
  Jane Loveless   (At home of John Booker)   W.J. Booker, MG

BOOKER, William B.   07-15-1838   John McClammy
  Martha Ann McClammy *   T.M. Riley, JP

BOOKER, William J.   08-09-1865   Willis L. Booker
  Martha J. Walker   F.A. Mason

BOOKER, W.L.   12-18-1866   J.H. Tatum
  M.E. Cato *   William A. Litz, MG

BOOKER, W.N.   01-28-1879
  M.B. Moody   (At home of Mrs Dowadey)   S.E. Ellis, JP

BORDEN, J.W.   12-19-1878   A.A. McMillan
  Jane Thompson   (At home of I. Thompson)   J.T. Bayles, MG

BOROUGHS, W.M.   12-22-1869   A.E. Jenkins
  Laura Jenkins   (At home of Doc Jenkins)   John McWilliams, MG

BOULWARE, H.W.   01-02-1873   Hugh McKinzie
  Nancy E. Hines *   (At home of Mrs. Hines)   J.L. Eddins, MG

BOULWARE, J.M.   04-17-1860   W. Lee
  M.M. Hixon *   Andrew Jay, MG

BOWDEN, Lemuel   09-02-1858   John DeLoach
  Caroline M. Daniel   (At Susan Daniel's)   George Watson

BOWDEN, Lemuel   12-22-1859   Dixon Hestle
  Sarah Dean   Elias Brown, MG

BOWDEN, Samuel   01-31-1839   Jacob Rhodes
  Caroline Rhodes   R.C. Parker, JP

BOWDEN, W.S.   02-08-1877   F.W. Jones
  Elizabeth Moore (At home of John Moore)   A.J. Lambert

BOYKIN, Erasmus   01-20-1853   Grace Thompson
  Mary Lambert   James Daniel, MG

BOYLES, Andrew J.   12-18-1877   C.W. Boyles
  Minnie Ferrell *   (At William Ferrell's)   A.J. Lambert, MG

BOYLES, D.H.   05-06-1874   J.F. Boyles
  Bettie C. Robbins   (At Pineville)   W.G. Curry, MG

BOYLES, James H.   05-28-1841   John Adcock
  Harriett Melton *   T. Burpe

11

```
BOYLES, James H.              06-24-1844           Reuben Hendrix
  Rhoda Pace                                       _____

BOYLES, J.D.                  12-01-1874
  N.M. Riley              (At home of T.M. Riley)  W.G. Curry, MG

BOYLES, Joel                  11-12-1836           James McClure
  Mrs. Elizabeth Barnett                             John J. Roach, Judge

BOYLES, John T.               12-31-1835           Lemuel Craps
  Elizabeth Wiggins *                                Cornelius Thames

BOYLES, Josiah F.             08-28-1842           A.B. Ward
  Christianna Lambert                                J. Withers

BOYMAN, William               12-29-1839
  Elvira T. Boyman *      ("Bond mislaid")         J.G. Wallace, JP

BOZEMAN, Jasper               09-03-1865           D.J. Morris
  Marsena Morris *        (At home of D.J. Morris)  M.M. Graham

BOZEMAN, Lewis                01-20-1839           Davis Bozeman
  Louisa Stacey *                                    T. Bryan, JP

BOZMAN, James                 09-26-1838           Davis Bozman
  Martha Morris                                      W.C. Faulk, JP

BOZMAN, W.T.                  03-07-1872           F.M. Wiggins
  Nancy J. Wiggins     (At home of Mrs. M. Wiggins) John McWilliams, MG

BRADBERRY, B., Jr.            12-23-1875           Z.R. Northcut
  Virginia Northcut *     (At James Northcut's)      W.G. Curry, MG

BRADBERRY, G.A.               04-02-1874           W.H. Bradberry
  Emma Gibson                                        T.M. Riley, Jr., JP

BRADBERRY, Joseph W.          03-12-1857           Thomas T. Lewis
  Susan W. Daggett *                                 A.J. Brown, JP

BRADBERRY, W.H.               02-02-1870           H.V. Helton
  Maryan Helton           (At home of H.C. Helton)   Hugh McKenzie, JP

BRADEE, Nathan                12-05-1833           William Hirst
  Matilda Hirst * (Hirt?)                          _____

BRADFORD, Thomas J.           02-02-1865           T.M. Riley
  Sophronia E. Riley *    (At Methodist Church       D.S. McDonald, MG
                          at Pineville)

BRADLEY, George S.            09-2101848           S.M. Kennedy
  Mary Ann Davis *                                  James Daniel, MG

BRADLEY, Gospnow              11-13-1849           David Nettles
  Sarah J. Finklea *                                 Evant Andress, JP

BRADLEY, James                11-17-1836           Adam O'Neal
  Ailsey Nettles *                                   Elias Brown

BRADLEY, Jesse G.             08-08-1843           Arthur Foster
  June W. Nettles                                    Evant Andress, JP

BRADLEY, J.J.                 11-22-1865           John Burns
  Caroline F. Sowell *  (At Mrs. Nancy Sowell's)    M. McCorvey, Judge

BRADLEY, John                 02-06-1861           J.W. Posey
  Martha O. Nettles *                                Eld. J.D. Kendrick

BRADLEY, Joseph W.            03-12-1857           _____
  Susan M. Doggett                                 _____
```

12

BRADLEY, Robert J. Hannah F. Miller	01-11-1866	_____ _____
BRADLEY, Samuel Nancy J. Nettles *	12-12-1854	John Bradley _____
BRADY, James Fannie M. Dees	01-30-1878 (At William Dees')	F.M. Hawkins Emanuel Cline, MG
BRAIDY, James F. Mary E. McMuller	01-27-1867 (At Elizabeth McMillan's)	Joel Dees Neil McMillian
BRANDENBURG, Jacob Mary S. Hall *	05-2-1852	James Gallespy W.H. Aldridge
BRANSFORD, Irvin F. Mary E. Middleton *	01-22-1871 (At the Middleton's)	Nathan Branford Hugh McKenzie
BRANTLEY, C.T. M.J. Calloway	08-14-1870 (At home of Enoch Morris)	H.H. Brantley Samuel Kelly, JP
BRANTLEY, Hilliard Emeline Stokes *	01-06-1848	George D. Dukes J.G. Wallace
BRANTLEY, John Tabitha Denmark (Dennard?)	10-26-1839	A.B. Kennedy T. Burrps
BRANTLEY, Joseph S. Nancy C. Tucker	12-18-1872 (At home of A. Tucker)	John DeLoach John Leslie, Judge
BRANTLEY, Walter Martha McMillan	01-16-1868 (At Elizabeth McMillan's)	W.W. Simmons Emanuel Cline, MG
BRANTLY, C.G. Nancy W. Robinson *	10-18-1870 (At the bride's fathers)	A.J. Hopkins David Adams, MG
BRAZELL, Kindred Sarah A. Greene	01-05-1865 (At Claiborne)	D.J. Morris N.W. Sugden, JP
BRAZIL, Joseph Kesiah Hobbs *	12-02-1876 (Near Lasanta Sampey's)	William Hobbs S.R. Kelly, JP
BRENT, John A. Ann Huzzey *	12-15-1841	Thomas Wilson Thomas Wilson, JP
BRENTON, Thomas J. Susan A. Giddins	10-15-1874 (At home of A. Giddins)	W.W. Giddens Robert Smith, MG
BREWER, T.C. Sarah V. Patterson	12-12-1867	John DeLoach W.W. Spence, MG
BRICKELLOO, John Sarah Ann Lee	07-27-1870 (At Phillip Owen's)	John Blackwell Joel Hardee, JP
BROOKS, Allen Melinda Mims *	03-27-1838	L. Sawyer H.E. Courtney, AGM
BROOKS, Charles Margaret Mims *	07-30-1848	James O'Neil John Fore, JP
BROOKS, Edward F. M.M. Gunn *	08-10-1873 (At the home of the bride's father)	Allen M. Gunn John Hardee
BROOKS, George W. Martha Harris	11-02-1860 (At home of J.R. Watson)	Evant Brooks J.R. Watson, JP
BROOKS, George W. Hulda A. Gunn	08-24-1873 (At bride's fathers)	John Hardee John Hardee, JP

13

BROOKS, John
  Elizabeth Grimes *
	10-16-1855	John DeLoach
		  S.A. Farmer, MG

BROOKS, John S. Narcis A. Skinner	09-12-1876 (At bride's mothers)	<u>John</u> Hardee, JP

BROOKS, J.S.
  Mary Jane Devin *
	08-19-1869
	(At home of Mrs Devin)
		W.H. Patrick
		  Joel Hardee

BROOKS, Samuel
  Eliza McClammy
	03-02-1851	W.H. Loveless
		  W.M. Longmire, JP

(He was the son of Sawyer Brooks and Rebecca Mitchell)
(She was the dau. of Mark McClammy, Jr.)

BROUGHTON, A.B.
  Susan E. Andress
	12-06-1855
	(At Evant Andress')
		J.L. Andress
		  Robert D. Thompson

BROUGHTON, Charles R.
  Mary Snell *
	12-10-1839	John O. Walker
		  Elias Brown, MG

BROUGHTON, James W.
  Martha J. Daily
	09-11-1853	C.R. Broughton
		  H.B. Farrish, MG

BROUGHTON, John W.
  Margarette Davison
	01-06-1852	C.R. Broughton
		  R.O. Connell, JP

BROUGHTON, Nathaniel
  Mary A. Way
	03-22-1866	James McKinzy
		  E. Andress, JP

BROWN, Andrew
  Tabitha Kearley
	10-17-1850	John E. Cunsion
		  Joel Hardee, JP

BROWN, Benjamin
  Elizabeth Bozman *
	11-28-1833	James Bozman
		  ————

BROWN, Charles
  Caroline Sheffield
	12-09-1857	Paschal Brown
		  W.W. Perry, Ord. Min.

BROWN, Charles H.
  Elizabeth McKinley
	12-05-1863	Dixon Hestle
		  ————

BROWN, D.T.
  Amanda Betts
	03-31-1858	E.E. Robison
		  ————

BROWN, Elias
  Texana Crawford
	12-05-1875
	(At bride's mothers)
		Eli H. Adkinson
		  W.C. Sowell, Judge

BROWN, George W.
  Nancy McClammy *
	01-10-1865	T.J. Gray
		  Nathan Coker, JP

BROWN, Henry C.
  Fannie Perrin *
	11-15-1865	John R. McCants
		  ————

BROWN, Jackson
  Elizabeth Beard *
	07-20-1837	Andrew Nettles
		  C. Thames

BROWN, James
  Laura J. Rowley *
	12-24-1875
	(At home of J. Rowley)
		Mathew Lambert
		  S.R. Kelly, JP

BROWN, James E.
  Martha L. Hightower *
	12-05-1860
	(At James A. Hightower's)
		George W. Fountain
		  R.O. Connell

BROWN, James E.
  Seana J. Baker
	09-12-1865	J.B. Griffin
		  A.W. Jones, MG

BROWN, James E.
  Elizabeth M. Nettles *
	11-18-1878
	(At Jackson Nettles')
		J.M. Brown
		  Burney Sawyer, MG

BROWN, James H.
  Emma Fountain *
	10-24-1878
	(At Andrew Nettles')
		J.E. Brown
		  Burney Sawyer

BROWN, Jasper N.   11-10-1856   William Middleton
  Angelina Hussy *   ─────────

BROWN, John   10-04-1838   John Tolbert
  Eliza Davidson *   C. Thames

BROWN, John B.   09-06-1859   John A. Simmons
  Emily Fore   T.E. Feagin

BROWN, John E.   10-10-1875   W.J. Hendrix
  Frances E. Enzer   (At home of B.N. Walker)   S.R. Kelly, JP

BROWN, John L.   01-10-1851   Phillip Owen, Sr.
  Mrs. Margaret Mims   B. Dulanecy

BROWN, John M.   09-23-1857   Samuel McClure
  Margaret M. McClure *   H.R. Farrish, MG

BROWN, John M.   04-09-B 76   J.M. Brown
  Martha C. Hammon *   (At Thomas Thompson's)   E. Cline

BROWN, John W.   12-23-1873   John Hardee
  Frances Tucker *   (At home of G.R. Scoggins)   G.R. Scoggins, MG

BROWN, Luke A.   12-09-1866   J.H. Simpson
  Martha J. Simpson   Elder J.E. Knighton

BROWN, Luke A.   09-29-1861   J.M. Brown
  Mary Ann Metts *   J.R. Miller

BROWN, M.H.   11-19-1876   H.R. Hood & B.L. Hubbard
  Alabama Killam (At home of bride's father)   W.C. Sowell, Judge

BROWN, M.M.   09-08-1870   J.A. Simmons
  Martha Sawyer   (At Ramsey Sawyers)   W.W. Simmons

BROWN, Moses   01-12-1843   William Dunn
  Mary Eliza Wilson   J.G. Holcomb, JP

BROWN, Nathaniel R.   07-28-1852   C.R. Broughton
  Martha E. Wallace   W.H. Aldridge, JP

BROWN, P.R.   02-13-1875   M.M. Brown
  Susan A. Dunn   (At the Court House)   W.A. Sowell, Judge

BROWN, Randal   01-02-1867   J.M. Brown
  Susan Thames *   J.E. Knighton

BROWN, Reuben   10-10-1877   J.W. Waters
  Matilda Brown   (At Kempville)   L.W. Duke

BROWN, Rufus A.   12-01-1833   Elijah B. Taylor
  Eliza Harbin *   Robert Warren

BROWN, Stephen *   12-12-1880   L.A. Brown
  Nancy Taylor *   (At Andrew Taylor's)   J.L. Eddins, MG

BROWN, Thomas   01-04-1852   Travis Simmons
  Elizabeth Houghman   James M. Davison, JP

BROWN, Thomas E.   01-17-1872   T.J. Watts
  Mrs. Ellen Blanton (At Ellen Blanton's)   Charles J. Torry, JP

BROWN, W.D.   11-25-1880   J.M. McCants
  Sallie Burgess   (At home of Mrs Jane McCants)   P.J. Cree, MG

BROWN, William   12-13-1855   W.W. Pridgeon
  Mary E. Brown   A.J. Lambert

BROWN, William A. Amanda Adkinson	12-08-1858	J.M. Brown George Watson, MG
BROWN, William D. Martha Crosby *	09-26-1854	W.G. Middleton ————
BROWN, William D. Catherine Zellers	03-16-1855 (At home of S. Byrd)	Elijah Pate S.A. Feagon
BROWN, W.W. Susan J. Biggs	11-06-1870 (At Randold Biggs)	M.B. East, JP
BRUMLEY, John Eliza Mann	12-23-1838	John G. Wallace John M. McWilliamsMG
BRYANT, Anthony Susannah Hammond	10-05-1865 (At C. Ha-mond's)	George P. Hammond M.M. Graham, MG
BRYANT, Ambrose M. Nancy A. Tuberville	11-18-1849	Richard Tuberville Evant Andress, JP
BRYANT, Asa J. Drusetta Stevens *	04-17-1853	A.A. Stevens W.H. Aldridge, JP
BRYANT, C. Martha Piner *	11-12-1865	George Hammond N.W. Synden, JP
BRYANT, Edmund S. Henrietta Nettles *	10-16-1856 (At Joseph M. Nettles')	Jeremiah W. Bryant Elias Brown, Elder
BRYANT, Jeremiah W. Mary Jane Stabler *	10-09-1856	Edmund S. Bryant W.W. Simmons, JP
BUCK, William Fanny Eubanks	10-20-1844	F.B. Long Samuel Kelly, JP
BULLARD, Joel Adelide A. Pettibone *	10-19-1858 (At Mr. S.M. Pettibone's)	E.E. Robison N. Goodwin, MG
BULLARD, Joseph Dora McClen	02-29-1880 (At home of R.C. Reaves)	J.L. Bullard J.M. Slaughter, NP
BULLARD, Pheasant Maria Fryer *	01-21-1837	Isaac Fryer J.H. Schroebel
BULLARD, Wesley Flora J. Lowery	10-07-1880 (At home of W.R. Lowery)	A.L. Lowery G.W. Salter, JP
BULLARD, William Elizabeth Austock	12-02-1847	R.C. Torrey Cornelius Thames, MG
BULLOCK, John Permelia A. Moody	11-20-1866	T.H. Maulden ————
BULLOCK, John Sarah T. Watson	12-31-1866	J.J. Flake F.P. Clingman, JP
BURGE, E.B. Marenie George	12-11-1878 (At home of John George)	B.J. Skinner, MG
BURGESS, Andrew F. Ann Holly *	10-30-1847	Richard Holly ————
BURGESS, James Laura T. Snell	12-28-1859 (At Capt. John Snell's)	Robert P. Rankin C.W. Hare, MG
BURGESS, John Sarah J. McCants	08-03-1866 (At home of Mrs. McCants)	Robert Burgess D.S. McDonald, MG

BURNETT, Frank L.W. Rutherford	11-24-1880 (At William Rutherford's)	M.B. Ritchie D.J. Wright
BURNETT, William H. Sarah Brown *	08-13-1835	Soloman Blackman Thomas Wilson, JP
BURNHAM, James M. Elizabeth Williams	10-12-1859	T.J. Filpott John Hardee, JP
BURNHAM, W.H. Catherine Archie	10-05-1869	J.A. Simmons J.M. Jordan
BURNS, B.M. M.J. Kemp	10-18-1860 (At P.M. Dennis' on Thursday) evening	P.M. Dennis Robert D. Thompson, JP
BURNS, George W. Mollie E. Hestle	11-18-1870 (At Lewis Millender's)	B.M. Burns W.G. Curry, MG
BURNS, John Minnie Stallworth	05-22-1866 (At the Methodist-Episcopal Church at Pineville)	B.F. Stallworth D.L. McDonald, MG
BURNS, ⸏⸏⸏⸏⸏ ⸏⸏ Elizabeth Parker *	12-28-1836	Soloman Parker ————
BURNS, Nathaniel S. Martha Himmington	03-25-1860	John S. Chunn ————
BURNS, S.A. Henrietta Ladd *	01-08-1878 (At home of J.T. Bayles)	J.E. Bayles J.T. Bayles
BURT, Jesse Jennet McMillan	01-20-1859 (At Murdock McMillan's)	Neil McMillan M. McCorvey
BURT, Richard S. Jane Watson *	08-28-1854	John D. Burt A.W. Jones, OMG
BURT, William K. Martha J. Brantley *	10-11-1865 (At Oren Brantley's)	N.M. McMillan Neil M. McMillan JP
BURTON, Wilaby Nancy Ann Fry	03-10-1843	Frances W. Miles Jacob Rall
BUSBY, William M. J.E.M. Chunn *	12-20-1845	Stephen Wiggins ————
BUSEY, Charles S.S. Watts *	09-19-1867	J.F. McCorvey E.S. Smith, MG
BUSEY, Samuel Nancy J. Andress	05-19-1858 (At Evant Andress' on Wednesday evening)	Robert D. Thompson Robert D. Thompson
BUSEY, Samuel J. Mollie E. Hurry *	05-08-1872 (At home of Mrs. Hurry)	J.A. Simmons John McWilliams
BUSSY, Samuel Lucinda J. Bivin *	01-25-1838	William Stevens Asa Hammond, JP
BUSSY, Samuel Isabella Umphrey	08-15-1844	C.H. Foster ————
BUTLER, James G. Mary Ann Allen	06-04-1840	A. Stevens Jesse ————
BUTLER, John W. Kate Riley	10-13-1875 (A- home of L.R. Riley)	F. Metts W.G. Curry, MG

BUTLER, T.J. Ella E. Thompson	12-19-1880 (At home of J.W. Carter)	J.W. Carter R. Buster
BYRD, Allen Louisa Woodham	08-08-1850	James M. Byrd T.E. Feagen, JP
BYRD, Allen Millie Ann Wiggins	12-22-1880 (At Adam Wiggins)	Adam Wiggins Joel Hardee, NP
BYRD, Harry J. Nancy Middleton	12-04-1865	W.J. Langham —————
BYRD, Henry I. S.A.E. Lawrence *	05-16-1869 (At Mr. Lawrence's)	Drury Lawrence James L. Eddins, MG
BYRD, Isaac Elizabeth Middleton *	10-26-1865	Thomas J. Duke William Robertson, JP
BYRD, James W. Francis Wiggins	04-18-1875 (At home of A. Wiggins)	Joel Hardee
BYRD, Jesstha Millie Ann Woodham	07-21-1839	Daniel Fore Charles P. Salter, MG
BYRD, John Emelia A. Middleton *	12-23-1856	H.H. Middleton Joel Hardee, JP
BYRD, Leonard Lucy Owens	11-04-1855 (At office of L.E. Feagin)	J.M. Byrd L.E. Feagin, JP
BYRD, Moses Mary Dikes *	07-28-1859 (At home of Moses Byrd)	John A. Simmons T.E. Feagin
BYRD, Moses B. Josephine Wsythe	12-31-1876	John Lester Joel Hardee, NP
BYRD, Patrick Mary Owen *	02-10-1851	James M. Byrd T.E. Feagin, JP
BYRD, P.C. Mary I. Jones	12-20-1875	S.M. Byrd Joel Hardee, NP
BYRD, Rufus Castilie Andrew	11-06-1879 (At Adam Wiggins')	J.B. Andrew Joel Hardee, NP
BYRD, S.A. Mary J. Brown	03-14-1880 (At Mrs Mary Ann Byrd's)	J.H. Byrd Joel Hardee, NP
BYRD, William Mary Ann Wright *	12-30-1869 (At C.H. Wright's)	J.H. Hardee Joel Hardee, JP
BYRD, W.J.W. Sarah E. Snowden *	01-02-1879	Isaac Byrd Joel Hardee, NP
CALLAHAN, Cuyler Sallie Jones	02-08-1866	J. Cloud J.B. Colley, JP
CALLAHAN, John Lucinda Fredericks	12-22-1849	James Drew T. Burpe
CALLAWAY, C.A. Rebecca J. Soloman	01-03-1877 (At Mrs Elizabeth Solomon's)	Miles McWilliams M.L. McWilliams
CALLOWAY, Joshua Margaret J. Morris	12-07-1859 (At Enoch Morris')	Joshua Page R.N. Burt, JP
CALOWAY, Clements Allice Powell	01-08-1-80	T.W. Coleman Joel Hardee, NP

```
CALOWAY, Oren                    09-02-1880
  Mary McMillan              (At home of W. McMillan)    D.C. Mims, NP

CAMPBELL, James T.                01-05-1879            J.B. Holt
  P.A. Bodiford             (At Mrs. Mary Holt's)         Burney Sawyer, MG

CAMPBELL, William L.              11-03-1865            George Watson
  Mrs. Martha E. Ethridge                               _____

CANNON, Nathaniel                 10-25-1835            David Cannon
  Saber Ann Kennedy                                       William Clark

CANTERBURY, A.K.                  04-09-1863            J.W. Posey
  Corolie E. Stabler        (At James Welch's on          Robert D. Thompson,JP
                             Thursday evening)

CAPERS, Joseph                    01-30-1855            J.G. Eubanks
  Margaret Callahan *                                     J.G. Eubanks, JP

CARLETON, Morgan                  04-01-1872            James O. Dickinson
  Fannie J. Gray            (At Pineville)                Neil Gillis

CARNELY, Jeremiah                 08-06-1872            John DeLoach
  Celia Odom                (At Judge's office)           John W. Locklin

CARNLINE, Daniel                  04-26-1838            Enoch Hendrix
  Rosanah Hendrix                                         D. Hestle, JP

CARNLINE, Lewis                   10-16-1853            Charles Casselins
  Elizabeth Roach *                                       T.S. Densler, MG

CARNLINE, William                 01-09-1857            George W. Stacey
  Martha Ann Stacey         (At George W. Stacey's)       R.D. Thompson, JP

CARR, E.P.                        02-12-1880            J.W. Sellers
  M.A. Sellers *            (At Joseph Sellers')          D.J. Wright

CARR, Thomas G.                   06-08-1880            John A. Simmons
  Susannah J. Pyrkin *                                    John Hardee, JP

CARRLINE, Milton                  02-07-1854            J. Carrline
  Sarah J. Stacie *                                       William C. Smith, JP

CARSON, Adam                      09-18-1841            William R. Stevens
  Seala R. Grey                                         _____

CARSON, Joseph                    11-08-1837            G.D. Greer
  Bathena Lambert                                       _____

CARSON, Major R.                  03-17-1845            James N. Boyls
  Pleceda Bradford                                      _____

CARSON, William F.                02-19-1846            Pinkney P. Powell
  Margaret Leslie                                         Rufus C. Torry

CARTER, B.F.                      01-01-1879            L.R. Carter
  J.V. Rikard               (At home of G.W. Carter)      L.W. Duke

CARTER, Charles B.                07-22-1850            W.W. McColl
  Adeline Carter *                                        F.E. Feagin, JP

CARTER, Charles M.                01-02-1867            W.J. Newbery
  Ellen Newbery *                                         J.E. Knighton

CARTER, Edwin (CATER?)            12-02-1834            Thomas S. Roach
  Clarissa H. Tarleton *                                  P.H. Schroebel, MG

CARTER, Frances B.                04-10-1839            A.B. Connell
  Sarah E.M.B.M. McConnell *                              T. Burps
```

CARTER, George W. Mary L. Thames	02-08-1855	D.T. Brown J. Lambert, MG
CARTER, Hazekiah Mary E. Daniel *	09-04-1856	John DeLoach A.J. Lambert
CARTER, H.E. C.E. Coleman	12-18-1862	C.C. Cleveland John A. Lee, MG
CARTER, H. Franklin Mosouri Pierce *	11-11-1870 (At her mother's house)	R.H. Rumbley, Jr. W.W. Simmons, JP
CARTER, James W. Mrs. A.C. Thompson	12-19-1866 (At home of N. Bell)	C.R. Broughton J. McWilliams, MG
CARTER, John W. * Mary C. Dogget	11-24-1870 (At home of C. Dogget)	B.B. Green H.J. Hunter, MG
CARTER, L.R. M.A. Boykin	01-01-B 79 (Near Claiborne)	G.W. Salter L.W. Duke, MG
CARTER, Richard H. Martha Childers	02-19-1841	William E. Carter Alger Newman, JP
CARTER, Stephen Eliza Andress	12-20-1838	J.M. Hawthorne Alex Travis
CARTER, Thomas J. Margaret Dunn	09-29-1864 (At Mrs. Walter Wingate's)	N. Thames A.J. Lambert, MG
CASEY, John L. Sarah J. Wallace	10-06-1853	J.M. Henderson J.P. Robbins
CASSELL, H.C. Mary E. Massey	04-26-1876	Miller Rutherford T.G. Abernathy, MG
CATER, William Margaret A. Sigler *	08-05-1858 (At Dr. R.A. Siegler's)	I.I. Roberts M. McCorvey
CATO, A.J. Sarah J. McPherson	12-20-1865 (At E.W. Cato's)	S.H. Dailey B. Bradbery, JP
CATO, Alex J. Elizabeth East	02-08-1865	John DeLoach ———
CATO, Elbert W. Sabrina Ann Booker	07-10-1840	William Booker ———
CATO, Lamenthurn W. Catherine Rawls *	05-06-1834	George Kyle J.H. Stroebel, JP
CATRELL, G.W. M.E. Little	02-18-1867	T.J. Duke N.L. McWilliams, MG
CATSETT, G.W. M.E. Little	02-18-1867	T.J. Duke M.L. McWilliams, MG
CAULFIELD, John Emily A. Wiggins	07-18-1834	Joseph O. Rawls B.F. Porter, Judge
CHANDRON, J.S. S.A. Lambert	06-23-1868	A.J. Sowell E. Andress, JP
CHANDSIN, Joseph Mary Wiggins	01-02-1879 (At home of M.E. Wiggins)	O.J. Wiggins Burney Sawyer, MG
CHAPMAN, Benjamin Elizabeth Forehand	12-28-1856	Asa Bryant W.W. Simmons, JP

20

CHAPMAN, George W.	02-07-1839	Elbert M. Rumley
Rosa Brown		J.A. Graham, JP
CHAPMAN, Simeon	09-95-1853	Pascal Brown
Susanna M. Brown		Elias Brown
CHAPPLE, John M.	11-05-1871	James L. Eddins
Mary Mims	(At home of James Maxwell)	James L. Eddins
CHAVERS, Frank	08-01-1867	T.J. Stephens
Ann Smith *		W.D. Garrett, JP
CHAVERS, Henty T.	06-15-1879	John T. Chavers
Mary C. Grimes	(At home of Allen Grimes)	Robert Smilie, MG
CHAVERS, John T.	05-20-1880	
Lucretia Rhoads	(At McKenzie Church)	A.C. Hensley, MG
CHAVERS, John W.	02-16-1879	J.T. Chavers
Mary A. Roach		D.C. Morris, NP
CHAVERS, Josiah	07-05-1868	U.R. Chavers
Mary Stanley		J.T. Daily, LMG
CHILDERS, James	12-20-1837	William E. Longmire
Elvina Curry *		
CHILDRESS, John	05-12-1870	John DeLoach
Martha F. Lott *	(At Mrs. M. Collun's &	J.B. Colley
	written consent by J.M. Curry)	
CHILDS, Willis M.	09-26-1867	Charles F. Branton
Mary J. Branton *	(At Robert Branton's)	J.L. Eddins, MG
CHILES, John G.	12-03-1862	J.B. Beard
Emeline Snowden *	(At Jacob Johnson's)	T.E. Feagin, JP
CHISHOLM, Elbert	04-05-1868	J.N. Watts
Francis Hawkins		W.W. Spence
CHISHOLM, Elbert	09-20-1877	H.F. Curley
Louisa Musgrove	(At Franklina Corley's)	B. Sawyer
CHISHOLM, John	02-28-1834	John Dubose
Matilda Curry		
CHRISTHOLM, Berry	01-28-1856	C.C. McArthur
Mrs. Mary J. Powell	(At Polly Harp's)	John T. Bayles, MG
CHUN, J.L.	12-27-1868	J.L. Hoyt
L.V. Hutto	(At home of Mrs. Hutto)	J.T. Bayles
CHUNN, E.B.	02-01-1877	
Annie Durden	(At home of J.W. Durden)	J.T. Bayles, MG
CHUNN, John S.	02-10-1848	John H. Finklea
Mary Boyles		Evant Andress
CHUNN, William	06-30-1842	James G. Butler
Sophia Wiggins		J.G. Holcomb, JP
CHUNN, William R.	06-25-1861	Wilson S. Wiggins
Catherine R. Simmons *		
CHUNN, William R.	03-10-1874	T.J. Rachels
C.E. Wiggins	(At home of W.S. Wiggins)	J.T. Bayles, MG
CLARK, Aldin	10-08-1839	Erasmus H. Crosby
Emily Hollingsworth		J.M. Williams

CLARK, Gilleam H. Margaret Lynch	01-09-1840	John H. Nichols N. Goodwin
CLARK, J.J. Claudine E. White	01-01-1879 (At home of J.F. White)	C.C. McWilliams John McWilliams
CLARK, Richard Elizabeth Bates	04-28-1846	Edmund C. _____
CLARK, William Martha Walker *	03-29-1842	James McColl Alger Newman, JP
CLAUSELL, Joseph B. Sarah A. Atkinson	12-16-1845	James S. English H.A. Smith, Minister
CLIFTON, Hawkins Matilda Renfro	04-22-1867 (At home of William Hall)	J.W. Stevens C.W. Hare, MG
CLINE, Emanuel Jeremiah McMillan	03-01-1838	A. McMillan Elias Brown
CLOTHIER, George Sarah M. English	08-31-1839	William H.S. Sampson _____
CLOUD, Jeremiah Mary Graham	01-27-1853	J.W. Foster G. Longmire, ODMG
CLOUD, Samuel G. Roseanna E. Travis	02-15-1836	William M. Cato _____
CLUCK, Dr. N.M. Martha J. Davison	09-05-1860	William Kilpatrick Elder J.D. Kendrick
COBB, J.W. Margaret F. Grace	12-03-1859	T.H. Coker John Hardee, JP
COBB, William R.A. Rowell	02-13-1867	J.J. Johnson I.F. Andress, JP
COGBURN, Henry W. Eastha Kidd *	04-25-1845	M.D. Kidd (Guardian) _____
COHAN, W.W. Sarah F. Brown	10-17-1869 (At Mrs Elizabeth Piearce's)	N.Z. Hardee Joel Hardee, JP
COKER, George W. Levitia House	07-07-1851	John W. Cobb N.A. Agee,JP
COKER, James M. Mary Ann Boney	02-02-1839	John Agee _____
COKER, Nathan Mrs. Mary Flake	05-01-1849	Isaac Betts Hugh Rankin, JP
COKER, Thomas Hamilton Epsey Ann Grace	02-28-1848	E.G. Betts _____

COKER, Thomas Hamilton (continued)
(He was the son of Nathan Coker)
(She was the dau. of Samuel Grace & Hettie Sawyer)

COLEMAN, Daniel Matilda Kennedy	03-13-1834	John J. Eubanks John McWilliams
COLEMAN, Menan Nancy S. Patrick *	12-13-1855	T.B. Thames John McWilliams
COLEMAN, Osburn Vicy Morris *	12-21-1837	Arthur W. Fort Elias Brown
COLEMAN, William S. W.D. Fountain	11-10-1865 (At Mrs. Martha Fountain's)	W.S. Wiggins William G. Curry, MG

COLESON, Wiley J.
  Katherine Riley *
	06-24-1841	W.M. Longmire
		  T. Bryan, JP

COLEY, Luke
  Saraha A. Crocker *
	08-03-1854	James Gallaspy
		  D.W. Kelly, JP

COLLEY, Allen
  Mary Dailey *
	11-24-1836	John S. Dailey
		  Joshua Peavy

COLLEY, James B.H.
  Elizabeth Rikard
	07-02-1843	James C. Rollins
		  _____

COLLEY, John B.
  Mary Curry *
	03-27-1842	Alden Clarke
		  Garrett James, OGM

COLLINS, G.M.
  Caroline Collins *
	01-11-1868	John Andrews
		  _____

COLLINS, Hiram F.
  Mary Daniel
	06-09-1864
	(At home of Mary Daniel)
		William Robinson
		  William Robinson, JP

COLLINS, Monroe
  Caroline Andress *
	01-29-1863	Phillip Owens
		  W.D. Garrett, JP

COLLY, John B.	03-24-1842	
_____		_____

COLTON, Benjamin C.
  Amanda Sawyer
	12-29-1842	Nathan Bell
		  J.G. Wallace, JP

COMANDER, Nathan
  Susan Rikard
	09-30-1845	J. McColly
		  _____

CONSWELL, Ned
  Mrs. Evie Perryman
	09-05-1866
	(At John Simpkins')
		J.F. McCorvey
		  W.W. Graham, MG

CONWAY, Aenol
  Ann Tatum
	05-04-1870
	(At home of Mr. Tatum)
		W.S. Wiggins
		  W.G. Curry, MG

CONWILL, Yates J.
  Nancy Hunter *
	11-08-1846	John C. Jones
		  J.G. Holcomb, JP

COOK, C.W.
  Allice Feagin
	09-19-1872
	(At home of J. Etheridge)
		E. Pate
		  Franklin Geter, MIN.

COOK, J.T.
  Ada Wright *
	10-28-1875
	(At home of John Wright)
		_____
		  Joel Hardee, JP

COOK, N.B.
  Tranquilla Thomas
	02-07-1859	J.M. Cook
		  _____

COOK, Thomas M.
  Susan S. Covin
	01-08-1875
	(At home of Mrs. Casky)
	(This marriage was crossed out)
		_____
		  Joel Hardee

COOK, T.M.
  Susan M. Covin
	01-08-1874
	(At home of Mrs Casky)
	(See marriage above)
		John Hardee
		  Joel Hardee, JP

COOK, Watson W.
  Mary J. McCants
	07-22-1865	James E. Cook
		  _____

COOK, W.S.
  Mary A.E. Mixon
	10-21-1874
	(At his father's home)
		Joel E. Mixon
		  John Hardee, JP

COOPER, Charles M.
  Sarah R. Killam
	02-15-1864	D. Hestle
		  William Peavy, MG

COOPER, J.C.
  Susannah Brantley
	11-12-1878
	(At William Brantley)
		Phillip Andress
		  Joel Hardee, NP

CORLEY, Daniel R.L. Leah Hendrix	06-19-1851	S.J. Corley J.G. Wallace, JP
CORLEY, Isiah M. Julia Ann Kelly	12-14-1843	John Reid J.G. Wallace, JP
CORNLEY, Charles J. Fanny L. Newall *	08-05-1856	James McCall ————
CORVEY, James W. Emily Johnston *	05-03-1838	A.H. Curry James Andress, JP
COSKNEY, James L. Margaret Preston *	09-11-1855	J.A. Rabb John D. Winsell
COTTON, James F. Delphia T. Martin	09-08-1859	W.B. Kemp ————
COTTON, James F. Susan F. Davison	03-23-1865	B.C. Cotten James M. Davison, JP
COTTON, J.B. Corine Davison	01-19-1876 (At home of H.E. Davison)	W.G. Curry W.G. Curry
COTTON, Johiel B. Mrs. E.A. Wallace	12-17-1855	W.R. Brown ————
COTTON, Whitman Mary E. Ross	05-04-1865	John DeLoach Hugh McKenzie, JP
COUCH, George Allachey Carry *	02-03-1834	William G. Curry ————
COUCH, Jackson Parmelia Couch	08-02-1839	Joshua Curry ————
COUCH, James Permelia Weatherford *	05-21-1836	Josiah Curry L.W. Lindsey
COUNTRYMAN, T.A. * M.M. Wiggins	01-18-1877 (At Mahala Wiggins')	J.C. Countryman I. Talbert, JP
COUNTRYMAN, W.R. Mary B. Barborow	06-23-1875 (At the bride's mothers)	J.H. Whisenhant L.W. Duke
COURTNEY, H.E. M.F. Knowles *	07-16-1866	A.P. Ledbetter ————
COURTNEY, John E. Sephronia M. Farrell *	06-20-1849	A.H. Curry L.W. Lindsey
COVEN, Charles Martha A. Ikner *	11-22-1866	Asden Middleton Elder J.E. Knighton
COVIN, Joseph L. Caroline Lumpkins (or Simpkins)	07-25-1847	E.D. Alford Joel Hardee, JP
COWEN, John A. Caroline E. Riley	11-24-1842	Wiley J. Cohom J. O'Neill, JP
COXWELL, Hilliary Mrs. Mary M. McArthur	11-10-1870 (At home of her father)	G.B. Coxwell W.W. Simmons, NP
CRAPPS, Greenberry Q. Amanda Sawyers *	12-22-1869	W.R. Lowery W.W. Simmons, JP
CRAPPS, Henry T. Frances Perry	12-30-1873 (At home of H. Perry)	George W. Salter John W. Leslie

CRAPPS, Reuben
  Christian Elizabeth Lowry
02-04-1841
Lemuel Crapps
  J.G. Wallace, JP

CRAPPS, W.A.
  Florence Bethae *
12-22-1869
H.T. Crapps
  W.W. Simmons, JP

CRAPS, Daniel
  Elizabeth A. Stevens
10-08-1833
("Burned")
James G. Clovis, JP

CRAPS, James W.
  Sarah T. Broughton
11-25-1849
Coleman O'Gwynn
  J.G. Wallace, JP

CRAPS, John
  Mary L. Bynum *
02-27-1834
L.W. Cato

CRAPS, Lemuel
  Elvira Massey *
04-28-1845
D.M. Massey

CRAIY, C.C.
  Unity Garner *
02-14-1861
(At home of Israel Garner)
Israel Garner
  R.O. Connell, JP

CRAWFORD, Bryant
  Nancy Jane Atkinson *
12-24-1839
Enoch L. Morris
  J.G. Wallace, JP

CRAWFORD, F.M.
  C.S. Rikard
09-14-1871
(At her father's home)
B.F. Giddings
  W.W. Simmons, NP

CRAWFORD, G.E.
  Marriah Maiben
09-25-1872
(At home of Dr. Maibens)
A. McCaskill
  A.C. Hundley

CRAWFORD, Henry D.
  Americas Salter
01-04-1873
("Void/Returned not executed")
N.R. Crawford
  John W. Leslie

CRAWFORD, James
  Adeline English
10-04-1834
Charles A. English
  T. Burgess

CRAWFORD, Mahabel
  Martha Wilson
02-07-1837
Thomas Wilson, JP

CRAWFORD, Mahalahed
  Sarah Finklea
11-19-1845
W.C. Ross
  William C. Ross, JP

CRAWFORD, Norvel
  Riabah J. Atkinson *
05-06-1840
Enoch Morris
  J.G. Wallace, JP

CRAWFORD, Seaborne
  Frances Salter
11-01-1842
Owen Shaw
  H. Fowler, JP

CRAWFORD, William B.
  Mary B. Stacey
06-?-1766
(At Philadelphia Church
on the fourth Sunday of June, 1866)
Thomas B. Green
  John McWilliams, MG

CRAWFORD, Willis
  Rebecca Ann Murray
12-24-1846
John C. Jones
  J.G. Holcomb

CRAWFORD, Uriah T.
  Nancy Watters
11-03-1872
(At home of W.G. Curry)
Needham Watters
  W.G. Curry, MG

CREE, Peter John
  Elizabeth Snell
08-11-1842
Ansley Sanders
  John McWilliams

CREIGHTON, Chapman L.
  Mary M. Helton
12-30-1844
James Wiggins
  John McWilliams

CREIGHTON, William W.
  Mrs. Hussey
01-13-1850
Thomas Thompson
  J.G. Holcomb, JP

CREW, Josiah L.
  Amelia Lockland
10-03-1839
Samuel G. Portis
  J.H. Schroebel, MG

CRIET, Gilford Louisa Galaspy	03-28-1842	John C. Downey J. Withers, LEMEC
CROCKER, David A. Margaret A. Reynolds (At Thomas Reynolds')	12-21-1865	S.H. Dailey N.W. Sugden, JP
CROMARTIE, A.B. Sarah L. Higdon	11-22-1873	J.H. Higdon ————
CROMARTIE, Alex R. Obedience T. Cunningham * (At John Cunningham's)	02-10-1856	H. Middleton Joel Hardee, JP
CROOK, D.L. Rebecca McDaniel	02-18-1874 (At home of W.B. Crook)	G.A. Watson Robert Smilie, MG
CROOK, George C. Pauline Moore	08-29-1866 (At Dr. L.R. Moore's)	W.S. Wiggins Dr. L.R. Moore, MG
CROOK, James Hortensia Moore*	11-22-1865	B.B. Kimbell William N. Peavy, MG
CROOK, James J.S. Moore	10-29-1873 (At the bride's fathers)	Charles L. Moore L.W. Duke, MG
CROOK, John W. Elizabeth Henderson	03-19-1869	J.F. McCorvey W.W. Spence, MG
CROOK, W. Mrs. C.F. Bradley	10-19-1871 (At the home of Mrs Bradley)	J.A. Simmons W.G. Curry, MG
CROOK, William Mrs. Martha A.W. Agee	03-10-1848	William Salle T. Burps
CROSBY, A.B. Martha J. McMillan	11-07-1878 (At Neal McMillan's)	D.R. McMillan Emanuel Cline, MG
CROSBY, Andrew Phebe Harp	02-07-1858	Thomas Harp W.W. Simmons, JP
CROSBY, Dennis Mary L. Johnson *	11-18-1846	J.J. Stallworth John Herrington, MG
CROSBY, Erastus H. Fidleia Hollingsworth	04-20-1837	Dem Royman H.A. Sterns, Clerk
CROSBY, William Frances Hollingsworth	01-17-1834	———— ————
CROSS, John Elizabeth R. Brown *	03-17-1870 (At home of Mrs. Brown)	Edward Watts J.M. Wood, MG
CROSSLAND, William B. Frances V. Black	06-12-1856 (At Claiborne)	W.M. Longmire N. Goodwin, MG
CROW, Josiah L. Elizabeth L. Marshall	06-27-1854	S.G. Portis N. Goodwin, MG
CRUM, D.L. Mary Jane Powell *	01-25-1860	W.H. Rhoad A.C. Ramsey, MG
CULPEPPER, G.L. S.C. Green	04-04-1867	D.F.C. Rhoad J.G. Bradley, JP
CUNNINGHAM, Abraham Lucretia Fore	11-10-1863	H.C. Middleton T.E. Feagin, JP
CUNNINGHAM, John Sallie Perryman	01-20-1876 (At Munsford Perryman's)	W.G. Curry W.G. Curry

CUNNINGHAM, William Sarah Fox	07-03-1844	_____ _____
CUREY, R.L. S.M. Gibson	04-23-1880 (At home of W.C. Gibson)	_____ G.W. Salter, JP
CURLEY, James M. M.A. Frye	12-06-1876 (At Joseph Frye's)	J.D. Frye S.R. Kelly, JP
CURRY, A.A. Susan Powell	03-31-1878 (At Mr. Pitman's home)	_____ B.J. Skinner, MG
CURRY, Allen H. Fanny Farnwell	08-13-1835	_____ _____
CURRY, D.C. Sarah Ellen Williams *	07-29-1869 (At Mrs Mariah Williamson's)	J.H. Hardee Nathan Bransford
CURRY, Hinchy L. Susannah Roberts *	11-30-1847	John Roberts W.H. Longmire
CURRY, Jesse M. M.J. Davis	07-14-1876	R.C. Pitman _____
CURRY, J.G. Mary Stringer	09-11-1856 (At Emery Stringer's)	A.T. Curry J.B. Colley, JP
CURRY, J.J. Almeda S. Raines	12-28-1833	_____ _____
CURRY, John Lula Hines	10-17-1878	D.I. McKenzie D.C. Mims, NP
CURRY, Levi, Jr. Susannah Farrell *	09-30-1845	Isaac Curry _____
CURRY, Levi B. Frances E. Curry	02-03-1857 (At Mrs F.E. Curry's)	J.W. Curry J.B. Colley, JP
CURRY, R.H. M.A. Hollerwy	03-02-1873 (At home of Allen Grimes)	John DeLoach Elder Joseph T Dailey
CURRY, William G. Charlsey Partridge	06-30-1842	John Lyon Garrett Longmire, MG
CURRY, William G. Ann M. Wiggins	07-01-1865 (At home of Mrs. E.M.Wiggins)	Samuel H. Dailey John McWilliams MG
DAGGETT, William S. Clarissa J. Rankin *	09-20-1855	S.F. Lewis L.M. Wilson
DAILEY, Alexander Martha A.D.C. Dailey *	12-23-1874 (At Beauna Vista)	Lewis Dailey W.G. Middleton, JP
DAILEY, F.S. Georgia M. English	09-19-1877 (At home of Mrs English)	John DeLoach W.G. Curry
DAILEY, George Pennelia P. Mason	08-19-188- (At home of F.A. Mason)	A. Dailey Joseph T. Dailey, PM
DAILEY, Hugh Sarah Griffith *	11-12-1850	David Dailey J.G. Holcomb, JP
DAILEY, Jacob Maria M. Rikard *	01-19-1837	William Dailey Thomas Wilson, JP
DAILEY, James Martha E. Jordan	04-17-1859	Henry Jordan T.E. Feagin

DAILEY, John Sarah Hawkins	09-20-1833 ("Burned")	Thomas Wilson, JP

DAILEY, Joseph A.
  Elizabeth Hawkins *
	08-10-1843	Jacob Rikard
		  J.G. Holcombe, JP

DAILEY, L.A.
  Leah R. Peebles
	02-14-1858	Richard Reaves
		  L.W. Lindsey

DAILEY, Levi Louisa Stacey *	12-17-1838	D. McNiel

DAILEY, Levi
  Elizabeth Ann Hendrix *
	08-20-1840	Nathan Hendrix
		  James Bynam, JP

DAILEY, Michall
  Elizabeth Ousley
	12-23-1850	H.R. Johnson
		  H.R. Johnson, JP

DAILEY, Samuel H. Mary R. Wiggins *	12-21-1875 (License never executed)	W.C. Sowell, Judge

DAILY, Alexander
  Mrs. Catherine A. Jones
	05-08-1848	C.R. Broughton
		  T.J. Foster, MG

DAILY, H.B.D.F. *
  Theany Riley
	11-30-1876
	(At home of G.W. Riley)
		W.J. Holder
		  C.W. Hare, MG

DAILY, Henry W.
  Evaline Garrett *
	12-16-1852	Silas Garrett
		  F.E. Feagin, JP

DAILY, Jacob Jr. Elizabeth A. Sessions	04-16-1856	Edward Helms

DAILY, John H.
  Mary Ronaldson
	05-04-1864
	(At M. Ronaldson's)
		J.F. White
		  John McWilliams, MG

DAILY, L.M.
  C.S. Drew
	08-12-1867
	(At home of James Drew)
		J.F. McCorvey
		  W.G. Curry, MG

DANIEL, Alexander
  Serena Leoftin
	04-02-1835	Alexander Lambert
		  J.H. Stroebel, MG

DANIEL, David
  Frances Jacobs *
	09-29-1859	John DeLoach
		  R.O. Connell, JP

DANIEL, F.B.
  Frances D. Williamson
	06-21-1860	Joseph L. Daniel
		  W.W. Simmons

DANIEL, George P.
  Rachel McCorkle *
	04-20-1838	Dixon Hestle
		  J.H. Schroebel, MG

DANIEL, Issac N.
  Rosanna M. Weatherford *
	07-14-1836	S.D. Parker
		  John S. Roach

DANIEL, John Martha Parker *	11-06-1841	J.J. Staples

DANIEL, John M.
  Martha J. Cooke
	08-09-1866
	(At home of John McCords)
		J.L. Marshall
		  A.J. Lambert

DANIEL, John M.
  M.C. Talbert
	12-15-1869
	(At home of Mrs. Talbert)
		W.T. Powell
		  John McWilliam, MG

DANIEL, Joseph
  Ann H. Harrison
	05-06-1852	Robert Lambert
		  Elias Brown

DANIEL, Joseph L.
  Amanda M. Daily
	12-08-1852	Thomas Thompson, Jr.
		  W.H. Aldridge

DANIEL, S.F. Elizabeth Thompson	01-29-1862 (At Jesse Thompson's)	J.L. Daniel R.O. Connel, JP
DARBY, J.W. M.J. Simpkins *	05-13-1867	John DeLoach W.W. Graham, Min.
DARR, Michael Rebecka Gaston	11-25-1837	Daniel Carmichael ————
DAVID, A.M. Fannie Bryans	12-20-1878 (At office of J.D. Weatherford)	A.J. Qualls J.D. Weatherford,NP
DAVIDSON, John Mary M. Craps *	02-12-1836	Lemuel Crapps Asa Parker, JP
DAVIDSON, William June McMillan *	08-13-1840	John McWilliams, MG ————
DAVIS, A.L. F.E. Davis	11-25-1880 (At home of bride's father)	W.C. Sowell, Judge
DAVIS, Alex Ann McKenzie	12-23-1867	W.D. Wainwright E. Andress, JP
DAVIS, E.S. Sarah P. Slaughter	10-03-1877 (At S.E. Powell's)	T.E. Powell George Watson
DAVIS, Franklin A. Gergia L. Newberry	05-08-1870 (At Mr. Tuberville's)	J.T. Perry J.G. Bradley, JP
DAVIS, Henry Jackson Rebecca Ann Locke *	12-22-1842 (In the evening)	Jeshinun Dunnam T. Burps
DAVIS, James Carolina Bullard	01-10-1834	C.D. McCall J.H. Schroebel
DAVIS, Jeremiah Nicey Hicks *	05-03-1835	Moses Hicks ————
DAVIS, John D. Mary J. McNeil	06-03-1839	B.M. McNeil ————
DAVIS, John F. Amanda Fountain *	03-27-1860	T.G. Fountain W.N. Peavy, Min.
DAVIS, John H. Mary Ann Brown *	01-05-1837	W.W. Bond ————
DAVIS, John J. Mary J. Johnson	08-26-1854	L. Bowden ————
DAVIS, John J. Mary Andress	05-17-1859 (At William G. Davis')	William G. Davis George Watson, MG
DAVIS, John T. Virginia J. Griffin	07-18-1866 (At Mrs. Griffin's)	John G. Johnson D.S. McDonald
DAVIS, J.S. Josephine Lowery *	02-18-1868 (At Mrs. Lowery's)	H. Brayford M.M. Graham, MG
DAVIS, Samuel G. Jane E. Johnson	04-07-1834	Henry G. Jones ————
DAVIS, William * Mary Curry	02-06-1879 (At William Curry's)	R.C. Pitman B.J. Skinner, MG
DAVIS, William G. Madeline L. McColl *	12-03-1854	J.M. McNeil ————

DAVIS, William W. Louisa P. McKenzie	01-06-1857 (At George S. Bradley's on Tuesday evening)	George S. Bradley R.D. Thompson, JP
DAVISON, B.F. Rachel Robbins	01-16-1878 (At Pineville)	W.B. Kemp L.W. Duke
DAVISON, George Mary A. McMillan *	01-25-1854	William McMillan H.A. Smith, MG
DAVISON, George W. Elizabeth Leslie	01-25-1837	John J. Roach John J. Roach
DAVISON, George W. Liza Nettles *	01-02-1844	William Lammonds John McWilliams
DAVISON, George W. Mary E. Dubose *	03-17-1853	Abner Deese Garrett Longmire, MG
DAVISON, Hugh Mary J. Andress *	01-21-1837	John Davison John McWilliams
DAVISON, Hugh E. Nancy George	06-07-1864	H.M. Andress D.S. McDonald, MG
DAVISON, James Martha Deason *	12-29-1843	Hugh Davison H.S. McMillan
DAVISON, James Jane Leslie	10-11-1843	Hugh Davison John McWilliams, MG
DAVISON, James V. Frances H.A.R. Porter *	01-09-1861 (At R. Porter's)	John DeLoach R.O. Connell, JP
DAVISON, John Martha Andress	07-07-1878 (At Isaac Andress')	J. DeLoach John McWilliams
DAVISON, John Elizabeth Nettles *	11-09-1838	G.M. Hunt T.M. Williams
DAVISON, John Nancy Bynam	01-01-183 7	John W. Smith ———
DAVISON, Miller Margaret C. McMillan *	03-16-1847	Edwin Holly H.A. Smith
DAVISON, Miller Julia McMillan	09-14-1870 (At Dr. W.W. McMillan's)	L.R. Wiggins Archibald Fadgen VDM
DAVISON, Newton Sallie F. Riley	12-14-1871 (At Col. Riley's)	J.S. Herrington D.M. Hudson, Min.
DAVISON, Stephen D. Kate B. Stallworth	04-05-1876 (At Pineville)	J.H. Hobdy J.L. Skipper, MG
DAVISON, T. Mary Nettles *	01-23-1840	William Nettles John McWilliams, MG
DAVISON, William Catherine McWilliams *	10-10-1836	Hugh Davison, Jr. F.F. Harris
DAVISON, William Eliza Daniel *	02-04-1844	Henry R. Johnson A.S. McMillan
DAVISON, William June McWilliams *	08-13-1840	——— John McWilliams, MG
DAVISON, William M. Masoney E. Powell *	11-16-1865 (At Mrs E.A. Powell)	W.T. Reaves John McWilliams, MG

DAW, Jeremiah Nancy A.H. Robinson	06-08-1848	Thomas Short J.G. Wallace, JP
DAWSON, Edward J. Sarah Taylor *	09-23-1846	Benjamin Dawson H. Fowler, JP
DEASON, John J. Mary J. Norwood *	11-25-1852	S.J. Norwood John O'Gwynn
DEASON, William Elizabeth Davison	01-09-1856	R.A. Pollard J.B. Colley, JP
DEE, William Ann E. Pace	11-06-1867	A.J. Mishut E. Andress, JP
DEEN, J.W. B.E. Lambert *	02-07-1878 (At home of W.D. Lambert)	W.F. Lambert J.M. Rothwell, NP
DEEN, Pierce Margaret C. Biggs *	12-21-1876 (At Winfrey Biggs)	John Biggs J.F. White, JP
DEEN, Sirmon Caroline Biggs *	12-16-1875 (At Elias Gosby's)	Elijah Golsby B.B. Green, JP
DEER, H.B. Matilda Eddins *	06-04-1845	David McColl ————
DEER, John L. Sarah M. Curry	09-13-1853	Eliphas Raines John DeLoach, JP
DEES, Abner Frances Hurry *	12-16-1852	W.L. Millender N.A. Agee, JP
DEES, Cornelius Nancy J. Robinson	02-04-1880 (At J.W. Robinson's)	J.W. Robinson Joel Hardee, NP
DEES, Daniel Celissa Bullard *	02-01-1849	W.R. Dees T.J. Foster, MG
DEES, Ezekial T. Jearsa Fortenberry	02-17-1836	John Davison Elias Brown
DEES, J.M. Eliza Biggs	12-15-1868 (At the bride's fathers)	Randall Biggs John McWilliams, MG
DEES, John F. Sarah W. Shriver	12-27-1847	D.B. Shriver ————
DEES, J.T. Mary J. Biggs	11-15-1866 (At Randolph Biggs')	W.J. Biggs W.G. Curry, MG
DEES, Richard Martha Wiggins	07-05-1858	J.J. Gordon William L. Gully, JP
DEES, Thomas H. Mary A. Jay	09-14-1865	William Dees ————
DEES, William C. M.E. Northcutt	12-20-1876 (At James Northcutt's)	J.R. Sawyer W.G. Curry, MG
DEESE, Ezra Elizabeth Lisinba	12-26-1880	Henry Billberry ————
DEESE, James Lucinda Lee	12-18-1878 (At home of Joel Deese)	Richard Deese S.R. Kelly, JP
DEESE, Joel Mrs. Elizabeth Hawkins	01-22-1856	J.J. Watson C.H. Foster

DEESE, Martin Elizabeth Kile	01-01-1852	W.H. Northup Jason Staples, JP
DEESE, William Clarissa H. Watson	09-09-1852	J.W. Philyan J.P. Robbins, MG
DEIVER, T.J. N.J. Brooks	12-13-1877 (At home of James Brooks')	J.S. Brooks Joel Hardee, NP
DEKLE, William Cytha G. Snowden	01-24-1872 (At John Snowden's)	J.W. Perrim James L. Eddins, MG
DELLETT, James Mary W. Womley	12-26-1842 (At Claiborne, "in the presence of many witnesses")	A.B. Cooper Thomas D. Lee, Pastor Elect
DELOACH, Armanias Amanda Middleton *	10-03-1854 (At Martin Middleton's)	W.P. East T.E. Feagin, JP
DELOACH, Anamias Caroline L. Middleton	12-16-1855 (At Martin Middleton's)	John DeLoach T.E. Feagin
DELOACH, John, Jr. Amanda Garret	02-29-1880 (At R.B. Middleton's)	John E. Parrett, JP
DENNIS, Irvin B. Junietta M. Kemp	10-11-1856	T.H. Coker
DENNIS, Pollard M. Henrietta Maria Kemp	01-27-1841	Thomas Mason T. Bryan
DENNIS, Robert B. Mary C. Davison	01-18-1866 (At William Davison's)	Thomas E. Dennis M. McCorvey, Judge
DENNIS, Thomas E. Eliza C. Davison	12-04-1872 (At H.B. Davison's)	W.B. Kemp W.W. Spence, MG
DEWBERRY, Thomas Posey Riley	05-09-1837	James Andress, JP
DEWIERS, David Frances E. Williams	03-13-1880 (At J.D. Weatherford's)	A.J. Qualls J.D. Weatherford, NP
DICKINSON, John S. Mary S. Stallworth *	11-30-1858 (At M.P. Stallworth's)	John Burns M. McCorvey
DIGGS, James B. Elizabeth A.D. Arthur *	05-05-1836	Duke W. Goodman Thomas S. Witherspoon, VDM
DIMOND, George Jane Lambert	08-31-1879 (At home of Mrs S. Lambert)	Andrew Lambert W.A. Locke, MG
DIXON, George W. Amanda E. Connell *	12-20-1860	Robert O. Connell W.W. Simmons, JP
DIXON, John A. Mary June Jordan *	05-20-1851	Joel Hardee
DIXON, Martin V. Sarah F. Connel *	04-04-1860	R.O. Connell W.W. Simmons, JP
DIXON, William B. Martha Hooks	04-21-1834	Daniel Hooks J.H. Stroebel, MG
DOGGETT, Benjamin F. Frances C. Morris	12-18-1872 (At home of E.L. Morris)	G.W. Carter B.B. Green, JP
DOGGETT, George Martha Bayles	12-20-1855	F. Lewis Hugh Rankin, JP

DOGGETT, Joseph Frances Cobb	10-15-1872 (At home of Mr. Johnson)	T.A. Johnston W.G. Curry
DOR, Joseph Ardelia Miles	12-26-1867 (At home of Mrs Nancy Miles)	Mr. Norris A.J. Lambert, MG
DOUGLAS, Daniel Mary A. Self	01-06-1870 (At home of Mrs. Self)	T.J. Hawkins Emanuel Cline, MG
DOWNES, Jesse M. Martha Gallahan	02-07-1854	John D. Smith W.H. Aldridge, JP
DOWNEY, Peyton F. Martha Weatherford	01-16-1837	David Gallaspy ————
DRAUGHON, Robert J. Elizabeth L.M. Howe	01-04-1849	E.E. Thames A. Travis, MG
DREADEN, William T. P.A. Moody	11-29-1767 (At home of P. McGlenn)	William Joiner P. McGlenn, JP
DREW, James Amelia Peebles	09-30-1845	J.L. Guild ————
DREW, Nervet Rebecca Henderson *	11-02-1834	Frederick Rhodes Ebenezer Hearn, MG
DRISCOLL, Daniel Eliza A. Black	05-11-1855	Nelson Smith H.A. Smith, MG
DRISKILL, Jerry Milly Byrd	09-18-1865	H.C. Middleton F.A. Mason
DUBOSE, David S. Fannie R. Baldwin *	11-15-1865	T.J. Stevens W.W. Spence
DUBOSE, John D. Mary Stallworth	06-23-1857	John A. Marshall ————
DUBOSE, John D. Laura F. Bradley	02-01-1872 (At W.T. Nettles')	W.F. Nettles Neil Gillis
DUBOSE, William E. Eleanor Andress	02-24-1834	John N. McLure ————
DUKE, Frank P. Mrs. Nannie Henderson	12-30-1874 (At the bride's home)	M. Sawyer W.G. Curry, MG
DUKE, George D. Sarah W. Lett	06-19-1860	George Watson, Sr. ————
DUKE, James H. Isabella McCoy	07-20-1871 (At home of Mrs. McCoy)	Jeff Knowle L.W. Duke, MG
DUKE, Walter N. Jane Knowles	05-21-1865 (At Mrs. William Green's)	George C. Nettles P.J. Carr
DUKE, William J. Isabella McColl	12-26-1848	William A. Pugh H.A. Smith
DUKE, W.N. Martha Jane Bird	02-03-1875 (At home of W.N. Duke)	D.H.C. Roach W.G. Middleton
DUKES, George L. Narcissa Watson *	10-25-1848	James M. Betts H.J. Hunter, Min.
DUMAS, Benjamin M. Martha Ann Miles	11-02-1843	Elias Lambert William R. Agee, JP

DUMAS, Jacob C. Drucilla Davis	08-09-1838	James Davis J.H. Schroebel, MG
DUMAS, James S. Ella J. Snell *	12-04-1873 (At home of bride's father)	B.F. Foxworth L.W. Duke, MG
DUMAS, Sanders C. Martha M. Agee	06-19-1838	John Agee J.H. Schroebel, MG
DUNAWAY, Felt E.M. Lambert *	12-25-1868 (At Andrew Lambert's)	M.L. Lambert A.J. Lambert, MG
DUNAWAY, William J. Drucilla Lambert *	02-13-1862 (At Andrew Lambert's)	H.M. Lambert A.J. Lambert, MG
DUNHAM, Elias F. Elizabeth Grimes	12-20-1872	J.K. Grillery ————
DUNN, Anthony W. Jane C. Brown	03-20-1848	William M. Dunn R.O. Connell, JP
DUNN, Elustus * Nancy Caroline Lloyd	08-08-1878 (At office of Judge)	I. Dunn W.C. Sowell, Judge
DUNN, Isaac William Ann Loyd	07-24-1879 (At Capt. James Lambert's)	Jacob Dunn John L. Marshall, JP
DUNN, Jacob Amanda Avery	11-04-1869 (At home of Mr. Avery)	L. Bowden A.J. Lambert, MG
DUNN, John May N. Jay	11-05-1874 (At the bride's fathers)	Isaac Dunn Eld. Joseph J. Dailey
DUNN, William Maria Brown *	11-10-1840	Elias Brown Thomas Wilson, JP
DUNN, William M. Georgia Ann Knowles	11-08-1860	John W. Snell ————
DUNNUM, James A. Sissy Isabella Watson *	11-30-1850	Robert B. Morris H.J. Hunter, MG
DUNNAM, John L. Louisa Butler	12-03-1857 (At Mrs. Sarah Butler's)	J.H. Colley J.B. Colley, JP
DUNOWAY, H. M.J. Lambert	12-23-1874 (At home of A.M. Lambert)	Andrew C. Lambert A.J. Lambert, MG
DURANT, Charles L. Nancy Hussey *	12-01-1852	D. McColl H. O'Gwynn, JP
DURDEN, C. Baker Ellen A. Swift *	01-23-1850	A.W. Gray ————
DURDEN, E.T. Elizabeth Barnes	06-22-1876 (At home of S. Barnes)	C.J. Torry J.T. Bayles, MG
DUVALL, Elisha Mary L. Lambert *	04-23-1850	B.B. Lambert T. Burps
EAST, West P. Angelina D. O'Neil *	12-24-1854 (At James O'Neil's)	D. McColl C.H. Foster, Judge
EASTEP, W.P. Delilah P. West	05-02-1858 (At Pine Grove Church)	John A. Simmons R.O. Connel, JP
EDDINS, James L. Ellen E. Soloman	10-24-1855	Riley Adams L.A. Farmer

EDDINS, William R. Patience Weatherford	05-06-1846 (Not executed)	E.T. Nethery ————
EDINS, Calvin L. Ruthy Daily *	12-21-1846	Christian Rikard J.G. Holcomb, JP
EDINS, C.S. A.B. Smith	05-30-1880 (At home of A. Smith)	———— J.L. Eddins, MG
EDWARDS, Gabriel J. Martha F. Rhoad *	09-01-1853	L. Boyden James M. Powell
EDWARDS, John W. Mrs. Mary J. Crum	02-23-1865	John S. Dickinson ————
EDWARDS, Napolean B. Elizabeth A. Agee *	05-31-1855	W.R. Crook L.M. Wilson
ELLIOTT, John F. Allin Pettibone	05-23-1866 (At the Protestant Episcopal Church in Claiborne)	N.W. Sugden F.W. Dumas, MG
ELLIS, Ephiram Rhody Rivers *	04-15-1849	G.D. Foster G.D. Foster, JP
ELLIS, Lowery Maria James	01-07-1848	William L. Lowery R.O. Connell, JP
ELLISON, William E. Lucy Adcock	10-06-1840	Thomas Ellison ————
EMMETT, W.H. Martha Jane Owens	10-29-1857 (At Jesse Owens' on Sunday evening)	W.C. Owens R.D. Thompson
EMMONS, Washington Martha Salter *	02-11-1841	M.E. Manning J.G. Wallace, JP
EMMONS, William Rachel Rumbley	01-09-1840	Wingate P. Rumbley J.C. Wallace, JP
ENGLISH, Charles A. E.A. Cleary	09-26-1834	Robert Bullard T. Burps
ENGLISH, Charles A. Mary G. Arthur	12-10-1863 (At home of John C. Arthur)	T.H. Cooper M. McCorvey, Judge
ENGLISH, John A. Mary M. Arthur *	11-29-1836	L.M. Harris Walker ————
ENGLISH, Johnathan D. Martha Kemp	08-01-1857	Daniel McColl ————
ENGLISH, Munson H. Anna L. Crawford	11-22-1859 (At the King's Residence)	Thomas C. English A.J. Lambert, MG
ENGLISH, Thomas J. Hattie Creighton	03-02-1867 (At home of Mrs. A. King)	F.M. Jones W.B. Philps, MG
ENGLISH, W.Z. Mary E. Byrd	01-21-1880 (At Mrs. Mary Byrd's)	J.H. Byrd Joel Hardee, JP
ENZOR, Jesse Eliza E. Frye	03-04-1875 (At Andrew Frye's)	John DeLoach S.R. Kelly
ETHERIDGE, George W. Mary E. Crometie *	01-08-1874 (At home of Mrs. Crometie)	John Hardee John Hardee, JP
ETHRIDGE, J.R. M.M. Mason	03-20-1870 (At home of J.H. Hardee)	J.R. Hixon Joel Hardee

EUBANKS, Ezunder Elizabeth Eubanks	02-19-1839	John M. Caskill William C. Faulk, JP
EUBANKS, J.B. Martha A. Newberry	09-30-1863 (At William Newberry's)	J.J. Eubanks M. McCorvey, Judge
EUBANKS, Jesse Julia Rawls	01-06-1848	R.O. Connell R.O. Connell
EUBANKS, Jesse A. Sarah A. Davison *	01-04-1866 (At home of Mrs Davison)	J.J. Eubanks M. McCorvey
EUBANKS, Jesse G. M. Catherine Rall *	10-05-1848	Malcom Graham J.G. Wallace, JP
EUBANKS, J.J. Prudence Hawkins	02-10-1880 (At home of the bride)	A. Packer G.W. Salter, JP
EUBANKS, John J. Eliza C. Walker *	02-12-1836	S.A. Dubose Asa Parker, JP
EUBANKS, John J. Mrs. Elizabeth Rikard	12-30-1849	David W. Kelly R.O. Connell, JP
EUBANKS, R.H. M.C. Holman	05-19-1865	G.W. Salter M.M. Graham, MG
EUBANKS, Thomas J. Laura Catherine Craps	02-10-1859 (At John Craps')	Daniel Craps R.O. Connel, JP
EUBANKS, William H. Adelade V. Craps	12-19-1867 (At home of Mrs. Bethea)	H.T. Craps W.B. Dennis, MG
EVANS, Gillman Dicey Tolbert	01-13-1837	Erwin Powell Elias Brown
EVANS, William N. Almira A. Haddox	06-19-1855 (At home of Charles Brooks)	Charles Brooks William Longmire
EVERATT, Wesley Mary A. Morris	02-10-1869	D.K. Burne J.D. Bradley, JP
EVERETT, Daniel W. Mary Jane Morris *	01-10-1878 (At W. Everett's)	R.W. Everett R.M. Tuberville, JP
EVERS, Jasper Sarah Solomon *	09-10-1846	Morgan Attaway Joel Hardee, JP
EVERS, John G. Frances A. Wilkerson *	12-05-1869 (At Asa Wilkerson's)	J.H. Hardee Robert Wilson, MG
EZELL, Andrew Martha Ann White	01-14-1843	Redmon H. Reynolds
FAIL, Osborne Emily Riley *	06-29-1842	Legrand Parker James O'Neal, JP
FAIRCLOTH, James K. Amy E. Langham *	08-17-1875	Joel Hardee, JP
FALKENBERRY, Colden Jennett Nettles *	11-05-1838	John Kearley Elias Brown
FALKENBERRY, William Margaret T. Ballard	01-13-1859 (At Mrs Jane Ballard's)	Chapman Falkenberry John T. Bayles
FALKENBURY, Joseph M. Arriane McClure *	02-10-1868	W. Falkenbury E.T. Andress, MG

36

FARISH, Dr. R.W. S.E. Burgess	07-20-1864 (At Mrs James Burgess')	James T. Parker D.S. McMillan
FARRAR, Abel Nancy Ann Salter	11-21-1852	F.R. Robbins H. Lee
FARRAR, Abel Martha J. McInnis *	05-19-1859 (At James McInnis')	Alexander McInnis R.N. Burt, JP
FARRAR, Frances Mrs. Mary R. Fore	12-28-1875 (At John McMillan's)	Lesten Hurry L.W. Duke, MG
FARRISH, Robert J. Susan C. Nichols *	08-12-1869	J.G. Johnson Thomas K. Armstrong MG
FARRISH, W.C. Virginia T. Thrush	04-23-1863 (At James Powell's near Bell's Landing)	J.A. McCaskey Anson West, MG
FAULK, J.T. J.A. Rawles *	06-16-1868 (At home of Joel Rall)	J.F. McCorvey M. McCorvey, Judge
FAULK, Seaborn J. Mary J. Rumbley *	01-18-1860 (At W.P. Rumbly's)	H.M. Graham M. McCorvey, Judge
FAULK, William J. Samanthy E. Rumbley	11-22-1865 (At W.P. Rumbley's)	T.J. Stevens M. McCorvey
FAULKENBERRY, Deason Eliza Holloway	12-04-1847	Daniel McColl John McWilliams, MG
FAULKENBERY, James C. America Talbert	10-03-1877 (At home of Mrs. Talbert)	John DeLoach L.W. Duke
FAULKENBERY, J.M. M.R. Helton *	12-18-1878 (Near Pineville)	C.J. Sawyer L.W. Duke
FAULKENBERY, Lestin Billie Helton	12-15-1875 (At J.F. Helton's)	J.R. Sawyer W.G. Curry, MG
FEAGIN, John W. Mary E. Dixon	02-15-1853	J.M. Bird Joel Hardee, JP
FEASTER, John Miss Chilis	05-05-1866	A. Padgett
FEASTER, John Roseline Byrd	11-06-1867	William Byrd W.D. Garrett, JP
FEASTER, Jordon Peggy Daily	01-24-1866	A.A. Padgett J.W. Feagin, JP
FERGUSON, William H. Rutha Pritchett	04-10-1851	Murdock McMillian J.G. Wallace, JP
FERRELL, William M. Sarah Ann Lambert *	05-10-1843	Perry Lambert J. Withers, LEMEE
FERSSELL, Benjamin Amanda Stacey *	04-14-1867 (At home of Amos Stacey)	Olin Bradshaw M.M. Graham, MG
FESTER, Ira Sophia Whittle	10-21-1877 (At home of Mrs. Whittle)	Andrew Fester J.A. Mason, Esq.
FEW, G.W. Dicy Stanley	08-16-1870 (At Pineville)	J.J. Simpkins Neil Gillis, MG
FEW, Jesse Mary Ann Casidy *	11-28-1858	T.E. Feagin T.E. Feagin, JP

FEW, Jesse Frances Barlow	07-13-1866	T.E. Feagin ———
FILER, G.W. Mrs. A.E. Powell	02-04-1858	W.G. Stovall H.B. Farrish, MG
FILLPOT, Thomas J. Mrs. Frances Luccas	08-28-1860	W.L. Willis ———
FINCH, Alfred A. Mary Smith *	12-20-1835	David Smith T. Burrps
FINDLEY, Buford Maria Hixon *	01-20-1857	John Hixon W.W. Simmons, JP
FINE, Perry D. Loucinda Black	08-09-1875	John Hardee T.M. Riley, Jr., JP
FINKLEA, Evander Alabama Grace	11-25-1877 (At Agrippa Grace's)	R. Cunningham J.S. Skipper
FINKLEA, Gadi Agnes C. Muldroe	02-09-1837	——— Thomas Wilson, JP
FINKLEA, Gadi Carrie Burgess	12-27-1871 (At Bell's Landing)	James T. Packer D.T. McCants, JP
FINKLEA, H.B. L.A. Nettles	12-17-1874 (At the bride's mothers)	J.J. Kinklea L.W. Duke
FINKLEA, J.C. Millie Finklea	04-24-1874 (At G.C. Nettles')	W.G. Middleton J.T. Bayles, MG
FINKLEA, J. Hardy Mary Hylert	05-07-1844	Mahala Crawford Thomas Wilson, JP
FINKLEA, John C. Mrs. Mary Wilson	02-06-1848	Elias Brown E. Brown
FINKLEA, John J. Lydia B. Nettles	09-15-1869	S.M.C. Middleton C.F. Sturgess, Pastor of Concord Ch.
FLAKE, J.J. Elizabeth F. Colvin	01-26-1860	J.J. Covin R.N. Burt, JP
FLEMING, Daniel Sarah F. Priner	12-11-1868	William Fleming W.W. Spence, MG
FLEMING, Thomas J. Mary Jane Ward	08-21-1873 (At home of Mrs. Ward)	William Fleming E. Cline, MG
FLEMING, Thomas W. Mrs. Mary Kennedy	12-08-1834	John M. Byers Thomas S. Wetherspoon
FLEMING, William H. Caroline J. Smith *	11-26-1833	William J. Morgan ———
FLEMING, William L. Mary Ann Owen	10-08-1857 (At Mrs Jesse Owen's on Thursday evening)	John Owen Robert D. Thompson JP
FLEMING, Yancy Ellen McArthur	08-27-1868	John McArthur J.M. Wood
FLEMMING, Francis A. Nancy Ward *	10-26-1876 (At home of M. Ward)	Madison Ward S.R. Kelly, JP

FLEMMING, John Mary E. Fry *	07-02-1867	William Flemming Z.D. Cottrell, LE
FLEMMING, William Henrietta Chamberlin	08-27-1863 (At Mrs. Nancy Foster's on Thursday evening)	B.F. Johnson R.D. Thompson, JP
FLETCHETT, A.C. Mattie M. Bone	06-16-1865 (At home of G.W. Bone)	D.S. McDonald D.S. McDonald
FLINN, Alex A. Martha Odom	12-22-1846	William Slaughter ————
FLOYD, T.C. Margaret Fleming	10-25-1877 (At Mrs. Fleming's)	Thomas Fleming W.R. Agee, JP
FONDA, Christopher Gates Mrs. Sarah L. Black	10-23-1838	Daniel Black James Wilson, JP
FORE, Daniel F. Mary R. McWilliams	01-07-1866 (At Zion Baptist Church)	J.F. Fore W.G. Curry, MG
FORE, Daniel W. S.E. Hixon	01-22-1873	Randall McDaniel John McWilliams, MG
FORE, James A. Mari Broughton *	12-14-1865 (At C.R. Broughton's)	Harry O'Gwynn John McWilliams, MG
FORE, James A. Annie Coleman *	09-13-1876 (At John J. Watson's)	J.I. Watson Thomas M. Fore
FORE, James E. Eliza A. Armstrong *	11-12-1860	Thomas M. Fore T.M. Lynch, Pastor
FORE, .Jbel Matilda McKinney	01-17-1838	John Fore James King, Elder
FORE, John Elifora Hutts *	01-02-1836	William Riley ————
FORE, Nelson Harriet Ann Andress *	02-09-1843	James Davison John McWilliams, MG
FORE, Peter Lucrisia Middleton	08-07-1850	————
FORE, Thomas M. A.C. Phillips	07-29-1860	J.E. Fore John Hardee, JP
FOREHAND, William Elizabeth Bryan	12-24-1837	Allen Gordy Elias Brown
FORREST, A.H. Judy Ann Bozeman	10-17-1833 ("Burned")	———— ————
FORT, Arthur W. Nancy Coleman *	12-11-1837	Osburn Coleman ————
FORT, Drury Mrs. Vicoy Finch	07-18-1855 (At Mrs. Finch's)	M. Patrick W.M. Longmire, JP
FORT, John C. Eliza Conwell *	12-20-1849	John W. Foster J.G. Holcomb, JP
FORT, N.M. M.E. Rikard	08-07-1860	William Fort ————
FORT, William Louisa Oman *	01-17-1848	Chris Brooks W.C. Monroe, MG

FORT, William Nancy J. Curry	04-07-1853	L.S. DeLoach William Longmire, JP
FORT, William Deborah G. Martin	08-20-1860	J. DeLoach T.M. Lynch, MG
FORTENBERRY, Chapman Mary M. Colvin *	12-14-1852	James J. Colvin John McWilliams
FORTES, Samuel G. Hattie Betts	11-23-1876	D.L. Neville James S. Rencher
FOSTER, Arthur Mary S. Williams	02-12-1851	George W. Foster J.S. Rabb
FOSTER, Charles K. Martha B. English	03-28-1839	John C. Arthur J.H. Schroebel, MG
FOSTER, George D. Elizabeth Johnson	10-22-1868 (At J.L. Johnson's)	J.S. Bradley J.H. Salter
FOSTER, George W. Jane E. Draughen	09-03-1844	William F. Andress Alex Travis
FOSTER, James Elizabeth Ann Roley *	05-07-1863 (At Mr. Roley's)	Alex Norris R.O. Connell, JP
FOSTER, John C. Josephine M. Megginson	06-20-1858 (At William R. Agee's) on Thursday evening)	A.J. Megginson A.J. Lambert
FOSTER, John W. Mrs. Mary Rawles	11-11-1841	Thomas S. Roach J.G. Williams, JP
FOSTER, William Nancy Daniel	11-24-1858	A.J. Smith
FOUNTAIN, George W. Zady A. Brown *	02-02-1860 (At J. Brown's)	J.M. Brown R.O. Connell
FOUNTAIN, Green K. Janie Y. Newby	04-20-1879 (At John Simpson's)	J.J. Simpson Burney Sawyer, MG
FOUNTAIN, Henry W. Gatsey A. Sawyer	03-22-1850	Thomas Newberr John McWilliams, MG
FOUNTAIN, H.T. M.S. Clingman	09-12-1878 (At Burnt Corn)	J. DeLoach John S. Frazer, MG
FOUNTAIN, H.W. Mary E. Smith	12-20-1874 (At bride's fathers)	Wiley Sawyer & D.I. Roberts; H.H. Hybert, JP
FOUNTAIN, John A. Mary Elizabeth Wiggins *	11-14-1850	Joseph Wiggins John McWilliams, MG
FOUNTAIN, Lewis S. Emily F. Carter *	10-12-1854 (At Col. H.T. Fountain)	G.R. Fountain C.H. Foster, Judge
FOUNTAIN, Thomas D. Issabella A. Roberts *	09-16-1856 (In the evening)	H.S. Fountain William C. Smith
FOUNTAIN, Thomas G. Sarah I. Dubose	12-03-1857 (At Mrs Sarah Dubose's in the evening)	W.A. Locke M. McCorvey, Judge
FOUNTAIN, Thomas G. Lydia Davison	10-11-1865 (At Mr. H.E. Davison's)	George W. Davison D.S. McDonald, MG
FOUNTAIN, William D. Martha Beard	01-17-1837	William W. Wiggins J. McWilliams

FOUNTAIN, William D. Nancy E. King	01-31-1866 (At home of Mrs. J. King)	M.M. Graham, MG
FOUNTAIN, William H. Mary E. McCorvey *	11-05-1855	J.S. Fountain H.A. Smith, MG
FOUNTAIN, William H.C. Harriet A. Tucker	12-11-1860 (At James Henderson's)	H.T. Fountain John McWilliams, MG
FOWLER, Allen C. Martha Andress *	09-22-1841	Hickman Fowler John McWilliams
FOWLER, Hickman Nancy Purvis	12-20-1835	S.R. Andress ————
FOWLER, William Willie Pullen	02-14-1879 (At home of M.M. Pullen)	J. DeLoach W.C. Sowell, Judge
FREDERICK, Marshall E.F. Griffin *	02-17-1845	Daniel McColl ————
FREDERICK, Peter K. Jane Davison	12-04-1842	James G. Butler Thomas S. Wilson, JP
FREDERICK, Stephen Mrs. Elizabeth Brooks	07-05-1852	B.C. Cotton Hugh Rankin, JP
FREEMAN, Boswell Rosanna Colbert *	03-02-1852	N.L. Murphy W.H. Aldridge, JP
FREEMAN, C.B. Mollie Simpkins *	09-07-1873 (At the bride's fathers)	C. Devane W.W. Walker
FREEMAN, William Martha E. Norwood	10-15-1874 (At the courthouse)	William Dees John W. Leslie, Judge
FRENKEL, Levi Caroline Metzger *	05-13-1854 (At Claiborne)	Soloman Metzger James J. Barklay, JP
FRY, E.W. Nancy E. Daniel	09-10-1857 (At Susan Daniel's)	S.F. Daniel R.O. Connell, JP
FRY, W.H. Mary F. Taylor *	12-11-1868 (At William Taylor's)	H.L. Crapp John W. Leslie, Judge
FRYE, Andrew Mary E. Brown	03-04-1875 (At Andrew Frye's)	G.W. Salter S.R. Kelly, JP
FRYE, David M. Rebeca Bayles	08-20-1845	George Holman ————
FRYE, John H. M.A. Parker	05-24-1866 (At home of Asa Parker, Esq.)	R.T. Kennedy M.M. Graham
FRYE, John W. Mary Hendrix	07-31-1856 (At Johnathan Hendrixon's)	George M. Frye R.O. Connell, JP
FRYE, Neal Mrs. Sarah J. Bradley	02-06-1860	William A. Locke W.W. Peavy, Min.
FRYE, Simeon Mary Jane Lowery *	02-08-1844	George Lowery J.G. Wallace
FRYE, W.L. S.J. Richardson	03-15-1880	———— ————
FULENWIDER, Daniel M. Mary Ann Leslie	12-22-1858	E.E. Robison H.A. Smith, MG

FULLER, George W.
  Sarah McClammy *
	03-14-1869	John Brooks
		  John Hardee, JP

FULLER, Joseph
  Tabitha Ann Pearce
	06-01-1845	James Lumpkin
		  ————

GAILLARD, Samuel F.
  Lucy S. Frye
	11-15-1853	E.L. Willison
		  William F. McKee

GAINES, Thomas
  Mary A. McDonald
	08-02-1866	Thomas D. Daily
		  Hugh McKenzie, JP

GALAWAY, J.T.
  M.A. Thompson
	03-16-1876
	(At Gus Thompson's)
		John DeLoach
		  J.M. Rothwell, JP

GALLASPIE, James M.
  Sinia Tignor
	11-06-1865	R.F. Cruit
		  ————

GALLASPY, George W.
  Margaret Maxwell
	11-17-1846	James M. Griffith
		  H. Fowler, JP

GANDY, Evander Sarah Newberry *	06-17-1841	Thomas Dewberry & George W. Coker; H. Fowler, JP

GANSE, Edward Alexander
  Katherine N. Hall *
	10-17-1860	Thomas R. Hall
		  ————

GARNER, Isreal
  Artimesia Hendrix
	01-15-1862
	(At James Hendrix's)
		Peter Hendrix
		  R.O. Connell, JP

GARRETT, John M.
  Sarah Carter
	10-18-1868
	(At home of Mrs. A. Carter)
		George W. Carter
		  Elder J.E. Knighton

GARRETT, Joseph
  Rachel Andress
	05-30-1872
	(At home of bride)
		Joseph Andress
		  G.W. Scoggins, MG

GARRETT, Silas
  Lucretia Sirmon
	12-16-1852	William Young
		  Joel Hardee, JP

GARRETT, Silas
  Margaret Grime
	09-11-1879
	(At home of Daniel Grimes)
		Jesse Dees
		  Robert Smilie, MG

GASKEY, Henry C.
  Tabitha Grace
	05-30-1838	John W. Smith
		  ————

GASQUE, James W.
  Caroline Coven
	03-15-1866	Joel Hardee
		  W.D. Garrett, JP

GATES, James M.
  Mary Hayles *
	09-16-1868
	(At the bride's fathers)
		W.E. Brooks
		  C.F. Stinges

GATES, Joseph
  Martha Powell
	05-08-1834	Samuel Crapps
		  E.P. McCoy, JP

GATES, Joseph
  Catherine Kennedy *
	02-11-1837	Thomas R. Kennedy
		  ————

GATES, W.C.
  Sarah Hayles
	01-17-1878
	(At William Hayles')
		W.C. Green
		  D.P.C. Rhoad, JP

GAYLE, Edward B.
  Mary C. Sowell
	04-27-1874
	(At Monroeville)
		J.F. McCorvey
		  Father Crowley

GELLENBERG, J.C.
  Isabella J. Caldwell
	06-05-1873
	(At Monroeville)
		John I. Watson
		  John W. Leslie

GENTRY, R.H.
  Elizabeth J. Snowden
	12-20-1868
	(At the bride's fathers)
		J.W. Snowden
		  Joel Hardee, JP

```
GENTRY, S.J.                    12-08-1866              T.J. Stevens
  Drucilla Lambert          (At Martha Lambert's)       A.J. Lambert, MG

GIBSON, Joseph                  02-02-1874              A.W. Wallis
  Maranda Wallis            (At the bride's home)       Joel Hardee, NP

GIBSON, Joseph                  02-07-1875              _____
  Maranda Wallis           (At Mrs. Maranda Wallis')    Joel Hardee
                        (This marriage was crossed out)

GIBSON, William                 12-24-1838              _____
  Susannah East *                                       _____

GIBSON, William C.              09-20-1855              W. Gibson, Jr.
  Mary J. Hemington                                     G. Longmire

GIDDINS, William W.             10-07-1869              G.A. Watson
  Mary M. Rikard                                        W.W. Simmons

GILL, William M.                10-29-1857              W.C. Owens
  Emily E. Owens            (At Jesse Owens' on         R.D. Thompson
                            Thursday evening)

GILL, William P.                12-20-1842              John W. Foster
  Louisa A. Furlow                                      Alger Newman

GILLIARD, John                  12-12-1834              C.T. McConnico
  Caroline Rachel Gordan *                              Thomas S. Wetherspoon

GILMER, Charles L.              06-22-1846              James J. Barclay
  Matilda Kile                                          T. Burpe

GILMRE, Edward H.               01-26-1847              L.L. Steele
  Mary A. Tarlton *                                     William McRee

GLOVER, Gailford                08-16-1837              Rawling Griffin
  Nancy Reaves                                          Phillip Owens, JP

GLOVER, John                    07-07-1846              W. Nutt
  Sophia Ann Johnson                                    Joseph L. Baughman,
                                                                        JP

GLOVER, Philip S. *             11-20-1838              John P. Torry
  Frances A. Torry *                                    J.H. Schrobel, MG

GODBOLD, William G.             04-17-1842              George W. Robbins
  Anabella Beard                                        Jacob Rall, JP

GODBOLD, Wyatt J.               12-21-1842              E.G. Betts
  Serena W. Betts *                                     Blanton P. Box

GODDARD, Abram                  01-23-1848              Thomas Hinson
  Elizabeth A. Rankin                                   J.G. Wallace, JP

GODELL, William                 12-29-1841              Mr. Davison
  Sarah Bell                                            Hickman Fowler, JP

GOLDSMITH, Jacob                02-13-1847              L. Myers
  Henrietta Hiller                                      G.D. Foster, JP

GOMILLUN, J.H.C.                11-21-?                 C. Fields
  Ellen Fields              (At Ireland, Ala.)          S.L. Ellis, JP

GOODE, Burton                   08-24-1865              S.H. Dailey
  Elizabeth H. Davis                                    W.N. Peavy, MG

GOODLOE, Turner                 01-15-1873              C.L. Moore
  Kathy S. Moore *          (At Dr. L.R. Moore's)       A.J. Lambert, MG
```

GOODWIN, Harwell H. Maria McColl *	06-28-1852	George H. Gray ————
GOODWIN, I.J. Mattie Fountain	07-02-1871 (At Col. H.T. Fountain's)	John DeLoach Eld. J.E. Knighton
GOODWIN, John M. Sarah R. Griffin *	01-11-1877 (At bride's fathers)	———— John Hardee, NP
GOODWIN, Norflet Mary Ann McColl	03-18-1842	———— Alex Travis
GOODWIN, William L. Mary J. Griffin *	02-12-1874	E.M. Joiner ————
GOODWIN, William L. Mary J. Griffin	02-12-1875 (At Reubin Stinson's)	———— Joel Hardee, NP
GORDON, Andrew J. Catherine Henderson	01-20-1834	James W. Gordon ————
GORDON, John J. Jane Andress	06-16-1859 (At home of Isaac Andress)	Silas Talbert George Watson, MG
GORDON, William L. Susanna M. Pitman *	04-28-1853	Jack R. Wilson A.G. Longmire
GORDY, John P. Martha Miller	08-20-1865	W.F. Andress M.M. Graham, MG
GORDY, William Henrietta Morris	02-20-1840	Daniel C. Hampton J.H. Graham
GORDY, William Agunepta Mims	02-20-1840	Daniel C. Thompson J.J. Graham, JP
GOULSBY, W.J. Helan McLain	12-31-1879 (At home of Alcy McLain)	J.T. White, JP J.T. White, JP
GRACE, Agrippa Elizabeth Davison	12-23-1841	Duncan McCall James McWilliams
GRACE, James R. Eliza Salter *	02-29-1852	William McColl Charles P. Salter, MG
GRACE, J.P. Nannie J. Grace	09-03-1879 (At Bell's Landing)	J.A. Grace Ed E. Owen
GRAHAM, H.M. Eliza Fowler	03-23-1870 (At home of Mrs. Fowler)	R.H. Rumley John W. Leslie, Judge
GRAHAM, Walter Amanda McIntosh *	04-22-1850	W.W. McColl H.J. Hunter, MG
GRAHAM, Walter R. Ann McIntosh *	12-21-1846	James McColl T. Burpe
GRAHAM, William A. Margaret Eubanks	07-25-1839	Robert O'Connell William C. Faulk, JP
GRANT, John H. Virginia Wsythe	11-22-1876	W.C. Hemp ————
GRANT, M.W. M.N.E.Garrett	10-03-1869	J.J. Flake T.E. Feagin, JP
GRAY, Ernest A. Mattie A. Guned *	08-08-1867	William Griffin C.W. Hale, MG

GRAY, George H.   05-21-1849   William J. Colvin
  Mary Jane Owen   N. Goodwin, MG

GRAY, John S.   12-27-1860   John J. Brown
  Willamina Frances Cromartie *   J.J. Simpkins, JP

GRAY, J.S.   01-22-1880   J.S. Pugh
  E.D. Burgainum   (At Joseph Wiggins')   Joel Hardee, NP

GRAY, Linon P.   10-27-1853   L.C. Lindsey
  Adaline H. Johnston   N. Goddwin, MG

GREEN, B.B.   11-21-1875   Thomas S. Wiggins
  Mary J. McMillan   (At Thomas Green's)   James S. Renchew

GREEN, B.B.   11-27-1866   W.L. Smith
  S.J. Burt   (At home of Mrs. Nancy Watson) W.B. Dumas, MG

GREEN, Christopher W.   11-27-1839   Alden Clark
  Frances Watson *   J.G. Wallace, JP

GREEN, George B.   09-11-1856   John A. Simmons
  Nancy A. Fountain   (At Mrs. Nancy Fountain's)   Uriah Atkinson, JP

GREEN, John O.   09-03-1868   Mike Boltz
  Mary S. McCaskey *   J.G. Bradley, JP

GREEN, J.W.   03-30-1860   William S. Millender
  Milly A. Young *   ————————

GREEN, L.J.   12-24-1879   J.C. Green
  N.J. Rhoad   (At the bride's mothers)   W.P.H. Cournerly, MG

GREEN, T.B.   09-26-1866   J.F. McCorvey
  Mrs. V.C. Mosely   (At W.B. Crook's)   M.M. Graham, MG

GREEN, W.B., Jr.   06-21-1865   D.K. Smith
  Susan D. Watson   (At Mrs Nancy Watson's)   Wesley B. Dennis, MG

GREEN, W.B.J.   01-27-1860   Richard Reaves
  Mrs. Caroline Pugh   ————————

GREENE, W.B.   04-25-1866   W.L. Smith
  Martha A.M. Watson   (At Mrs. N. Watson's)   M.M. Graham

GREGG, James M.   01-06-1869   S.S. Loe
  Amanda Hartin *   (Executed at office)   John W. Leslie, Judge

GREGG, James S.   11-30-1865   John DeLoach
  Permelia Childers * (At Mrs. Nancy Riley's)   W.G. Curry, MG

GRIFFIN, Andrew   01-28-1869   M. McKinley
  Frances J. Dees   (At home of E. Dees)   W.G. Curry, MG

GRIFFIN, Benjamin F.   09-07-1848   Richard Holly
  Matilda Chrisholm *   ————————

GRIFFIN, Davis   08-17-1855   J.M. McColl
  Elizabeth Branton *   (At R.L. Branton's)   L.A. Farmer

GRIFFIN, D.R.   12-14-1879   John Hardee
  Margaret Brooks   (At John Hardee's)   John E. Parrett, JP

GRIFFIN, Frank *   07-07-1879   T.L. Sowell
  Nora Powell   (At office of W.E. Sowell) W.W. Sowell, Judge

GRIFFIN, H.C.   12-28-1879   T.L. Griffin
  Josephine Tuberville   (At R. Tuberville's)   I. Talbert, NP

45

GRIFFIN, John E. Eliza Chancely	05-24-1853 (on Tuesday)	T.E. Feagin T.E. Feagin
GRIFFIN, John M. Ann E.E.L. McKinley	12-30-1868	A. McKinley Francis Walker, MG
GRIFFIN, Samuel S. Mary E. Coleman *	11-18-1877 (At B.S. Hardee's)	J.E. Griffin John Hardee, JP
GRIFFIN, T.L. M.A. Tuberville	08-24-1873 (At Rilland Tuberville's)	W.C. McKinley Isaiah Talbert, JP
GRIFFIN, William Martha Gaskey	12-09-1844	John Holloway ———
GRIFFIN, William H. Melissa Ann Ballard *	07-17-1845	Daniel McColl ———
GRIFFIN, Z.T. Susan Bayley	10-05-1877 (At home of Mrs. Griffin)	J.E. Griffin John Hardee,NP
GRIFFITH, Abner Martha McLain	07-17-1857	James Griffith James Daniel, MG
GRIFFITH, Daniel Mary Salter	10-05-1854	James M. Griffith Hugh Rankin, JP
GRIMES, Allen, Jr. Mary A. Fore	01-01-1860	C.C. McMillan A.D. Anderson, JP
GRIMES, B.B. Narcissa Jones	04-17-1868 (At the bride's mothers)	W.C. Jones P.J. Crew, MG
GRIMES, Caleb L. Margaret J. Parker	12-04-1871	J.E. Henderson Hugh McKenzie, JP
GRIMES, Daniel M. Frances A. McMillan *	12-04-1852	D.A. Anderson ———
GRIMES, Dorson Margaret Andress *	09-22-1859	Hugh McKenzie A.C. Ramsey, MG
GRIMES, John Asseneth Mims *	11-16-1846	Duncan McKenzie ———
GRIMES, John Permelia A. Lambert *	12-06-1869 (At Joseph Lamberts')	J.A. Simmons A.J. Lambert, MG
GRIMES, William Mrs. Elizabeth Grimes	07-03-1879 (At Mr. Grimes')	D.C. Mims, NP
GRIMES, William Avarilla Mims *	01-04-1847	David Mims ———
GRISSETT, John D. Susan Isabella Travis *	04-25-1845	Edward Grissett ———
GRISSETTE, W.J., Jr. B.J. McCorvey	01-15-1874 (At Neil McCorvey's)	J.F. McCorvey J. Mentor Crane, MG
GROOM, H.M. Susan L. Banchman *	06-28-1868	John A. Simmons W.D. Garrett, JP
GROOM, William E. Elizabeth J. Rhoad *	12-11-1856	T.E. Powell James M. Powell, JP
GROSS, David Olivia Kinsey	08-16-1853	S.D. Hestle Jason Staples, JP

GULLY, James   01-12-1859   Samuel Dailey
  Sarah N. Dailey   (At John H. Dailey's)   J. McWilliams, MG

GULLY, James K.   11-29-1866   William L. Gully
  Nancy E. Wiggins   (At Cooper Wiggins')   M.M. Graham, MG

GULLEY, James L.   10-22-1849   W.L. Gulley
  Eleanor Nettles *   J.J. Sessions, MG

GULLEY, William   03-21-1845   Joseph Nettles, Jr.
  Caroline Nettles *   _____

GULLEY, William L.   02-19-1857   John DeLoach
  Frances E. Jones *   James M. Davison, JP

GULSBY, Elijah   11-27-1873   W.J. Downs & T.L. Downs
  Polly Rikard   (At J.F. White's)   J.F. White

GULSBY, L.D.   09-16-1880   J.W. Biggs
  Jennie McClure   (At William Andress')   John McWilliams, MG

GUNN, B.B.   12-15-1870   J.S. Thompson
  Sarah A. Lee   (At home of I.F. Andress) J.T. Bayles, MG

GUTHERY, J.V.   02-05-1874   John Hardee
  Catherine Herrin *   T.M. Riley, Jr., JP

GUTHRIE, A.C.   04-11-1869   James E. Griffin
  Isabella Ross   John Hardee, JP

GWATNEY, J.H.   07-11-1867   F. McCorvey
  Catherine Hopkins *   (At Mrs. Hopkins')   Hugh McKenzie, JP

HACKETT, William H.   01-26-1847   A.R. Arthur
  Martha A. Parsons *   Thomas S. Witherspoon

HADDOX, W.S.   11-04-1874   J.T. Dailey
  S.E. Bohannon   (At home of A. Bohannon) Eld. Joseph F. Dailey

HAINES, James W.   07-01-1866   F.M. Rigby
  Nancy A. Rigby   J.E. Knighton, LMG

HALE, Asa   05-22-1860   John Jay
  Mary Williamson   (At Jesse Hale's on   Robert D. Thompson
                            Tuesday evening)

HALE, Bagby   03-08-1866   E.A. Gray
  Mary J. Hale   (At Judge's office in   M. McCorvey, Judge
                            Monroeville)

HALE, James F.   10-14-1858   M. Stacey
  Mary J. Stacey *   S. Helburn, MG

HALE, John   03-08-1867   William Sage
  Sarah Lambert   S. Andress, JP

HALE, John H.   07-15-1870   W.S. Wiggins
  Alcy Ann Dimond   (At the Judge's office)   John Leslie, Judge

HALL, G.B., Jr.   06-01-1870   J.M. Little
  E.A. Cartrat   (At home of Mr. Little)   Franklin Peters, Min.

HALL, George T.   01-01-1874   J.E. Bayles
  Bettie Lee   (At William Lee's)   J.T. Bayles

HAMBLETON, William   10-06-1855   W. Ousley
  Nancy A. Lowe *   _____

HAMBRICK, Thomas   11-23-1834   Veilsey Mosley
  Cinai Brown *   J. McWestan

47

```
HAMBRICK, William               09-10-1880
   Elizabeth Williams        (At judge's office)        W.C. Sowell, Judge

HAMILTON, B.G.                  06-08-1867              John DeLoach
   Sophonia Stacey            (On Thursday)             Z.D. Cottrell, LE

HAMILTON, Blassengain           01-15-1842              John Barton
   Margaret Ann Elizabeth Segler                        Elias Brown

HAMILTON, Zedekiah              09-01-1850              Edward Hamilton
   Amanda C. Daniels                                    Evant Andress

HAMMOND, G.P.                   02-18-1864              D.C. Stanford
   Mary J. Stanford *                                   M.M. Graham, MG

HAMS, Nelson                    04-13-1880              W.F. Lambert
   Dicey Jay           (At Mrs. Elizabeth Hayles') J.M. Rothwell

HANCOCK, Charles W.             12-27-1853              William S. Reaves
   Mrs. Ann E. Bateman                                  James M. Davison, JP

HANNER, John                    12-22-1841              Robert Lambert
   Polly Taylor                                         Alger Newman, JP

HANSON, Jacob G.                01-21-1869              T.J. Duke
   Elo Jones *                                          T.E. Feagin, JP

HARDEE, Bryant S.               06-02-1864              James Brooks
   Jane Patrick                                         Nathan Coker, JP

HARDEE, Joel                    06-12-1851              Samuel G. Ports
   Elizabeth A. Devane *                                T.E. Feagan

HARDEE, John                    02-15-1834              Joel Hardee
   Sibithi Brooks *                                     _____

HARDIN, John T.                 05-04-1854              G.E. Longmire
   Mrs. Henrietta M. Parker (At Mrs. Parker's)          William Longmire, JP

HARDY, Joel                     06-01-1835              George W. Coker
   Isabella Coker *                                     _____

HARGIS, Robert B.S.             01-21-1846              Neal Beard & Neal
   Susan C. Horton *                                    McCorvey; _____

HARPE, Mannin                   01-17-1877
   Martha Booker       (At home of W.B. Booker, Sr.) J.H. Raines, JP

HARPER, Adam                    04-02-1876
   Matilda Bryant            (At Ramah Church)          J.H. Raines

HARPER, Henry                   09-23-1860              J.W. Billings
   Mary E.J. Billings *                                 W.W. Simmons, JP

HARPER, Henry C.                09-17-1865              S.H. Dailey
   Sarah Kirby               (At Moab Kirby's)          M.M. Graham, MG

HARPER, J.B.                    04-16-1871              W.W. Simmons
   Caroline Cowan       (At Patrick McGlinn's)          W.W. Simmons, NP

HARPER, Noah S.                 01-16-1870
   Martha Waters *                                      J.B. Harper

HARRINGTON, James               04-27-1841              Henry A. Dubose
   Susan Andress                                        J. Bryan, JP

HARRIS, Charles                 10-03-1837              N.R. Adams
   Amanda Foster                                        Asa Parker
```

HARRIS, George W. Delilah E. Kelly *	10-20-1853	William Kelly J.P. Robbins, MG
HARRIS, James M. Mary A. Connley	03-22-1866	Richard Provost E. Andress, JP
HARRIS, John W. Edith A. Loftin *	01-31-1856 (At William Loftin's)	J.H. Loften R.D. Thompson, JP
HARRIS, Robert Sarah A. Hayles *	11-24-1853 (At Jesse Hayles')	W.D. Lambert R.D. Thompson, JP
HARRIS, William H. Jane Barlow	04-22-1879 (At office of J.D. Weatherford)	Adam Hollinger J.D. Weatherford
HARRISON, Benjamin H. Elizabeth Daniel *	09-06-1846	Joseph Daniel Elias Brown, MG
HARRISON, Benjamin H. Mary E. Carter	09-25-1866	D.N. Roberts E. Knighton, LM
HARRISON, James E. Nancy Smith	12-22-1867 (At home of John Smith)	L.D. Harrison Francis Walker, MG
HART, John L. Mary E. Coker *	04-10-1851	Elisha Reynolds Joel Hardee, JP
HARWELL, William F. Levelita Weatherford	04-11-1842	C.C. Sellars T. Burps, Ord. Min.
HASS, Issac Levitice H. Hollinger	12-17-1844	Green Brown ————
HASSKEW, Peter Ann E. Withers *	12-15-1840	Nathan Hendrix T. Burpe, MG
HATHCOCK, James F. Matilda Poltson	10-15-1866 (At Mary Connley's)	T.H. Maulden Emmanuel Cline, MG
HATHCOCK, John Rose Maphee *	06-30-1853	Thomas L. Hathcock Charles Foster, Judge
HATHCOCK, Simeon Julia McArthur	07-01-1855	John M. Langham Stephen Hillburn
HAWKINS, Edward Anna B. Conwell *	01-28-1835	Daniel G. Conwell Thomas Wilson
HAWKINS, Jacob L. Susan Blanton	02-19-1862 (At home of R.O. Connel)	George W. Salter R.O. Connel, JP
HAWKINS, John N. Mary R. Brooks *	02-11-1865	Robert J. Pugh Nathan Coker, JP
HAWKINS, Thomas Martha M. Young *	04-22-1842	J.A. Dailey J.G. Holcomb, JP
HAWKINS, T.J. G.A. Bird *	02-12-1868 (At Alferd Bird's)	Daniel Douglas Emanuel Cline, MG
HAWKINS, William Caroline McClammy *	10-20-1844	A.L. Witherington ————
HAWKINS, William A. Anna McDonald *	12-20-1860 (At Henry McDonald's)	William Robinson T.E. Feagin, JP
HAWLEY, William L. Susan Ellis	05-04-1838	William R. Agee John C. Baldwin, VDM

HAWTHORN, George Adeline Matilda Anderson *	03-06-1834	Joseph J. Childs Alex Travis
HAWTHORNE, J.M. Nancy Andress *	10-13-1836	J.W. Pipkins Blanton P. Box
HAWTHORNE, J.R. S.H. McCorvey	07-24-1866	J.A. McCreary C.W. Hare, MG
HAYDEN, Isaac Elizabeth Loftin (Saften?)	08-08-1844	Daniel McColl G.F. Foster, JP
HAYLE, John H. Jo Anna Hendrix *	11-29-1850	David Hendrix J.B. Rabb
HAYLES, Brown Emily Lambert	02-09-1875 (At Matt Lambert's)	Lewis Hayles J.M. Rothwell, NP
HAYLES, Harman C. Nancy Young	11-02-1865 (At home of Mr. Davis)	William H. Stanley John T. Bayles, MG
HAYLES, Lewis Margaret Rhodes *	01-04-1836	John J. Roach T. Burps
HAYLES, Lewis, Jr. Susan Grimes	12-23-1874 (At home of G.W. Stacey)	W.B. Hayles J.M. Rothwell, NP
HAYLEY, F.D. M.L.D. Richardson	02-25-1880 (At bride's fathers)	C.A. McNiel W.R. Maxwell, JP
HAYNES, Jesse Polly Talbert *	05-18-1837	Richard Talbert E. Brown
HAYS, Charles H. Leah R. Gray *	01-03-1850	A.B. Dishman N. Goodwin, MG
HAYS, Charles W. Sarah R. Wood *	10-15-1865	A.H. Hays W.N. Peavy, MG
HAYS, J.W. Lucinda A. Anderson	12-21-1856 (At Matthew Anderson's)	William J. Bullock T.E. Feagin, JP
HEAP, W.C. Augusta A. Grant	03-02-1876	John Wright Joel Hardee, JP
HEARN, L.F. Barbara A. Barnett	11-21-1859	J.H. Barnett ————
HEATHERINGTON, John H. Rebecca J. Kyle *	01-26-1840	James Wiggins ————
HEATHERINGTON, John M. Margaret A. Broughton * (At C.R. Broughton's)	10-06-1867	H. O'Gwynn M.M. Graham, MG
HELBUN, Francis M. Sarah Whatley	04-03-1851	Walter R. Whatley W.H. Aldridge, JP
HELMS, Alexander Sarah A.M. Hundley	11-10-1836	James Holder
HELMS, Daniel Mrs. Susan Riley	12-08-1852	William Riley M.B. East, JP
HELTON, J.D. * M.L. Waters	10-11-1878 (At Mrs. Polly Waters!)	C.W. McClure S.E. Ellis
HELTON, Henry C. Betty Gibson *	03-18-1867 (In the church at Turnbull)	John DeLoach Hugh McKenzie, Esq.

HELTON, Issac M.   03-28-1858   George S. Bradley
  Nancy M.A.E. McInsey   (At George S. Bradley's)   Robert D. Thompson,JP
                           on Sunday evening

HELTON, James   02-15-1880   D.W. Fore
  M.V. Hixon   (At home of Webster Fore) W.R. Maxwell, JP

HELTON, James M.   12-29-1874
  Henrietta McClure   (At Joseph Falkenbery's)   W.G. Curry, MG

HELTON, James M.   03-05-1867   Henry Helton
  R.J. McAliston   (At home of John Sanders) W.G. Curry, MG

HELTON, Jeremiah   01-07-1857   Samuel Daily
  Martha M. Sawyer *   A.J. Brown, JP

HELTON, John A.   05-20-1866   J.F. McCorvey
  Sallie J. Bolling   W.D. Garrett, JP

HELTON, Joseph   02-22-1871   W.J. Helton
  Susomi Biggs   (At home of Randall Biggs) Hugh McKenzie, JP

HELTON, William   04-30-1843   Hasten D. Wainwright
  Mary Ann White *   John McWilliams, MG

HELTON, William   12-18-1852   James Graham
  Mariam Graham *

HEMPHILL, Wade   12-17-1844   Albert Curry
  Jinny Curry

HENDERSON, Frank L.   11-07-1867   S.H. Daily
  Fannie E. Tucker   (At A.B. Tucker's)   M. McCorvey, Judge

HENDERSON, G.A.   09-25-1879   R.J. Hudson
  Missoria Kirley   (At James Kearley's)   James T. Daily, MG

HENDERSON, G.A.   08-13-1873   W.M. Riley
  Susan F. Hicks *   (At Sam Hicks')   James L. Eddins, MG

HENDERSON, James   02-17-1853   Joseph H. Ryland
  Caroline S. Tucker   John McWilliams, JP

HENDERSON, James E.   02-21-1850   Travis B. Thames
  Martha Ann Wiggins

HENDERSON, John T.   04-05-1842   Joel B. Malden
  Mary A. Malden   John McWilliams, MG

HENDERSON, Nathaniel   01-22-1846   Othinel Parker
  Sarah Ann Avery *   J.G. Wallace

HENDERSON, Robert P.   11-27-1878   F.J. Powell
  L.C. Packer   (At home of J.B. Packer)   T.J. Abernathy,Clergy

HENDERSON, Samuel E.   12-27-1865   T.H. Maulden
  Nancy Mosley   (At the bride's fathers)   George L. Lee, MG

HENDERSON, Wiley   04-30-1873   J.W. Grant
  Vina Bizzell *   (At W. Langham's)   F.C. Johnson, Min.

HENDERSON, Williamson   10-27-1853   R. Hixon
  Georgiana Pridgeon   R.D. Thompson, JP

HENDERSON, Willis R.   01-30-1851   Robert O. Maldin
  Mary Jane Rall   (At William James Henderson's) J.G. Wallace, JP

HENDERSON, Z.G.   12-21-1859   R.R. Mosley
  Martha H. Stearns   W.C. Morrow, MG

HENDRIX, Aaron Mary Hixon	08-23-1839	Daniel McCall John J. Roach
HENDRIX, Eli Margaret Hendrix *	08-19-1840	James Bynum, JP Levi Dailey
HENDRIX, Enoch Sarah A. Sampey	01-07-1841	Daniel McColl Dixon Hestle, JP
HENDRIX, E.P. Margaret Hendrix *	08-18-1840	Levi Dailey James Bynam, JP
HENDRIX, Henry H. Catharine Sampy	07-15-1849	Eli E. Hendrix R.O. Connell, JP
HENDRIX, James Chloe M. Walker	01-05-1854	R.O. Connell W.H. Aldridge, JP
HENDRIX, Jesse B. Martha P. Wiggins	12-05-1872 (At the bride's fathers)	J.M. Newberry S.A. Keley, JP
HENDRIX, Noah B. Nancy D. Corley	11-22-1871 (At Isah Corley's)	G.W. Salter John W. Lockin, Judge
HENDRIX, Joseph Mrs. Eliza Galloway	07-09-1863 (At Robert D. Thompson's on Thursday evening)	C.R. Broughton Robert D. Thompson
HENDRIX, L.A. Missouri E. Porter *	11-09-1865	J.B. Hendrix M. McCorvey
HENDRIX, Martin L. Mary E. Morris	10-19-1854 (At home of Daniel Morris)	Daniel J. Morris Robert D. Thompson
HENDRIX, P.A. Susan Roberts	08-18-1865 (At Daniel Roberts')	John DeLoach M.M. Graham, MG
HENDRIX, William J. Mary A. Walker	01-18-1871 (At home of B.N. Walker)	C.W. Massengill J.M. Woods, MG
HENRY, Osborne Elizabeth Sessions	01-31-1868	S.M.C. Middleton ————
HENSON, William Maria Heathcock	02-02-1839	Thomas L. Heathcock ————
HERRIN, Soloman Samantha E. Guthery	05-20-1874 (At Turnbull)	———— T.M. Riley, JP
HENNINGTON, Charles A. Mary C. Andress	01-20-1869	M. Frederick J.L. Hoyt, JP
HENSIN, T.J. Ellen Boutwell *	12-20-1876 (At Mrs. Emma Henson's)	C. Watson E. Cline, MG
HEOLT, A.J. Louise Lowery *	03-21-1880 (At Mrs. Betsey Lowery's)	G.W. Bodiford Burney Sawyer, MG
HERRINGTON, John S. Sallie E. Stallworth	12-06-1871 (At S.A. Barnett's)	J.J. Stallworth W.G. Curry, MG
HESTER, Ephriam Mary J. Stanton	12-23-1841	John Stanton, Sr. Daniel Fore, JP
HESTLE, L.D. Mattie E. Riley *	02-05-1874 (At G.W. Riley's)	T.J. Robbins C.W. Hare, MG
HESTLE, William P. Mary E. Mullender	11-04-1847	E.G. Betts J.C. Wallace, JP

HESTLE, W.M.	11-04-1847	E.G. Betts
Cornelia H. Lindsey		J.C. Wallace, JP
HETHERINGTON, Franklin K.	02-04-1869	C.R. Broughton
S.E. Andress	(At home of Betsy Andress	John McWilliams, MG
HETHERINGTON, W.G.	01-15-1868	C.R. Broughton
S.M. Broughton	(At C.R. Broughton's)	P.J. Cree, OMG
HEYDEN, B.T.	12-04-1878	Elihu Mixin
Margaret E. Hardee	(At Joel Hardee's)	J.S. Gray, LP
HEYDEN, Royall B.	10-07-1833	
Nancy Ivey	("Burned")	Robert Warren
HIBBARD, B.L.	05-01-1873	J.F. Fore
Sallie B.V. Leslie	(At Hon. John W. Leslie's)	W.G. Curry, MG
HICKS, Delaney L.	01-08-1843	Allen T. Gordy
Elizabeth Forehand *		Evant Andress, JP
HICKS, Enoch	07-18-1855	Charles Brooks
Frances Brooks		William Longmire, JP
HICKS, Jesse	08-15-1857	J.R. Youngblood
Apenath Grimes		W.M. Longmire
HICKS, John W.	08-20-1866	W.H. Hicks
Amanda Grimes *		
HICKS, Isiam	06-27-1869	W.H. Hicks
Susan Chappell	(At James Chappell's)	Hugh McKenzie, JP
HICKS, Lewis C.	06-04-1845	
Ellen Douglas		William A. Tarlton
HICKS, Moses	12-18-1845	Daniel Welch
Precilla Welch *		Garrett Longmire, Jr.
HICKS, W.H.	08-18-1867	P.H. Davis
Amanda Mims		E.S. Smith, MG
HICKS, Willis	10-20-1854	Josiah Hicks
Sarah J. Mims	(At Jesse & Willis Hicks')	William Longmire, JP
HICKS, Willis	06-25-1856	Drury Fort
M.E. Riley *	(At home of E. Riley)	S.A. Farmer
HIGDEN, C.R.	11-14-1878	J.F. Mixon
Edna Robinson *	(At home of Mr. L. Robinson)	J.T. Bayles, MG
HIGDON, William F.	03-10-1862	E. Whatley
Mary Taylor *	(At Edward Taylor's on Thursday evening)	R.D. Thompson, JP
HIGHTOWER, James A., Jr.	09-12-1866	James A. Hightower, Sr.
Mary J. House		B.A. Sigler, JP
HIGHTOWER, James A.	06-14-1838	E.L. Moore
Nancy Umphrey		J.H. Schrobel
HILBUN, James	01-10-1852	David F. Cothand
Elizabeth Whatley		N.A. Agee
HILBUN, Thomas	12-23-1879	
Irena Jay	(At Watson's Hotel)	W.C. Sowell, Judge
HILLBURN, William	07-03-1855	Joseph C. Lambert
Susan E. Beard		

```
HINES, Hudson                           06-13-1860      John DeLoach
   Catherine D. Grimes                                     T.M. Lynch, Pastor

HINES, Joseph H.                        06-11-1865      G.W. Northcut
   Mary E. Northcut      (At Mrs. Northcutt's)             D.S. McDonald

HINES, Joseph Steele                    10-15-1873      G.W. Butler
   Hattie S. Savage      (Bride was from Claiborne)   William Brittan,
                                                          Rector of St. Mary's

HINSLEY, Calvin                         01-21-1840      James Hicks
   Sarah Hammond                                          Thomas Mercer Riley, JP

HINSON, William                         12-11-1860      Andrew Parker
   Matilda Parker        (At office of the Judge)       M. McCorvey, Judge

HIRSHFELD, Philip                       04-27-1853      L. Mayers
   Amelia Metzger                                         N.A. Agee

HIXON, Allen                            10-01-1840      Nathan Wiggins
   Susan Newberry *                                       C. Thames, MG

HIXON, C.R.                             12-16-1874      D.W. Fore
   F.E. Fore *           (At home of Mr. H.A. Fore)    John McWilliams, MG

HIXON, George                           09-03-1846      Daniel Helms
   Amanda M. Grace *                                      J. McWilliams

HIXON, John                             01-08-1835      Johnathan Thames
   Sarah Thames *                                         James Newberry

HIXON, Richard                          02-06-1851      Nathaniel Henderson
   Margaret A. Henderson *                                John McWilliams, MG

HIXON, Robert                           05-10-1849      James E. Henderson
   Mary J. McDonald *                                     C. Thames, MG

HIXON, William E.                       10-07-1874      J.M. Heatherington
   Nancy Broughton       (At Capt. C.R. Broughton's) John W. Leslie, Judge

HOBBS, Thomas J.                        09-26-1880      J.D. Weatherford
   Eugenia E. Sizemore   (At Mrs. Sizemore's)           J.D. Weatherford

HOBBS, William                          04-30-1880      P.R. Brown
   Lucy A. Brown         (At home of Pad Brown)         S.R. Kelly, JP

HOBDY, John H.                          05-21-1876      J.S. Dickinson
   Annie Bragg           (At Mrs. J. Stallworth's)      L.W. Duke

HOLCOMB, Thomas J.                      07-19-1847      John DeLoach
   Susan Jones                                           _____

HOLDER, William                         10-25-1836      Alex Helms
   Elizabeth Lindsey                                     _____

HOLLAND, Lewis R.                       04-14-1836      A.J. Taylor
   Mrs. Emily A. Caulfield                               J.H. Schroebel, MG

HOLLEY, James D.                        01-18-1849      A.S. Burgess
   Susan C. Etheridge *                                  B.A. Sigler

HOLLEY, John L.                         04-17-1870      W.C. Thompson
   Ella Duke             (At home of W.J. Duke)         L.W. Duke

HOLLEY, Richard                         07-29-1850      John Norwood
   Julia Ann Myers *                                     James M. Davison, JP

HOLLINGER, Adam                         10-23-1861      Richard Roley
   Virginia McGee        (On or near the dividing    Robert D. Thompson, JP
                          line between Conecuh, Baldwin, & Monroe Co.)
```

```
HOLLINGER, Adam                    01-18-1870    John Robin
  Patsey Taylor      (At Thomas Dees')             A.J. Lambert

HOLLINGER, Alexander               12-26-1850    W.R. Agee
  Caroline Gaston                                  N.A. Agee, JP

HOLLINGER, Jefferson               11-11-1852    James W. O'Neil
  Mrs. Elizabeth Sizemore                          N.A. Agee

HOLLINGER, William                 08-28-1861    Franklin Taylor
  Josephine Sizemore *             (At office)     M. McCorvey, Judge

HOLLINGSWORTH, Thomas A.           01-11-1843    E.H. Crosby
  Pheaney Caroline Lindsey                         J.G. Wallace

HOLLOWAY, James A.                 05-12-1850    Malachi Nettles
  Martha A. Nettles *                              Elias Brown

HOLLOWAY, John                     10-12-1842    Isaac Falkenberry
  Eliza Nettles *                                  John McWilliams

HOLLOWAY, Mattie                   01-16-1877    S.H. Nettles
  Annie Rikard       (At home of Sarah Rikard)    Joseph T. Dailey, GM

HOLLOWAY, Templeton M.             12-06-1842    Duncan McKenzie, Jr.
  Eliza Grimes *                                   William Holloway, JP

HOLLOWAY, T.M.                     01-20-1856    J. DeLoach
  Caroline Cunningham                              T.E. Frazier, JP

HOLLOWAY, W.C.                     09-11-1879    J.C. Waymen
  G.A. Waymen        (At home of W.C. Waymen)     Joel Hardee, JP

HOLLOWAY, William                  09-15-1835    Wingate P. Rumbley
  Milly A. Nutt                                    Thomas Wilson

HOLLOWAY, William                  01-05-1858    James O'Neil
  Martha Bonds                                     Joel Hardee, JP

HOLLY, Edwin                       01-02-1841    James M. Graham
  Mary Boyles                                      T. Burpe

HOLLY, John                        05-29-1837    Miller Davidson
  Martha Lee                                       _____

HOLLY, John                        11-19-1868    R. Reaves
  R.J. Wiggins       (At home of Robert Wiggins)  J.T. Bayles, MG

HOLLY, Malachia                    01-25-1852    Henry Middleton
  Penny Middleton *                                Joel Hardee, JP

HOLLY, W.H.                        02-27-1879    L.R. Wiggins
  T.Z. Broughton     (At J.W. Broughton's)        W.C. Sowell, Judge

HOLMAN, George                     10-26-1840    W. Holman
  Rebecca Frye                                     C. Thames, MG

HOLMAN, M.A.                       12-25-1861    G.W. Salter
  Mary C. Davison    (At J.L. Davison's)          R.O. Connell, JP

HOLMES, John C.                    12-01-1864    B. Bultard
  Catherine Ballard *                              Francis Walker, MG

HOLOMAN, Ashley                    12-16-1874
  Cora J. McCants    (At the bride's fathers)     L.W. Duke, MG

HOLT, A.T.                         01-12-1860    Robert Owens
  Alvira S. Thompson * (At Mrs. Anna Thompson's    Robert D. Thompson
                       on Thursday evening)
```

HOLT, J.B.   05-22-1879   _____
  Adella Killam   (At home of Mrs. Killam)   Burney Sawyer, MG

HOLT, R.D.   12-11-1872
  Saleanear Lowry *   (At Mrs. Lowery's)   W.W. Spence, MG

HOOKS, Charles   10-21-1837   William Autry
  Mary A. Carter   Asa Parker

HOOKS, David J.   01-01-1839   William Autry
  Sarah A. Carter   D. Hestle, JP

HOPKINS, W.G.   01-30-1878   W.T. Gully, J.K. Gully
  M.J. Kimbel   (At J. Holloway's)   & Asa Parker
                                                         John McWilliams, MG

HOUSE, James   12-04-1837   A. Taylor
  Caroline Hoyle   _____

HOUSEFORD, Claiborne   10-12-1871   S.H. Dailey
  Ann E. Ferth   (At home of A.J. Lambert)   A.J. Lambert

HOUSS, W.A.   07-16-1870   W.R. Hollinger
  Martha E. Lambert   (At the church)   A.J. Lambert, MG

HOWARD, Thomas   01-15-1805   John H. Moore
  Mary L. Moore *   N. Goodwin, MG

HOWARD, William B.   12-01-1840   James W. Parsons
  Elizabeth O. Gaillard *   Alex Travis, Minister

HOYT, John L.   08-23-1863   B.F. Stallworth
  Fannie E. Hurry   _____

HUDGINS, Thomas   06-30-1868   H.M. Graham
  Sallie Pruett *   (At M.H. Pruett's)   Hugh McKenzie, JP

HUDSON, A.S.   10-03-1880   Burell Purvis
  Lucy Ward   (At Pleasant Hill Church)   W.A. Locke, MG

HUDSON, Charles H.   11-20-1854   James Henderson
  Eveline Tucker   John McWilliams, MG

HUDSON, Hilany   03-27-1879   J.B. McMillan
  M.A.F. Ryland   (At the bride's mothers)   W.C. Sowell, Judge

HUGANUSS, Isaac   01-28-1840   Jesse Ward
  Sarah Simpkins   M.D. Dickson, JP

HUGGINS, Evan   01-19-1834
  Henrietta Kennedy   G.D. Williams, GM

HUGGINS, James B.   08-23-1858   J.W. Perrin
  Mary Jane Nettles *   _____

HUGGINS, John S.   10-16-1859   J.G. Harper
  Mary C. Harper *   W.W. Simmons

HUGH, Robert J. (Pugh?)   02-15-1834   Joel Hardee
  Elizabeth A. Riley *   _____

HUGHES, A.F.   09-25-1879
  Eliza Driver   John T. Chavers, MG

HUGHES, J.A.   03-08-1876   J.E. Creighton
  Elizabeth Gilmore   (At J.E. Lunshaw's)   Joel Hardee, NP

HULL, William A.   01-17-1839   Washington E. Hull
  Elizabeth A. English   J.H. Schroebel, MG

56

HUMPHREY, W.J.   01-03-1856   E.W. Searcy
   Azline Flemons *   R.D. Thompson, JP

HUNT, Charles B.   12-25-1856   John DeLoach
   E.A. Hunt   (At home of Mrs. M.J. Colburn) William C. Smith, MG

HUNT, Lovlas   12-22-1878
   Josephine Tatum   (At Owen Tatum's)   S.L. Ellis, JP

HUNZER, James   02-19-1860   L. Bowden
   Susan Eliza Lee *   Elias Brown, MG

HURRY, John W.   12-06-1852   J.M. Gafford
   Margaret D. McCants *   _____

HURRY, Richard H.   11-20-1851   William S. Millender
   Margaret McWilliams *   N. Gordan, MG

HURRY, William D.   01-20-1848   Daniel Fore
   Lucienda Fore   J. McWilliams, MG

HURST, William W.   11-11-1844   James McColl
   _____ *   _____

HURTEL, Alphonse   12-06-1855   S.S. Gaillard
   Catherine M. Gaillard *   H.A. Smith, MG

HUSHFIELD, Soloman   04-22-1851   Lazarus Mayer
   Hannah Sanders   J.T. Rivers

HUSSEY, Andrew J.   12-23-1834   William B. Sanders
   Mary Ann Rachels *   Thomas Wilson

HUTTO, C.L.   01-09-1879   R.T. Chunn
   Ida Riley   (At home of T.M. Riley, Sr.) B.J. Skinner

HUTTO, C.L.   11-25-1869   J.A. Grace
   Laura Coker   (At the bride's mothers)   Thomas Armstrong, MG

HYBERT, Henry H.   02-28-1872   J.M. Davison
   J.C. Posey *   (At Monroeville)   James Watson

HYBERT, W.L.   03-26-1872   J. DeLoach
   Foscillina Wheeler *   (At J. Wheeler's)   D.J. Wright

IKNER, Jacob S.   09-22-1841   Duncan McColl
   Sarah Middleton *   J.D. Foster

IKNER, Joel C.   03-23-1875   J.F. Fore
   Mary L. Lloyd *   (At Mrs. Lloyd's)   J.M. Rothwell, NP

IKNER, J.S.   02-12-1880   Chesley Ikner
   Mary Morris *   (At home of Mrs. Morris)   R.M. Tuberville, JP

IKNER, W.W.   12-23-1873   Jacob S. Ikner
   Juranda A. Whisenhant * (At W.A. Whisenhanet's)   J.G. Bradley, JP

IVEY, James   10-31-1833
   Elizabeth A. Stanton   ("Burned")   John McWilliams, VDM

IVEY, John M.   02-12-1840   James Ivey
   Nancy Stanley *   Thomas Wilson, JP

IVEY, Richard   05-01-1861   Robert D. Thompson
   Martha J. Reynolds   (At Thomas Reynolds' Robert D. Thompson
                         on Wednesday evening)

IVEY, Robert   12-16-1873   Neil McMillian
   Americas Brantley *   (At Oran Brantley's)   Emannuel Cline, MG

IVEY, William Elizabeth Dailey *	09-01-1836	Jacob Dailey Joshua Peavy
IVY, James A. Sarah Ray	05-05-1845	W.W. McColl
IVY, William Mary E. Justice	03-18-1868	Samuel Cornwell Neil Gillis, MG
JACKSON, Abner Isabella Baggett	07-09-1842	D.R. Rankin
JACKSON, James A. Amanda A. Knowles	04-10-1852	Dave Knowles R.O. Connell, JP
JACKSON, James A. Mary J.E. Gordy	08-21-1859	Jackson McKinley William N. Peavy, Min.
JACKSON, William J. Melinda Stringer	11-27-1850	Stephen Gibson W.M. Longmire, JP
JACOBS, Wesley Missouri Davison *	11-11-1863 (Near Monroeville at Mrs. Davison's)	John DeLoach M. McCorvey
JAOBY, Jacob Elizabeth Maynor	03-04-1844	Jones Mayner
JAMES, Alagrande Ann Peoples	06-14-1843	John W. Foster
JAMES, Burwell B. Sarah J. Humphrey	08-16-1853	Joseph W. Humphrey James J. Barclay, JP
JAMES, C.E. Ida L. Lambert *	12-16-1880 (At A.J. Lambert's)	T.G. Hestle A.J. Lambert, MG
JAMES, George E.V. Ray	12-28-1871 (Near Claiborne)	William J. Newberry John Thames, JP
JAMES, Henry B. Caroline H. Meigs	06-26-1843	William B. Crook E.O. Martin, MG
JAMES, Jay Elizabeth A. Stainton	10-31-1833	
JAMES, John Mahala McClure	01-20-1834	James McClure
JAMES, Joseph J. Leucinda Bemus	03-26-1835	John J. Eubanks Thomas S. Witherspoon
JAMES, Martin Mrs. Polly Cliver	02-21-1834	Robert G. James
JAMES, Peter Lenora Rawles *	10-11-1871 (At her mother's)	George James W.W. Simmons, NP
JAMES, Peter G. Jane McLeure *	12-29-1834	James McLeure
JAMES, Robert A. Annie E. Fountain *	11-12-1874 (At the McNeil's)	W.S. Wiggins H.H. Hybert, JP
JAMES, Samuel Harriet E. Williamson *	11-23-1865 (At John Williamson's)	S.D. Williamson N.W. Sugden, JP
JAY, David A. Mary A. Curley	12-23-1880 (At Claiborne)	W.R. Jay N.C. Thames

JAY, Jackson   03-05-1846   Johnathan Aldridge
  Eliza Curry   J.G. Holcomb, JP

JAY, John   09-14-1858   James F. Hale
  Martha Hale   (At the home of Jesse Hayle) R.D. Thompson, JP

JAY, John S.   12-31-1876   Jacob Dunn
  Mary Everage   (At home of J. Dunn)   J.D. Weatherford, JP

JENKINS, John   12-28-1843   Emanuel Cline
  Martha McMillan   James Jenkins, EMP

JENKINS, Thomas   09-04-1845
  Marcia Bradley   ‾J.G.‾ Travis

JENKINS, William H.   11-24-1846   W.P. Leslie
  Sarah T. Colburn *   William R. McRee

JENNINGS, James S.   01-07-1864   E. Mills
  A.E. Fonda   (At home of Mrs. Fonda)   Issac H. Salter, MG

JERNIGAN, James S.   06-15-1866   A.J. Sowell
  Maggie Lee   (At Mrs. Nancy Sowell's) M. McCorvey, Judge

JOHNS, Jacob S.   02-07-1848   James Snowden
  Elizabeth Snowden *   ‾‾‾‾‾‾‾

JOHNSON, A.H.   09-25-1867   J.F. McCorvey
  S.A. Foster   (At home of Arthur Foster)   J.H. Salter, MG

JOHNSON, Alford   12-14-1873   John Hardee
  Marintha Beadingfield (At Jarett Johnson's)   John Hardee, NP & JP

JOHNSON, B.F.   07-23-1863   W.J. Humphrey
  Mary Fleming *   (At Robert D. Thompson's) Robert D. Thompson

JOHNSON, Charles L.   07-13-1870   G.G. Johnson
  Fannie B. Foster   (At Mr. A. Foster's)   Thomas H. Armstrong

JOHNSON, H.C.   11-08-1872   A.H. Johnson
  Mary F. Richie   (At the bride's father's)   J.W. Duke, MG

JOHNSON, Henry R.   09-13-1838   H.H. Daily
  Milly Dailey   Thomas Wilson, JP

JOHNSON, James   05-15-1859   John DeLoach
  Mrs. Mary E.D. Devall   Jason Staples, JP

JOHNSON, James M.   10-14-1854   William Ousley
  Laura A. Black *   ‾‾‾‾‾‾‾

JOHNSON, James M.   10-16-1874   J. Bozeman
  Amanda M. Ledkins (At the bride's fathers)   H.H. Hybert, NP

JOHNSON, John G.   10-17-1842   John B. Powell
  Ann Barrett *   Joshua Peavy

JOHNSON, John L.   09-10-1835   John W. Leslie
  Margaret E. Bradley *   Thomas Wilson, JP

JOHNSON, John P.   10-26-1865   James M. Johnson
  Sarah Flemming   M. McCorvey, Judge

JOHNSON, J.S.   11-25-1855   W. English
  Julia Bender *   A.J. Lambert

JOHNSON, Lewis   09-04-1844   Robert Johnson
  Beatrice C. Session   N. Goodwin, MG

JOHNSON, N.T. Ann Grimes *	08-17-1871 (At her mother's house)	John Johnson W.W. Simmons, NP
JOHNSON, Peter L. Mrs Caroline E. Murray	11-04-1852	John P. Deer ————
JOHNSON, William Sarah Hausey	08-21-1844	J.G. Butler ————
JOHNSON, William Mrs Leanor Hamilton	04-04-1853	Thomas Hawkins ————
JOHNSON, William R.W. Frances Emma Ledkins*	11-04-1875 (At J.W. Ledkins')	W.S. Wiggins & J.B. McWilliams; J.M. Rothwell NP
JOHNSON, William W. Mary M. Sather	10-3-1872 (At bride's home)	J.R. Betts J.B.F. Watts, Min.
JOHNSON, W.H. Lucinda Wall	02-18-1880 (Never Executed)	T.S. Wiggins ————
JOHNSON, Zachariah L. Frances Andress	10-31-1878 (At Harriet Crosby's)	I. Talbert, NP
JOHNSTON, Bethel R. Mary Matilda Ross *	03-25-1858 Near Claiborne)	John Ross J.J. Barclay, JP
JOHNSTON, Hamilton Susan C. Hawthorne	09-05-1860	Thomas Gibson A.D. Anderson, JP
JOINER, E.M. Susan R. Griffin *	05-09-1869	J.A. Simmons J.B. Colley, JP
JONES, Benjamin J. Christian Cobb	02-13-1845	W.W. McColl Mr. Fowler, JP
JONES, Berthel Elanor Simpkins *	11-28-1833	Samuel McQueen Daniel P. ?
JONES, B.M.M. N.E. Haddox	08-05-1844	S. Haddox James A. Rall, JP
JONES, Charles Hettie Northcutt	06-03-1877 (At J.L. Skipper's)	J.L. Skipper, MG
JONES, Edwin S. Hannah Mallett	07-31-1839	George J. Daniel James P. Wilson, JP
JONES, F.M. Mrs. M.E. Avery	10-03-1867 (At A.J. Gordon's)	J.F. McCorvey A.J. Lambert, MG
JONES, Henry C. Sarah Davis *	05-16-1834	Soloman W. Portis Thomas Wilson, JP
JONES, Hugh G. Mary Ann Finklea *	09-21-1848	Enos Finklea P.J.G. Holcombe, JP
JONES, Hugh G. Margaret Odom	06-13-1871 (At Mrs. M.D. Odom's)	E.R. Cannon P.J. Cree, MG
JONES, Hugh G. Sarah Eliza Dailey	08-25-1857	Thomas Jones ————
JONES, John Elizabeth Miller	06-21-1847	E.T. Broughton M.D. Dixon
JONES, John C. Elizabeth Crosby	01-13-1849 (Not executed)	M. Dailey ————

JONES, Nelson   12-03-1860   William T. Nettles
    Sarah S. Curry *   _____

JONES, Samuel F.   09-11-1878   _____
    Martha Holley   (At Mrs. Penny Holly's)   Joel Hardee, NP

JONES, Soloman   05-12-1839   William Ellison
    Mary Cobb   T. Burrps

JONES, Stephen   06-15-1853   Samuel Jones
    Lucinda Ward   T.E. Feagin, JP

JONES, Thomas   12-12-1833   Joseph O. Rawls
    Martha A.E. Burton *   _____

JONES, Thomas   10-07-1851   T.G. Holcomb
    Elizabeth A. Lacy *   Joel Hardee, JP

JONES, W.B.   12-20-1867   B.H. Harrison
    Laura T. Powell *   (At Mrs. Powell's)   A.J. Lambert, MG

JONES, William R.M.   04-17-1849   John Robinson
    Mary Avery   G.W. Foster, JP

JONES, W.W.   11-29-1857   H.T. Fountain
    Leah Louisa Collins (On Sunday at Mrs. Collins') M. McCorvey, Judge

JORDAN, David S.   12-24-1846   David Grose
    Elizabeth M.D. Pitman *   Josiah (Torn out)

JORDAN, J.B.   01-12-1865   William Jordan
    Julia Devane   J.F. Burson, MG

JORDAN, Samuel C.   12-20-1855   L.M. McKinsey
    Elizabeth A. Hines *   Hugh McKenzie

JORDAN, Isaac   11-01-1838   William Gordon
    Elmira Powell   J.H. Schroebel, MG

JURDON, Henry   02-23-1859   Caswell Garrett
    Mary M. Garrett   T.E. Feagin

JUSTICE, John H.   04-13-1848   William Talle
    Mary A. Crook *   T. Burps

KATES, Hiram   12-13-1860   John Ward
    Martha Ward *   T.E. Feagin, JP

KEARLEY, C.S.   06-13-1875   J. DeLoach
    Ellen C. Bethea   W.G. Middleton, JP

KEARLEY, John   01-26-1876   John DeLoach
    Tabitha Faulkenberry (At Mr. Faulkenberry's) L.W. Duke

KEARLEY, J.S.   12-24-1879   T.L. Sowell
    Geneva Rikard   (At Frank Rikard's)   W. Rothwell, JP

KEARLEY, Thomas J.   10-11-1865   James A. Fore
    Louisa Powell *   (At home of Mrs. E.A. Powell) John McWilliams, MG

KEARLY, James   01-03-1848   Joseph Snell
    Ellen Rikard *   J. McWilliams

KEARLY, John Mary Powell	06-15-1852	C.S. Sessions W.W. Simmons, JP
KEARLY, John Elizabeth Powell	11-28-1867 (At Mrs. E. Powell's)	J.A. Simmons John McWilliams, MG
KEARLY, Joshua Amanda Rikard	12-28-1848	James Kearly J.G. Wallace, JP
KEARLY, W.H. A.E. Courtney *	12-18-1867	Thomas Kearly ————
KEARNEY, John Susan Falkenberry *	02-26-1839	Colden Falkenberry T. Bryan, JP
KELLER, Henry Elizabeth Gallaspy	06-17-1860	J. McWilliams Robert R. Roberts, LP
KELLEY, John S. Mary Holder	02-07-1865	J.M. Cook ————
KELLEY, N.D. Lucy Ann Hendrick	05-19-1869	T.D. Hendricks W.W. Simmons, JP & NP
KELLY, Henry Mary E. Gallaspy *	08-03-1854	James Gillispie D.W. Kelly, JP
KELLY, Henry A. Mary M. Kelly *	12-24-1857 (At Samuel Kelly's)	Neil Salter M. McCorvey, Judge
KELLY, J.A. Nancy M. Owens	05-25-1865	S. Kelly J.W. Posey, JP
KELLY, Rollin H. Mary E. Herbert	04-28-1864 (At Monroe Springs)	John DeLoach John Miller, MG
KELLY, Samuel R. Annie E. Owens	11-16-1865	B.B. Kimbell M. M. Graham, MG
KEMP, W.B. Frances Davison *	10-12-1859 (At H.B. Davison's)	T.H. Coker M. McCorvey, Judge
KEMP, William B. Mary F. Phillips *	09-24-1856	M.B. East ————
KENDRICK, Robert Mrs. Martha R. Dean	06-08-1850	M.F. Fuller ᐟM.H. Aldnedy, JP
KENNEDY, Bartlett M. Susan Sawyer *	01-04-1849	McDuff Mann D. Hestle, JP
KENNEDY, B.B. Sarah A. Chance	04-26-1871 (At home of B.B. Kennedy)	W.H. McMillan E. Cline
KENNEDY, James B. Lydia V. Fountain *	01-19-1860 (At Mrs. Jane Fountain's)	John DeLoach John McWilliams, MG
KENNEDY, Robert S. Elizabeth G. Parker *	01-10-1855	A. Parker H.A. Smith, MG
KENNEDY, R.P. Minnie Watson	12-26-1880 (At Pineville)	D.L. Neville John Burns, Jr.
KENNEDY, Stephen Mary Ann Caldwell	02-18-1839	George Coker Daniel Fore, JP
KENNEDY, Sterling M. Melinda A. Marion *	09-24-1835	Theodore P. Marion Asa Parker, JP

KERLEY, J.M. Monty E. Roley *	12-25-1870 (At her father's)	John Roley W.W. Simmons, NP
KERNEY, Thomas Martha A. Medlock	02-15-1835	Moses Medlock Edwin Cater, JP
KERR, E.G. Mary Stifflimire *	10-08-1856	M. McMillan John J. Longmire, JP
KERSEY, J.H. Mrs. F.J. Stacey	03-02-1871 (At Mrs. Nancy Riley's)	John DeLoach Hugh McKenzie
KIDD, Andrew J. Cornelia Brannan	07-17-1837	James McDonald John J. Rouch, JC
KIDD, Harvey L. Carolina Fort	05-29-1838	David Cannon John L. Roach, Judge
KILE, Daniel W. Mary Bradford	02-21-1875 (At James Qualls')	A.J. Qualls J.D. Weatherford
KILE, N.W. Elizabeth Henderson	08-12-1847 (At Mt. Pleasant)	P. Stryder James A. Clemons
KILLAM, Henry E. Mollie A. Campbell	10-12-1865	William A. Shomo W.N. Peavy, MG
KIMBELL, B.B. Mrs. E.A. Edwards	05-12-1863	William B. Crook Frances Watt, JP
KIMBERT, John C, Elizabeth J. Nettles *	01-06-1848	C.R. Broughton John McWilliams, MG
KING, A. E.A. Wiggins	01-23-1868 (At home of Robert Wiggins')	J.F. McCorvey M.M. Graham, MG
KING, Benjamin Nisa Brown *	01-21-1836	John King Elias Brown
KING, James R. Mary Ann McWilliams	07-21-1858 (At W.L. McWilliams')	William M. Atkinson ————
KING, Stephen R. Mrs. Mary O. English	12-18-1838	John J. Roach Elias Brown
KING, William H. Sarah A, Branson	03-30-1852	James A. Mitchell Samuel McClure, JP
KIRKSEY, Isaac M. Emily C. Stanford	12-31-1857 (At D.N. Stanford's)	D.N. Stanford R.O. Connell, JP
KIRKSEY, N.J. Mary J. Bartlett	11-09-1860	James T. Rasco W.W. Simmons, JP
KNOWLES, J.H. Isabell Hendrix	02-18-1872	Isreal Garner Samuel R. Kelly, JP
KNOWLS, J.B. June Kearly	09-24-1878	J.H. Duke ————
KYLE, John W. Matilda Tarlton *	02-19-1835	T.P. Marion J.H. Stroebel, MG
KYLE, Webster Emeline Murphy	01-29-1878 (At office)	T.H. Dees W.C. Sowell, Judge
LACEY, Edward D. Sarah F. Colley *	04-04-1865	S.H. Dailey ————

LADD, James A.	12-31-1872	John DeLoach
Mary Jane Norwood	(At J.F. Bayles)	J.T. Bayles, MG
LADD, John W.	02-09-1871	J.H. Bayles
E.J. Bayles	(At J.T. Bayles')	W.A. Locke, MG
LAMBERT, A.C.	12-08-1875	W.J. Newby
Lucy Newby *	(At Mrs. E. Newbey's)	A.J. Lambert, MG
LAMBERT, Andrew	07-22-1842	Benjamin M. Dumas
Martha June Dumas *		————
LAMBERT, Andrew	10-10-1878	Thomas S. Wiggins
Elizabeth Cross	(At home of Mrs. Brown)	Burney Sawyer, MG
LAMBERT, Andrew J.	07-28-1857	Abner Dees
Josephine H. Shamfield *		————
LAMBERT, Barry	03-15-1846	Perry Lambert
Martha Adcock *		————
LAMBERT, Berry B.	08-28-1857	Daniel McColl
Martha Lambert		Jason Stap___
LAMBERT, Calvin W.	06-30-1863	William Emmons
Sarah A. Thompson	(At Robert D. Thompson, Jr.	Robert D. Thompson
	on Tuesday evening)	
LAMBERT, Carwell	03-25-1856	H.M. Lambert
Mary C. Jackson		A.J. Lambert
LAMBERT, C.W.	12-09-1868	T.J. Duke
Ella Solomon		T.J. Duke
LAMBERT, Elias	01-02-1860	J. DeLoach
Elizabeth J. Newberry		James Daniel, MG
LAMBERT, Elias Jr.	12-03-1859	J.J. Lowremoure
Sarah A.L. Lowremoure *		S. Hilburn, EL
LAMBERT, Ely	04-03-1867	H.M. Lambert
Mary Rogers *		E. Andress, JP
LAMBERT, Harvey M.	10-06-1846	William Thompson
Mary A. Miles *		————
LAMBERT, James	12-21-1843	Andrew Ormand
Nancy Hannah		William H. Agee
LAMBERT, James Jr.	12-16-1858	John DeLoach
Amanda Demarias Higdon *	(At Mr. Higdon's)	R.D. Thompson
LAMBERT, Jasper D.	12-19-1861	Edward Davis
Cenieth C. Davis *	(At E. Davis')	R.D. Thompson, JP
LAMBERT, John	04-08-1848	William R. Slaughter
Mrs. Susan Vincent *		G.D. Foster, JP
LAMBERT, John D.	04-13-1848	William Thompson
Mary Ann Young		Elias Brown
LAMBERT, John D.	06-03-1879	————
Mary Wiggins	(Near Claiborne)	L.W. Duke
LAMBERT, John M.	12-02-1869	M. Edgar
Florence C. Godwin *		Francis Walker, MG
LAMBERT, Joseph C.	09-13-1851	Elias Lambert
Mary Ann Beard *		N. Alfred Agee

LAMBERT, Joseph C. Mary E. Carter	11-06-1856 (At W.E. Carter's)	A. Osmand James Daniel, MG
LAMBERT, Lawrence Lula Soloman	12-23-1875	W.B. Hayley Joel Hardee, JP
LAMBERT, Madison M.C. Rhoad	12-08-1864 (At H.M. Lambert's)	John M. Thompson Robert D. Thompson, JP
LAMBERT, Mathew Sarah Ann Miles	06-25-1840	William Dunn Elias Brown
LAMBERT, Mathew Martha Brown	02-10-1870 (At Mary E. Brown's)	J.M. Lambert J.M. Wood
LAMBERT, M.D. Harris Sawyer *	12-18-1867	J.D. Frye W.W. Spence, MG
LAMBERT, Perry Caroline V. Withers	12-05-1844	Daniel McColl T. Burrps
LAMBERT, R.A. M.V. Busey	04-22-1867	M.D. Lambert ————
LAMBERT, Robert J. Eliza N. Turner *	05-17-1856	Alex Lambert A.J. Lambert
LAMBERT, Seaburn Sarah Ann Lowry	03-01-1838	A. Reed J.H. Schrobel, MG
LAMBERT, Thomas Cassindra Bowden	01-09-1867	C.W. Lambert B.A. Sigler, JP
LAMBERT, William Martha Lambert *	09-06-1843	Berry B. Lambert R.F. Withers, JP
LAMBERT, William D. Mary J. Hayles *	11-24-1853 (At home of Jesse Hayles')	Robert Harris R.D. Thompson, JP
LAMBERT, William D. Lizzie Vick	01-25-1877 (At Lewis Slaughter's)	———— J.B. Anderson, Min.
LAMBERT, William F. Malisa Jane Deen	03-07-1878 (At home of S.L. Deen)	J.W. Deen J.D. Weatherford, JP
LAMBRECHT, Simeon Rebecca S. King	02-24-1874 (At Mrs. R.O. King's)	Samuel H. Slaughter A.C. Hundley, MG
LANE, John C. Adaline Lee	05-29-1838	David Dodwell J.H. Schroebel, MG
LANE, William Aldereara Criet	12-27-1868	J.M. Gallaspie E. Cline, MG
LANGHAM, Jackson Cynthia Middleton *	11-08-1860 (At Jepotha Middleton's)	M.V. Middleton T.E. Feagin, JP
LANGHAM, James T. Rebecca A. Wright	03-27-1866	Thomas & W.J. Langham ————
LANGHAM, J.J. L.G. Langhen	09-14-1879 (At home of Joel Hardee)	G.M. Langhen Joel Hardee, NP
LANGHAM, John M. Margaret Jones		Joel Hardee Joel Hardee, NP
LANGHAM, J.T. Rebecca A. Wright	12-25-1866	W.J. Langham J.F. Burson, MG

LANGHAM, J.W. M.F.Owens	12-19-1878 (At Phillip Owens')	John Owens Joel Hardee, NP
LANGHAM, William Louisa G. Bezzell *	01-12-1868 (At S.A. Solomons')	J.F. McCorvey James L. Eddins, MG
LaPEER (?), S.S. Ciney C. Lambert	04-12-1877 (At Ed Davis')	John DeLoach J.M. Rothwell, NP
LARSON, John Martha Holder	09-27-1865 (At home of Mrs. Holder)	B.F. Stallworth C.W. Hare, MG
LATHERWOOD, John W. Martha McCarty	09-08-1852	W.P. East William N. Peavy, OM
LAW, Luke C. Martha Pipkins	08-20-1842 (By affidavit)	N.S. Graham James McColl, Clerk
LAWLEY, Thomas Matilda Hicks	12-11-1837	C.H. Foster ————
LAZENBY, James E. Lizzie Green *	11-19-1873 (By consent of guardian, at bride's grandmother's)	M. Purifoy Rev. A.R. Purifoy
LEA, Thomas D. Catharine Rose	11-22-1843 (At Gov. St. Presbyterian Church in Mobile)	————
LEAMBERT, Alexander Sina Leoftin *	05-02-1835	James Davis J.H. Schroebel
LEAPORTE, John Hannah Smith	09-11-1834	———— T. Burps
LEAVEY, George W. Mrs. Amanda Booker	10-29-1848	Levi Foster G.D. Foster, JP
LEDBETTER, A.P. Mary Commander *	08-09-1865	H.C. Rickard ————
LEDBETTER, Seaborn Mary Ann Bradley *	07-02-1835	Charles L. Bradley ————
LEDKINS, James F. Rosie Johnson *	12-23-1875 (At John Johnson's)	George Johnson J.M. Rothwell
LEE, Daniel Eliza J. Wood	02-23-1858 (At John Marshall's of Turnbull)	A.B. Davis M.M. McCorvey, Judge
LEE, George L. Nancy C. Henderson	10-11-1838	Samuel Henderson J.H. Schroebel, MG
LEE, James C. Mrs. Jane Paulk	06-05-1870 (At Liberty Church)	John Blackwell Joel Hardee, JP
LEE, J.W.D. Martha A. Holloway	02-11-1872 (At the bride's mothers)	W.C. Thompson M.L. McWilliams
LEE, Robert A. Missouri Henderson *	04-25-1862	J.M. Henderson George Lee, MG
LEE, William Mary Vinson *	01-22-1840	Samuel R. Thompson N.W. Broughton, JP
LEE, William Caroline Thompson *	12-17-1844	Duncan McCall ————

LEE, William R. Amanda Grimes	03-15-1879 (At home of D. Grimes')	Robert Smilie, MG
LEEONARD, Alexander D. Mrs. Elizabeth McDonald	04-25-1835	Wright Mims
LeN___(?), W.B. Ida Gunn	05-16-1877 (At John Chavers')	J.L. Skipper
LENOIR, William B. Ella Neville	10-03-1866 (At M.M. Graham's)	D.J. McCants M.M. Graham, MG
LENOIR, W.R. Mrs. Mary Odom	12-27-1870 (At home of Mrs. Odom)	W.W. Simmons John McWilliams, MG
LEONARD, George P. Margaret E. McNeill	12-17-1861	J.W. Posey
LESLIE, John W. Sarah L. McCorvey	09-07-1875 (At M. McCorvey's)	James T. Packer W.G. Curry
LESLIE, William Mary Ann Agee *	04-22-1847	Andrew Henshaw William F. McRee
LETT, H.H. Goode King	12-22-1874 (At Bell's Landing)	F.L. Sewall B.F. Riley, MG
LETT, James E. Elizabeth B. Hunter *	01-11-1845	R.H. Puryear Alex Travis
LEVY, James D. Ann E. Ballard *	12-05-1854	John G. Johnson J.W. Leslie, JP
LEVY, Soloman Henrietta Metzgar	06-04-1846	L. Mayarc G.D. Foster, JP
LEWIS, Benjamin M. Elizabeth H. Perry *	12-25-1860 (At Hamilton Perry's)	Harvey Phillips W.W. Simmons
LEWIS, John W. Catharine E. Forbes	10-18-1838	W.B. Rikard D. Hestle
LEWIS, N.F. Catherine Hendrix	01-08-1867 (At office)	T.H. Maulden M. McCorvey, Judge
LEWIS, Philip H. Melinda Roberts	01-15-1839	Warren Aiken T.M. Riley
LEWIS, Thomas F. Martha A. Doggett	07-24-1867 (At Chapman Doggett's)	Walter Brantley W.G. Curry, MG
LEWIS, Thomas T. Hannah Manerva Bradley *	01-15-1857	H. Rankin, Jr. A.J. Brown, JP
LEYHOM, James M. Sarah ___	08-06-1874	C.M. Beasley T.M. Riley
LIDDELL, Henry R. Elizabeth J.P. Bruner *	12-02-1852	D.A. Bonner Evant Andress, JP
LIDDELL, Henry R. Isabella P. Bonner *	01-10-1855 (At Mrs. Bonner's)	R.J. Bonner R.D. Thompson, JP
LIDDELL, M.L. R.S. McCoy	12-20-1877 (At Buena Vista)	B.S. Hubbard L.W. Duke
LIDDELL, Robert F. Ann E. Ballard *	12-27-1852 (Returned not executed)	H.R. Liddell

LIDDELL, William
  Paulina J. Stevens *
	10-20-1853	J.J. Seigler
		  Elias Brown

LINAM, B.J.
  Sarah Childs
	10-14-1867	G.I. Childs
		  ————

LINAM, Elijah
  Elizabeth Coleman
	01-21-1846	William L. Rivers
		  ————

LINAM, William J.
  Mrs. Jane Shiers
	07-19-1855
	  (At John Mirick's)
		S.A. Farmer
		  S.A. Farmer

LINDIN, Elijah
  Sarah A. Coleman *
	05-13-1851	John T. Beard
		  ————

LINDSEY, Caleb
  Jane D. Williams *
	10-04-1838	John Marshall
		  Greer Malone, MG

LINDSEY, Caleb
  Almira Mason
	01-13-1842	James G. Butler
		  T. Bryan, JP

LINDSEY, James E.
  Ann Crawford *
	11-04-1847	William A. Haynes
		  J.G. Holcomb, JP

LINDSEY, James M.
  A.R. Draughon
	06-03-1849	John W. Lindsey
		  Alex Travis

LINDSEY, James M.
  Mary Ann Lliza Draughon *
	05-09-1843	William P. Leslie
		  J.H. Schrobel, MG

LINDSEY, J.M.
  Ruth J. Watkins
	12-01-1874
	  (At J.M. Lindsey's)
		W.C. Sowell
		  John McWilliams

LINDSEY, John D.
  Clairemond E. Duke
	12-05-1852	J.W. Perrin
		  J.J. Sessions, MG

LINDSEY, Samuel
  Henrietta M. Longmire *
	12-02-1844	————
		  ————

LINDSEY, William R.
  Harriet Newell Wiggins *
	12-05-1852	J.W. Perrin
		  J.J. Sessions, MG

LINTON, William
  Nancy Smith
	12-08-1873	Lemuel Smith
		  T.M. Riley, Jr., JP

LIPKEY, Elias
  Rose Wolff *
	10-12-1854
	  (At A. Wolff's)
		L. Meyers
		  Robert D. Thompson, JP

LISINBA, J.W.
  Eliza Booker
	12-26-1880
	  (At Mrs. Burkett's)
		J.M. Bass
		  Joel Hardee, NP

LITTLE, Jefferson
  Evaline Cunningham
	12-08-1859	Jonas Little
		  John Hardee, JP

LOCKE, James J.
  Francis Sampey
	12-22-1850	Daniel McColl
		  J.P. Robbins

LOCKE, W.A.
  A.E. Kennedy
	11-25-1863	John W. Locke
		  W.N. Peavy, MG

LOCKHART, W.H.
  Nannie A. Flake *
	12-02-1875
	  (At bride's mothers)
		— W.C. Sowell

LOCKLIN, Charles W.
  Martha B. Moore
	08-25-1853	L.P. Gray
		  N. Goodwin, JP

LOFTIN, James M.
  Elizabeth Williams
	05-17-1865	James W. Barden
		  ————

LOFTIN, J.M. Susan M. Hayle	04-13-1871 (At the Courthouse)	W.W. Simmons W.W. Simmons, NP
LOFTIN, Green Ann Curry	05-17-1845	George Lowry ————
LOFTIN, William C. Abigail Lambert *	09-28-1856	James Black James Daniel, MG
LOFTON, Eli Elizabeth Aarons	09-26-1839	John Lambert J.H. Schroebel, JP
LONG, James S. Louisa E. Ferrell *	06-02-1852	W.M. Ferrell James M. Boyles
LONGMIRE, Garrett E. Margaret L. Ridd	08-13-1850	William Longmire Garrett Longmire, MG
LONGMIRE, James Mrs. Julia Hathcock	02-16-1867 (At W.W. Simmons' in Monroeville)	John D. McArthur M. McCorvey, Judge
LONGMIRE, William M. Sarah T. Lyon *	09-02-1838	———— ————
LOVALLET, J.T. Mary L. Sharp *	10-11-1857 (In Claiborne)	W.P. Clay A.J. Lambert
LOVELESS, Wilson H. Mary F. McClammy	03-23-1851	Samuel Brooks W.M. Longmire, JP
LOVIS, John W. Catherine E. Forbes	10-18-1838	W.B. Rikard D. Hestle
LOW, John Emily Rogers	07-27-1837	John G. Lowe Thomas Wilson
LOWELL, Andrew Mary A. O'Neil *	09-30-1852	R.F. Rawls C. Foster, Judge
LOWERY, A.L. N.M. Frye *	12-06-1877 (At the bride's mothers)	W.R. Lowery N.W. Sowell, Judge
LOWERY, Alexander B. Mary J. Kennedy	11-18-1847	B.M. Kennedy ————
LOWERY, B.T. * Addie Holt	03-23-1879 (At Mr. A. Lowery's)	J.M. Galloway J.L. Marshall, JP
LOWERY, Christopher W. Tricia Smith	01-27-1859 (At home of J. Smith)	Reuben Craps R.O. Connell
LOWERY, James June Hendrix *	01-17-1850	Jeremiah Crapps J.G. Wallace, JP
LOWERY, John A.M. Henrietta Rawls *	05-19-1880 (At Peter James')	J.L. Eddins, MG
LOWERY, Thomas M.B. Angelina H. Smith	11-17-1858 (At home of J. Smith)	Thomas McDaniel R.O. Connell, JP
LOWERY, William T. * Orra Ann Hendrix	12-03-1874 (At Eli Hendrix's)	Eli E. Hendrix & W.R. Lowery; S.R. Kelly, JP
LOWREMORE, John Mary Ann Reins *	03-25-1858 (At John Reins')	John Riley R.O. Connell, JP
LOWREMOURE, James Eliza E. Graham	01-04-1864 (In Monroeville)	Jacob Rabb M. McCorvey, Judge

LOWRY, George Elizabeth Canady	12-11-1844	James Thompson
LOWRY, William Nancy Taylor	01-16-1851	S.P. Taylor J.G. Wallace, JP
LOY, William Martha O. Armfield	12-13-1870 (At Dennis Crosby's)	James L. Smith William G. Curry, MG
LOYD, Thomas W. Sarah J. Melvine *	01-22-1880 (At Judge's office)	G.W. Melvine W.A. Sowell, Judge
LUCAS, Milton Mary W. McDonald	01-11-1859	H.B. McDonald T.E. Feagin, JP
LUDD, John M. Priscilla J. Bayles	06-23-1858 (On Thursday)	W.S. Wiggins H. O'Gwynn, JP
LUNDY, William A. Margaret L. Broughton *	12-07-1852	N.W. Broughton William C. Smith
LUYMANN, Fritty Emelie L. Henberger	03-14-1869	John S. Scwartz N. Feibleman
LYMAN, William H. Martha Prewett	03-08-1840	Joseph Rivers
LYNN, George Jennie Lacy	10-23-1879 (At home of Alan Lacy)	T.M. Riley, Jr. B.J. Skinner, MG
LYON, Robert L. Billie Jenkins	03-30-1876 (At the bride's fathers)	L.W. Duke
MAAS, Leopold Theresa Metzger	01-26-1857 (At home of S. Levi)	Elias Lepky R.D. Thompson, JP
MABLEY, James B. Martha O. Morris	05-03-1854 (At Joseph Barefield's on Wednesday evening)	R.C. Torry R.D. Thompson
MADDOX, James M. Elizabeth S. Anderson *	09-14-1847	C.L. Anderson
MADDOX, W.J. Eliza Enzer *	06-30-1878 (At home of Mr. Enzer)	J. DeLoach W.R. Agee, JP
MADISON, John Eliza Monroe	05-29-1875 (At Samuel Monroe's)	J.E. Boon W.H. Jennings, JP
MAGEE, William Julia Magee	09-11-1877 (At Monroeville)	W.A. Sowell
MAHASSEY, George Catherine Wiggins	06-06-1867	Alex Ross W.D. Garrett, JP
MALDEN, Tyne H. Emily Betts	09-08-1847	Willis R. Henderson T. Burp
MALDEN, Robert O. Caroline Beard	11-23-1854	T.H. Malden L.M. Wilson
MALONE, James B. Henrietta W. Steele *	11-03-1847	C.G. Richards T. Burps
MANLEY, C.J. Nancy Stinson	01-11-1873	John DeLoach
MANLEY, S.M. Martha J. Broughton *	11-05-1857 (At N.W. Broughton's on Thursday evening)	Robert D. Thompson R.D. Thompson

MANN, M. Duffe Mary A. Demanas Henderson *	05-07-1846	Alex Autry & Eld. Roberts John M. Williams, OMG
MANNING, Andrew Amarinta Daniel *	11-30-1854	R.O. Connell John J. Eubanks, JP
MANNING, E.M. Bethany Cahall *	12-10-1840	Manning Mann Dixon Hestle, JP
MANNING, Jasper Amanda Thames	02-06-1879 (At home of M.F. Thames)	Wade Massey Burney Sawyer, MG
MANNING, Milburn E. Martha E. Masson *	05-14-1843	Manning H. Masson H.C. Morrow
MANNING, R.A. Mary J. Brewton	10-22-1876 (At Pine Grove Church)	John S. Stanton Burney Sawyer, MG
MAPLES, Drewry Margaret Holly	03-20-1839	Thomas S. Roudi ————
MARION, Theodore P. Mary F. Rauls *	01-04-1835	S.A. Dubose F.F. Harris
MARONEY, John W. Nancy P. Pollard *	01-30-1849	W.A. Murphy M.R. East, JP
MARRIOTT, Cary M. Emma P. Barr *	11-08-1867	Thomas C. Barr W.W. Spence
MARSHALL Augustin J. Ann Robbins *	11-10-1854	J.W. Northcutt L.W. Lindsey
MARSHALL, Augustine Texas Dennard	10-25-1864	J.B. Colley Francis Walker, MG
MARSHALL, Francis P. Rachel D. English *	02-11-1851	John Marshall C.M. Hare, Minister
MARSHALL, Frank E. Martha J. Coskey	08-28-1879 (At home of Mrs. Dubose)	H.A. Marshall B.J. Skinner, MG
MARSHALL, H.A. V.E. Croskey	12-12-1871 (At Pineville)	J.D. Nettles ————
MARSHALL, J.L. G.E. Pleasant	04-30-1871 (At Dr. M. Lindsey's)	J.M. Slaughter A.J. Lambert, MG
MARSHALL, John A. Louisa Phillips *	09-24-1856	William B. Kemp ————
MARSHALL, John L. Jean R. Williams *	01-24-1840	D.N. Crane T. Burps, MG
MARSHALL, John S. Fannie Holloway	12-02-1880 (At home of J.A. Rabb)	Henry A. Marshall B.J. Skinner, MG
MARSHALL, Robert E. Sarah E. Dennerd *	10-15-1856	John A. Marshall Walter C. Harress, MG
MARSHALL, T.W. Annie B. McCorvey	07-23-1873 (At Monroeville)	W.G. Robinson J. Meuton Crane, MG
MARSHALL, T.W. Ida A. Fountain	11-04-1880 (At W.H. Fountain's)	Robert Maiben B.J. Skinner, MG
MARSHALL, William A. Martha E. Dubose *	11-24-1849	John Marshall ————

MARTIN, Alexander Susan Hunt	02-14-1839	Seitn (?) Mish John C. Baldwin, VDM
MARTIN, Daniel Laura Geck	03-19-1868 (At John Geck's, the bride's father)	J.F. McCorvey C.F. Sturges
MARTIN, E.L. O.E. Holman	05-23-1875 (At the bride's father's)	George Holman W.A. Sowell
MARTIN, Isaac Irena Bryant	01-22-1880 (At Ramah Church)	S.L. Ellis, JP
MARTIN, Joseph Elinda Partin *	03-11-1837	W.A. Graham H.S. Rauls, JP
MARTIN, S.B. Frances Gwatney *	04-14-1867	John DeLoach F.A. Mason
MARTIN, Thomas L. Julia S. Mann *	01-01-1843	Anderson B. Manning J.G. Wallace, JP
MARTIN, T.P.W. Missouri Andrews *	09-18-1877	Joseph Andrews
MARTIN, William Mary Patrick	09-25-1861 (At home of Mrs. Patrick)	T.H. Coker Stanford Mims, JP
MARTIN, Willis C. Susan J. Roggers *	07-06-1862 (At Willis Rogers')	R.F. Stallworth C.W. Hare
MASINGALL, J.T. M.A. Lambert *	11-01-1877 (At Mrs. Lambert's)	F.M. Masingall S.R. Kelly
MASINGILL, F.M. Georgia A. Wiggins *	12-17-1866 (At home of the bride)	John Masingill J.E. Knighten
MASINGILL, William W. Mary A. Brown *	04-05-1865	James B. Miller James B. Miller, OM
MASON, D.L. Bettie Rankin	02-10-1878 (At T. McKenzie's)	J.L. Eddins, MG
MASON, Elisha A. Amy Ann Brant	01-01-1857 (At home of A. Brant)	Bryant Rachels John T. Bayles
MASON, Franklin A. Melinda Ross *	02-19-1852	John Ross W.M. Longmire, JP
MASON, J.D. Nancy E. Garrett	11-06-1874 (At Caswell Garrett's)	C. Garrett James L. Edins, MG
MASON, Samuel Mrs. Elizabeth Black	05-31-1835	William C. Faulk William C. Faulk
MASSENGILL, C.W. Isadora V. Walker	06-18-1871 (At B.N. Walker's)	W.J. Hendrix J.M. Woods, MG
MASSEY, Andrew J. Martha A. Asberry *	07-13-1854	Henry Asberry W.H. Aldridge, JP
MASSEY, Arthur W. Amanda M. Bradley	12-05-1848	W.R. Graham Evant Andress, JP
MASSEY, Calvin Nancy Ann Aldridge	12-09-1834	James Boatwright
MASSEY, D. B.D. Bowden	12-17-1874 (At home of L. Bowden)	D.A. Massey H.H. Hybert, NP & JP

72

MASSEY, Dasliny Fannie Kolb	02-23-1879 (At Alma Cowart's)	D.A. Massey J.L. Eddins, MG
MASSEY, Drewry Jr. Louisa Wiggins	11-17-1874 (At J.T. Wiggins')	A.H. Burgess Isiah Talbert, JP
MASSEY, Elias W. Ailsey L. Thompson	04-18-1861 (At Samuel Thompson's)	John E. Bayles John McWilliams, MG
MASSEY, Francis M. Martha A. Downes *	10-12-1848	B.N. Walker J.G. Wallace, MG
MASSEY, George W. Mary Frye	05-15-1856 (At Robert O. Connell's)	C.H. Foster Robert O'Connell, JP
MASSEY, James Caroline E. Pugh *	10-03-1843	P.H. Pugh T.J. Foster, MG
MASSEY, John N. Martha A. Smith	02-02-1854	C.S. Simmons John McWilliams, MG
MATHEWS, George G. Sarah J. Hybert *	02-20-1850	N.S. McColl R.A. Sigler, JP
MATHEWS, Stephen Henrietta Holt	12-27-1877 (At May Holt's)	G.W. Salter, JP
MATTHEWS, George G. Jane R. Ferrell *	12-11-1857	Robert Parker A.J. Lambert, MG
MATTHEWS, Jesse A. Milly M. Young	02-19-1854	Thomas Hawkins J.T. Dailey
MAXWELL, Isaac G. Rebecca Helton	07-12-1848	George W. Gallaspy John McWilliams, MG
MAXWELL, Thomas L. Martha L. Doggett	11-03-1865	James H. Barnett ————
MAXWELL, William R. Martha A. Davison	10-14-1866	B.M. Burns John McWilliams, MG
MAYSON, N.M. Mattie Rankin	09-21-1875 (At home of Mrs. Rankin)	D.L. Neville W.G. Curry, MG
McALISTER, Hugh Frances Watts	08-28-1844	John Lindsey James H. Rabb, JP
McARTHUR, Charles Susan Chisholm *	05-02-1847	William McArthur C. Thames
McARTHUR, George M. Missouri M. Lowrey *	12-31-1863	George Frye Rev. M.M. Graham
McARTHUR, John O. Anna Chisholm	04-19-1866 (At W.W. Simmons' in Monroeville)	E. Chisholm C. Shannfield, JP
McARTHUR, William J. Julia Frye	05-02-1841	Willoughby Burton Jacob Rall, JP
McCALL, Charles Susan C. Boney *	06-02-1836	William J. Morgan J.H. Schroebel, MG
McCALL, James Mary E. Ganse	08-23-1844 (In the morning)	Daniel McColl ————
McCALL, John Mildred L. Stiggins	09-18-1866 (At Joseph Stiggins')	Jenne Cloud George Watson, MG

McCANTS, Charles Emma R. Cree	03-20-1878 (At Peter J. Cree's)	R.W. McClure Peter J. Cree, OMG
McCANTS, Charles E. Willie D. Stiggins	03-25-1878 (At Joseph Stiggin's)	_____ A.J. Colman, MG
McCANTS, David T., Sr. Mrs. Nancy Thompson	09-03-1876 (At John Thompson's)	A.T. Howard J. Talbert, JP
McCANTS, James M. Rosa Snell	10-16-1874 (At W.J. Snell's)	George C. Nettles L.W. Duke, MG
McCANTS, Robert W. Maggie McDuffie	01-22-1879 (At the McDuffie's)	W.L. Stallworth T.Y. Abernathy, Clergy
McCANTS, Thomas Mary A. Burgess	11-26-1845	_____ W.C. Ross, JP
McCANTS, Thomas J. Elizabeth Longmire *	11-29-1855	G.E. Longmire H.B. Farish
McCANTS, William J. Martha E. Johnson	12-17-1879 (At J.G. Johnson's)	M.B. Ritchie J.T. Payles, MG
McCANTS, William R. Rebecca McCrary	03-16-1834	John E. Murray Thomas Wilson, JG
McCANTS, W.J. Sallie J. Leslie	10-21-1874 (At J.W. Leslie's)	H.H. Hybart J.L. Skipper, MG
McCATNZ, Thomas Margaret Jane Burgess	12-17-1833	J.E. Murray Thomas Wilson, JP
McCARTHY, James J. Lucinda Adcock *	02-18-1849	S.D. Beard T. Burps
McCASKEY, James G. Ann A. Lyphrit	02-09-1854 (At John Lyphit's)	James Powell James M. Powell, JP
McCASKEY, John A. Elizabeth Lynch *	03-03-1837	Benjamin Lynch _____
McCSAKILL, John Caroline Eubanks	01-18-1838	B.N. Walker William C. Faulk, JP
McCLAMMY, John Martha Scoggins *	10-16-1839	Winston Pugh T. Bryan
McCLAMMY, John Jr. Sarah A. Booker *	09-06-1866	J.F. Salter Patrick McGlenn, JP
McCLAMMY, William Mary E. Snowden *	01-05-1865	John DeLoach T.E. Feagin, JP
McCLEAN, Hector R. Sarah S. Murphy	12-21-1846	Edward Gaillard W.F. McRee
McCLELLAN, Willie Mrs. Susan A. McMillan	01-22-1880 (At Mrs. Susan McMillan's)	William McMillan Joel Hardee, NP
McCLELLAND, J.J. Mary McCreary	04-26-1869	C.W. Hare C.W. Hare
McCLURE, C.W. M.S. Helton	01-21-1874	J.M. Faulkenberry W.G. Curry, MG
McCLURE, Eli Louisa Aldridge	11-23-1837	Daniel McColl Asa Parker

```
McCLURE, J.A.                    09-17-1865          J.P. Gordy
  Sarah A. Miller       (At the home of Mrs. Miller)  B. Bradberry, JP

McDONALD, Charles J.             10-06-1853          John Avery
  Martha A. Thames                                     John McWilliams

McCLURE, James                   07-15-1837          S.D. Parker
  Elizabeth A. Mitchell                                John Roach, JCCMCTY

McCLURE, Samuel                  02-22-1846          W.M. Busbey
  Louisa McClure                                       William W. Simmons, JP

McCLURE, William W.              04-17-1859          E.T. Andress
  Elizabeth M. Andress (At Mrs. Andress')              John McWilliams

McCOIN, James                    02-26-1866          T.J. Duke
  Epsey Smith                                          M. McCorvey, Judge

McCOLL, Daniel                   11-04-1849
  Almira J. Sowell *                                 ‾‾‾‾‾‾‾‾‾‾‾
                                                       J.G. Wallace, JP

McCOLL, Duncan D.                11-29-1854          D.R. Rankin
  Eliza Ivey *                                         Joel Hardee, JP

McCOLL, Nathaniel S.             02-20-1850          George G. Mathews
  Maria A. Hybert *                                    R.A. Sigler, JP

McCOLLISON, Thomas F.            10-11-1855          M.W. Raines
  Mrs. Mary M. Walker                                  J.B. Colley, JP

McCORVEY, J.E.                   11-05-1879          D.R. McMillan
  C.R. Nettles          (At William Nettles')          William H. McAutry

McCORVEY, John                   09-08-1847          Neal McCorvey
  Mrs. Lydia E. Wiggins                                H.A. Smith

McCORVEY, Murdock                04-07-1834          John J. Roache
  Lydia A. Ronaldson *                               ‾‾‾‾‾‾‾‾‾‾‾

McCORVEY, Neal                   12-19-1835          Daniel McColl
  Sarah Jane Beard *                                 ‾‾‾‾‾‾‾‾‾‾‾

McCORVEY, Neill                  11-03-1867          J.F. McCorvey
  Mrs. M. Fountain      (At William Coleman's)         W.G. Curry, MG

McCORVEY, Thomas M.              01-14-1864          J.W. Thompson
  Mary E. Byrd *                                       T.E. Feagin, JP

McCOY, H.C.                      05-21-1867          W.A. Fountain
  Bettie Fountain       (At home of W.A. Fountain)     John McWilliams

McCOY, John                      09-18-1841          Arthur Davis
  Sarah Davis                                          H. Standenmire, MG

McCOY, William P.                12-29-1853          W.A. Whissenhunt
  Mary A. Whissenhunt * (At Mrs. Whissenhunt's         R.D. Thompson
                         on Thursday evening)

McCREARY, John C.                04-02-1859          James Cunningham
  Sarah Stallworth                                   ‾‾‾‾‾‾‾‾‾‾‾

McDANIEL, John                   11-29-1871          B.R. Ramey
  E.S. Hunt             (At home of Allen Hunt)        W.G. Curry, MG

McDONALD, John                   10-24-1848          James Searcy
  Nancy Jane Searcy *                                  M.B. East, JP

McDONALD, L.M.                   12-19-1855          J.S. Coleman
  Louisa A. Womack *                                   L. Seward, MG
```

McDONALD, Ronald C. Marian Stainton	06-18-1864 (At Mrs. Marian Stainton's)	W.W. Simmons John McWilliams, MG
McDONALD, Thomas Mary S. Watson *	07-28-1859 (At Josiah Watson.'s)	H.M. Graham R.O. Connell, JP
McDUFFIE, Archibald Nancy Johnson	12-20-1849	L.A. Kidd H.A. Smith, MG
McDUGALD, H.F. Mary C. Wormley	10-25-1859 (At H.G. Scott's in Claiborne, Ala.)	Robert G. Scott A. Minneas, Rector of St. James Parish
McGEE, Alexander Elizabeth Rolin	05-04-1868 (At Office)	T.J. Duke M. McCorvey, Judge
McGLINN, Patrick Emma J. Stacey	02-10-1858 (At Mrs. Sarah Stacey's)	Joseph T. East M.B. East
McINNIS, Alex C. Sarah F. Doggett	12-20-1865	D.A. Rankin M.M. Graham, MG
McINNIS, John W. Nancy J. Doggett *	12-20-1865	D.A. Rankin M.M. Graham, MG
McINTOSH, William Mary Bonner *	02-09-1835	James M. Black ————
McKENZIE, Aaron Mahala Tuberville *	03-01-1850	Joel Boyles Evant Andress, JP
McKENZIE, Aaron Isabella Tuberville	11-25-1874 (At Claiborne)	W.R. Medlock J.M. Rothwell, NP,MG
McKENZIE, Angus Mary T. Mims	09-20-1845	C.H. Foster ————
McKENZIE, Duncan Christian Thompson *	01-24-1835	Duncan Thompson ————
McKENZIE, Duncan Mary Grimes	11-03-1840	W.H.E. Pierce William Holloway, JP
McKENZIE, Duncan, Sr. Elmira McKinney	11-21-1855	Sam McClure Joel Hardee, JP
McKENZIE, D.W. Frances A. Mason	12-14-1876 (At Richard Mims')	F.M. McKenzie Joel Hardee, NP
McKENZIE, Francis M. Adaline Grimes *	07-24-1859 (At Mr. Grimes' on Sunday morning)	John A. Simmons Robert D. Thompson, JP
McKENZIE, Frank Cynthia Mims	12-18-1867	J. Richardson C.W. Hare, MG
McKENZIE, James Mary Bennett *	07-20-1853	C.A. Thames James J. Barclay, JP
McKENZIE, John Amanda Bethea	09-04-1855 (At Claiborne)	J. DeLoach James J. Barclay
McKINLEY, A.G. Sarah A. Sellers	11-15-1872 (At Joseph Sellers')	Elbert McKinley D.J. Wright
McKINLEY, A.J. C.B. Frye	03-18-1880 (At home of Mrs. S.J. Frye)	C.L. Frye J.T. Bayles, MG
McKINLEY, Ambrose Asenath McKinley *	05-27-1855 (At Isom McKinley's)	P. McKinley John Bayles, MG

McKINLEY, A.N.   06-29-1873   J. McKinley
  Sarah L. Tuberville (At Joseph McKinley's)   J.G. Bradley

McKINLEY, E.F.   04-05-1860   William McKinley
  Willa E. Gramling *   W.W. Peavy, MG

McKINLEY, Elbert   04-30-1839   George Chapman
  Mrs. Malissa C. Chapman   J.H. Graham, JP

McKINLEY, Elbert   01-12-1845   David Stabler
  Mary A. Stabler   ‾‾‾‾‾

McKINLEY, George M.   09-12-1861   Elbert McKinley
  Martha J. Cobb *   W.W. Peavy, MG

McKINLEY, G.L.   12-09-1875   E. McKinley
  Margaret I. Thompson (At S.R. Thompson's)   I. Talbert, JP

McKINLEY, Isham B.   02-22-1866   John G. Johnson
  Henrietta D. Coleman   J.G. Bradley

McKINLEY, Harrison *   09-10-1878   Aaron McKinley
  Margaret Brown   (At home of J.A. Wall)   T. Talbert, NP

McKINLEY, H.N.   07-01-1866   E.B. Johnson
  Florence Autery *   (At Mrs. Walter McKinley's) J.E. Knighten

McKINLEY, James   06-01-1861   N. Gramling
  Hugine V. Gramling * (At Lewis Gramling's)   ·   Lewis Gramling, JP

McKINLEY, James M.   12-31-1860   Joseph McKinley
  Phebe Rogers *   ‾‾‾‾‾

McKINLEY, J.M.   05-22-1879
  Lucy A. Daniel   (At Mrs. Crawford's)   I. Talbert, NP

McKINLEY, John L. *   11-21-1872   Elbert McKinley
  Eliza J. Frye   (At Hopkins Frye's)   D.J. Wright

McKINLEY, Joseph   01-04-1838   Drewry Massey
  Mary Rowel   Elias Brown

McKINLEY, Joseph   09-08-1877   W.C. Tuberville
  Lucy Stabler   (At Joseph McKinley's)   T.J. Crew, MG

McKINLEY, Joseph E. *   05-13-1873   Joseph McKinley
  Jane Stabler *   (At Joseph McKinley's)   J.G. Bradley, JP

McKINLEY, Madison   01-05-1846   Stephen Rowell
  Rachel Rowell   ‾‾‾‾‾

McKINLEY, Madsion   02-02-1871   Elbert McKinley
  Melissa A. Griffin (At Mrs. M.A. Griffin's)   John McWilliams, MG

McKINLEY, Madsion W.   04-17-1860   Lewis Gramling
  Martha M.E.M. Gramling (At Lewis Gramling's)   W.N. Peavy, MG

McKINLEY, Manon *   12-20-1870   A.J. McKinley
  Bettie Griffin   (At home of Mrs. Griffin)   W.A. Locke, MG

McKINLEY, Patterson   10-17-1860   Elbert McKinley
  Sarah J. Ballard * (At William Ballard's)   J.T. Bazlet, MG

McKINLEY, W.B.   01-26-1871   M. McKinley
  Susan A. Shannon * (At Harget Shannon's)   Joseph T. Dailey, MG

McKINLEY, W.C.   05-20-1870   A.J. McKinley
  Mrs. Virginia J. Davis (At the bride's, by   Francis Walker, MG
                      written consent of Madison McKinley)

McKINLEY, William Julia A. McKinley	01-18-1855 (At Walton McKinley's)	Jackson McKinley John L. Bayles, MG
McKINNEY, Green W. Rebecca Sanders *	02-21-1849	Daniel Sirmon Rev. William McCracker of Wilcox County
McKINNSIE, Thomas H. Henrietta H. Roach	02-02-1865	R.N. Murphy ————
McKINZIE, Aaron Mahalah Bohanon	08-26-1874 (At I. Tolbert's)	W.C. Turberville Isiah Talbert, JP
McKINZIE, Daniel Sarah Brooks *	04-15-1834	Rolling Griffin Daniel P. Wright, JP
McLAURIN, L.M. Josephine McLane *	11-18-1874	H.H. Hybert H.H. Hybert, JP
McLEOD, John Mrs. C.R. Williams	01-03-1872	I.S. Williams W.W. Spence, MG
McLEOD, William Sarah Stacey	06-23-1865 (At Pleasant Hill Baptist)	John DeLoach A.J. Lambert
McMILLAN, A.A. Emogene McCall *	12-21-1871 (At M.E. McCall's)	Williamson McMillan James U. Ruhen
McMILLAN, Archibald S. Polly Chisholm	06-01-1845	Daniel McColl ————
McMILLAN, Caloway Mary C. Faulk *	01-16-1847	E.G. Betts J.G. Wallace, JP
McMILLAN, H.G. Mary McCormick	12-26-1878 (At Allen McCormick's)	D.L. Neville B.J. Skinner, MG
McMILLAN, James Lucinda Watson *	02-17-1845	Mrs. Watson ————
McMILLAN, James Felitha Parish	06-31-1874	Z. Parish Hugh Rankin
McMILLAN, John Adaline Hawthorne	05-06-1860	Williamson McMillan A.D. Anderson, JP
McMILLAN, Murdock M. Celia Ann Salter *	06-27-1836	Daniel McColl Asa Parker, JP
McMILLAN, R.N. W.F. Pritchett	03-09-1871 (At his mother's)	John DeLoach W.W. Simmons, Notary
McMILLAN, S.J. Francis S. Brantley	01-24-1872 (At Oren Brantley's)	D.L. Nevill Emanuel Cline, MG
McMILLAN, Thomas Nancy Watson	01-02-1855	D. Giddings ————
McMILLAN, Thomas B. Susan A. Thornton	11-?-1860	———— ————
McMILLAN, W.H. Turnicay Faulk	12-30-1845	Drury McMillan ————
McMILLAN, William Jemima Blackwell	08-10-1871 (At her mother's home)	J.A. Brady W.W. Simmons, Notary
McMILLAN, W.W. Eugene E. Morton	10-22-1868 (At home of T. Morton)	J.C. Arthur W.G. Bussy, MG

McMILLIAN, C.C.	09-12-1869	Richard McMillian
N.J. Thomas	(At home of Mrs. Russell)	D.M. Hudson, Minister
McMURPHY, Alex	02-12-1852	Jacob Rickard
Sarah Ann Cosby *		John O'Gwynn, JP
McMURPHY, Daniel K.	12-05-1850	Wiley Corley
Nancy J. Corley		H.B. Farrish, MG
McNEIL, C.A.	12-24-1879	T.D. Hayles
J.A. Reaves	(At home of Mr. L. Reaves)	W.R. Maxwell, JP
McNEIL, Charles R.	08-03-1854	J.W. Broughton
Elizabeth Davis	(At home of Joan Davis)	L.S. Berry, MG
McNEIL, Daniel M.	10-18-1842	_____
Lucy Booker		
McNEIL, D.M.	06-22-1879	John Hardee
Elizabeth Jordan	(At the bride's home)	John Hardee, JP
McNEIL, James	06-11-1839	Richard R. Moseley
Mary A.M. Laris		_____
McNEIL, James E.	05-27-1869	William O. Kennedy
Martha E. Stanley	(At Mrs. Stanley's)	Thomas K. Armstrong, MG
McNEIL, James N.	11-01-1876	John DeLoach
Emily C. Whisenhent	(At W.A. Whisenhent's)	John McWilliams, MG
McNEIL, William R.	06-12-1870	H.M. Graham
Sallie Ross	(At home of D. McNeil)	G.W. Riley, JP
McNEILL, A.D.	10-24-1869	Marcus Cater
M.C. Cater		E. Cline, MG
McNEILL, D.W.	11-27-1867	John Avery
Mary A. Henderson	(At Mrs. Sarah A. Henderson's)	John McWilliams
McNIEL, James N.	03-03-1842	T.J. Foster
Elizabeth Middleton *		T.J. Foster
McPHERSON, Cornelius	02-02-1878	_____
S.F. Furgison *		_____
McPHERSON, Cornelius	01-16-1880	Wesley McPherson
Amanda DeLoach	(At John E. Parrett's)	John E. Parrett
McPHERSON, Louis	09-25-1869	J. DeLoach
M.F. Gordon	(At home of Nancy Riley)	Hugh McKenzie, JP
McPHERSON, Wesley	03-28-1873	William Graham
Pollie Abney		T.M. Reiley, Jr., JP
McPHERSON, William	02-24-1840	Daniel C. Thompson
Mary Seawright	(See below)	Levy A. Kidd, JP
McPHERSON, William	02-24-1840	Daniel C. Thompson
Mary Seawright	(At John S. Johnston's)	Leroy A. Pitts, JP
McPHERSON, William	10-26-1873	T.M. Riley, Jr.
Anna Abney *		T.M. Riley, Jr., JP
McWILLIAMS, Drury	12-25-1834	William C. Faulk
Elizabeth W. Faulk *	(or McMillan?)	J.J. Roach, Judge
McWILLIAMS, James	03-25-1847	R.R. Morris
Elvina Morris *		Hugh Rankin, JP

```
McWILLIAMS, James M.              10-16-1865         D.T. Fore
   Sarah A. Henderson * (At S.A. Henderson's)         John McWilliams, MG

McWILLIAMS, James W. *            11-20-1876         J.J. McWilliams
   Sarah June Watson    (At J. McWilliams')           B.B. Green, JP

McWILLIAMS, Wooten D.             02-26-2843         David McCorvey
   Elizabeth Ann Fore *                               C. Thames

MEDARES, Malachin                 01-24-1852         George Bradley
   Mrs. Mary Hassy

MELVIN, G.W.                      05-27-1880         C. Ikner
   Nancy A. Morris *      (At W.R. Smith's)           R.M. Tuberville, JP

MERCER, Samuel                    10-15-1841         James W. Downes & Daniel
   Eddy Massey                                        Chisholm; J.G. Holcomb,JP

MERRITT, J.C.                     12-06-1859         William Morris
   Mrs. Vicy Coleman                                  Elias Brown, MG

METTS, George W.                  12-07-1865         E. Rigby
   Adaline Sellers                                    William N. Peavy, MG

METZGER, Myer                     07-30-1847         Lazarus Myers
   Frederika Myers                                    William R. Agee

METZGER, Soloman                  02-24-1857         William L. Gulley
   Hannah Myer *         (At Claiborne)               James J. Barclay, JP

MICHARD, Joseph                   08-15-1847         A.B. McDonald
   Eliza Parrish                                      H.P. Wainwright, JP

MIDDLETON, A.J.                   11-12-1869         Jeptha Middleton
   Sarah J. Rogers     (At A. Wilkinson's)            G. Boyett, Elder

MIDDLETON, A.Z.                   12-27-1866         Jeptha Middleton
   Margaret Anderson  (At Mathew Anderson's)          Jesse Hays

MIDDLETON, C.H.                   07-22-1857         John DeLoach
   Nancy A. Childress  (At George Kelly's)            J.B. Colley, JP

MIDDLETON, H.H.                   12-08-1861         J.A. Holloway
   Martha J. Holloway   (At J. Nettles')             J.B. Miller, Ord. Min.

MIDDLETON, James                  05-24-1857         Ananias DeLoach
   Rachel L. Owens                                    John Knighton, MG

MIDDLETON, Jeptha                 02-04-1880         J.L. Langhams
   Janie M. Carter    (At Hubard Carter's)            Joel Hardee, JP

MIDDLETON, J.H.                   01-12-1876
   Sarah J. Wilkinson  (At D.G. Wilkinson's)          Joel Hardee, NP

MIDDLETON, John G.                02-20-1845         Mr. Fore
   Eliza Fore *                                       Daniel Fore, JP

MIDDLETON, John M.                01-14-1858
   Mary E. Cromartee                                  T.E. Feagin, JP

MIDDLETON, J.W.                   05-29-1870         M.W. Middleton
   E.S. Cunningham    (At home of J.J. Little)        Joel Hardee, JP

MIDDLETON, Martin                 10-21-1858         John DeLoach
   Mary Holloway                                      T.E. Feagin, JP

MIDDLETON, M.B.                   01-13-1880         S.M.C. Middleton
   Lou Deese        (At home of Willis Deese)         John McWilliams, MG
```

```
MIDDLETON, M.W.                    09-16-1866        C.R. Anderson
  M.A. Middleton        (At Mathins Anderson's)       Jesse Hays, JP

MIDDLETON, R.B.                    11-12-1865        Thomas J. Duke
  Ann E. Coven *                                      J.J. Simpkins, JP

MIDDLETON, S.M.C.                  08-24-1861        W.G. Middleton
  Mrs. Frances E. Finklea                            _____

MIDDLETON, Stephen                 12-13-1866        John DeLoach
  A.E. Brantley                                       T.W. Posten

MIDDLETON, Stephen J.H.            12-15-1858        Willis Middleton
  Millisa A. Anderson *                               Joel Hardee, JP

MIDDLETON, Thomas                  12-30-1875
  Harriet Byrd                                       _____ Joel Hardee, NP

MIDDLETON, William                 01-18-1860        J.C. Kimbil
  Sarah Ann Tolbert                                   Elias Brown, MG

MIDDLETON, William                 10-03-1866        J.F. McCorvey
  Martha Jones            (At Thomas Jones')          C.F. Sturgis

MIDDLETON, William A.              01-06-1858        Willis Finklea
  Sarah C. Rhodes *                                  _____

MIDDLETON, Willis                  02-25-1875        J.G. Middleton
  Mrs Caroline Massengale (At Willis Middleton's) Joel Hardee, NP

MILES, Francis W.                  03-31-1848        George Holman
  Nancy A. Stiggins *                                _____

MILES, John S.                     08-06-1835        Isaac Fryer
  Nancy E. Fryer                                      J.H. Schroebel

MILLENDER, William L.              12-23-1852        Abner Dees
  Nancy Hurry                                         John McWilliams

MILLER, George                     01-12-1866        H.H. Middleton
  Lucretia J. Middleton *                            _____

MILLER, James H.                   04-28-1858        Samuel J. Atkinson
  Sarah E. Atkinson *                                 H.B. Farrish, MG

MILLER, John J.L.                  11-04-1863        Frank Droxler
  Mary E. Jennings                                   _____

MILLER, Jesse                      05-21-1834        G.D. Foster
  Pricilla A. Bradford *                             _____

MILLER, K.S.                       10-28-1858        D.J. Morris
  Sarah A. Morris *        (At Daniel Morris')        Neil Gillis, MG

MILLER, J.M.                       04-25-1878        R.I. Bradley
  Mary Mishut              (At Claiborne)             J.M. Rothwell, NP

MILLER, William M.                 02-27-1846        R.L. Rogers
  Mary F. Rogers *                                   _____

MILLS, Edward C.                   01-25-1857        J.S. Jenkins
  Flora Grissett         (At Claiborne Church)        A.J. Lambert, MG

MILLS, G.H.                        01-24-1872        W.R. Mills
  C.V. Masons *      (At home of Richard Mims)       James L. Eddins, MG

MILNER, J.B.                       12-23-1869        B.B. Kimbell
  S.E. Miller            (At A. Millhouse's)          P.S. Millner, MG
```

MIMS, David Margaret Smith *	07-02-1846	Ruffin Mims ————
MIMS, D.C. Nancy Watts	12-21-1870 (At John Watts' in Pineville)	T.J. Duke J.B. Colley, JP
MIMS, Frank Jane McMillan	11-22-1874 (At Ramley Chapel)	T.F. Williams
MIMS, Henry Caroline Grace *	08-10-1835	Wright Mims ————
MIMS, Hilliard Mary Mims *	04-09-1835	William G. Curry ————
MIMS, Ruffin Emily Mims *	10-24-1846	David Mims ————
MIMS, Slayton Perthanea McCurry *	07-02-1839	T.M. Riley T.M. Riley, JP
MIMS, W.L. Mary D. McKenzie	01-07-1866 (At Hugh McKenzie's)	H. McKenzie D.S. McDonald, MG
MIMS, Wright Sarah Hammons	08-25-1835	Alex D. Leeonard ————
MIMS, Wright Matilda Riley *	12-28-1837	E. Riley Alex Travis, VDM
MINER, George Levita Coker	02-25-1855 (At home of K. Fowler)	Thomas Hinson Uriah Atkinson, JP
MIRES, John H. Jane Norwood	07-21-1839	Marshall Frederick Thomas Wilson, JP
MITCHELL, John Mary Hollinger	11-08-1836	William Hollinger (Her father) Daniel M. Wright, JP
MIXON, Abbot Martha A. Snowden *	10-03-1846	W.J. Colvin Stanford Mims, JP
MIXON, A.C. D.E. Anderson	10-30-1873 (At Martha Anderson's)	I.J. Anderson J.L. Skipper, MG
MIXON, James R. Julia McClammey *	06-27-1869 (At John McClammy's)	Joel Mixon Joel Hardee, JP
MIXON, Joel E. Mary Middleton *	10-24-1856	Samuel Langham Joel Hardee, JP
MIXON, John Cassinda Middleton *	11-25-1847	Martin Middleton Joel Hardy, JP
MIXON, John Lucinda Leason	01-19-1854	Joel Hardee ————
MIXON, Morgan W. Cusinda Riley *	06-30-1845	Thomas Dewberry ————
MIXON, W.W. E.B. Durden *	(At Jacob Duncan's)	J.L. Skipper, MG
MONELL, John J. Elizabeth A. English	05-01-1841	Walter R. English T. Burpe
MONK, J.D. Mrs. A.J. McColl	12-11-1860 (At William C. Sowell's)	William C. Sowell A.J. Lambert

MONTGOMERY, Joseph H. Mary L. Langham	03-02-1859 (At William Langham's)	Joseph Montgomery M. McCorvey
MONTGOMERY, Phillip Flora Peebles *	02-23-1836	William H. Fleming J.H. Schroebel, MG
MONTGOMERY, Robert M. Laura A. Pugh *	11-26-1850	William J. Duke George Clothier, JP
MOODY, Thomas N. Elizer Hurt	12-30-1879 (At home of John White)	S.S. Ellis, JP
MOONEY, Andrew J. Nancy E. Pearce	07-04-1865	Whitman Cotten William Robinson, JP
MOONEY, Andrew J., Jr. Almeda R. Griffin	07-12-1865	Whitman Cotten William Robinson, JP
MOORE, Edward L. Mrs. Mary Longmire	07-04-1843	Thomas B. Clausell Garrett Longmire, Jr
MOORE, E.L. Lucinda Thompson	02-26-2867 (At the office)	A.J. Mims M. McCorvey, Judge
MOORE, Vicen Ada Williams	11-11-1879 (At home of the Justice of the Peace)	T.J. Daniel R.M. Tuberville, JP
MOORE, W.J. N.H. White	01-11-1877 (At home of Mrs. A.A. White)	W.W. Giddins B.B. Green, JP
MORGAN, John W., Jr. Nancy Anderson	06-13-1861	F.J. Lance J.J. Simpkins, JP
MORISON, Patrick Sarah E. Stacey	12-31-1865 (At home of P.M. Glen)	Patrick Carr B. Bradberry, JP
MORRIS, A.J. Ann E. McKinley *	05-20-1873 (At J.E. Bradley's)	H.W. McKinley J.E. Bradley, JP
MORRIS, A.M. Louisa Steadman	12-12-1878 (At Louisa Steadman's)	Asa Morris R.M. Tuberville, JP
MORRIS, Andrew J. Eliza J. Spencer	01-07-1855 (At Mrs. Morris')	W. Morris R.D. Thompson, JP
MORRIS, Asa Mary Deese	01-16-1879 (At Mrs. Martha Deese's)	E. Rigby John McWilliams, MG
MORRIS, Eli J. Lucy Ann Turberville*	01-26-1876 (At R.M. Turberville's)	John W. Watts J.G. Bradley, JP
MORRIS, J.B. Sarah Ann Harrison	10-20-1880 (At James L. Eddins')	James McKenzie James L. Eddins, MG
MORRIS, Jesse Secily Mahala Bryant *	11-24-1850	William Gordy Evant Andress, JP
MORRIS, Jesse Mary Ann Brent *	01-06-1858	William Gordon W.W. Simmons, JP
MORRIS, J.W. Ellander Haynes *	03-25-1869 (At Mrs. Elizabeth Haynes')	William Morris E. Cline, MG
MORRIS, Perry E. Mary B. Boseman *	04-09-1871 (At Jasper Boseman's)	Jasper Bowman Emanuel Cline, MG
MORRIS, Robert B. Mary McInnis *	01-21-1847	Zach Watson H. Fowler, JP

```
MORRIS, Walter D.                05-19-1865          John Roley
  Permelia J. Owen          (At the Watts' home)      M.M. Graham, MG

MORRIS, William                  06-22-1844          Arthur Talbert
  Martha Coleman *                                   _____

MORRIS, William                  06-20-1852          Jackson Morris
  Mrs. Nancy M. Bivin                                Evant Andress, JP

MORRISETTE, George G.            08-04-1858          N.J. Robinson
  Cornelia C. Robinson (At F.E. Richardson's)         M. McCorvey, Judge

MORRISSETT, F.S.                 12-20-1868          C.L. Hutto
  Annie A. King *              (At Mrs. King's)        J.H. Salter, MG

MORROW, William C.               06-24-1844          Dixon Hestle
  Martha A. McCraery *                                _____

MOSELEY, Richard F.              12-12-1876          R.W. Moseley
  S.E. White              (At home of J.F. White)     John McWilliams, MG

MOSELEY, Robert W.               12-18-1872          H.T. Fountain, Jr
  S.E. Duke               (At home of A.J. Duke)      W.G. Curry, MG

MOSLEY, Asa R.                    03-27-1862          R. Fowler
  Virginia Crook      (At W.B. Crook's on Thurs.) M. McCorvey, Judge

MOSLEY, Edward L.                03-19-1862          James E. Lott
  Mary Watkins                                       W.C. Morrow, MG

MOSLEY, Elijah                   01-04-1843          William S. Warren
  Martha Barlow                                      Daniel Fore, JP

MURPHY, Daniel                   11-30-1848          Robert Morris
  Eliza Green *                                      H.J. Hunter, Ord. Min.

MURPHY, Frank                    12-21-1876          E.T. Andress
  Margaret A. Andress  (At Evant Andress')            John McWilliams, MG

MURPHY, James                    02-22-1849          James Hamilzon
  Lucinda Hamilton *                                 C.T. Thames, MG

MURPHY, James M.                 07-23-1874          W.L. Murphy
  C.A. Sikes          (At bride's brother-in-laws)   B.B. Green, JP

MURPHY, John                     11-21-1875
  Mrs. Mary Rogers                                   ‾W.G. Middleton, JP

MURPHY, John M.                  11-25-1841          W.S. Cerman
  Rhoda Presnal                                      Joseph Tolbert, MG

MURPHY, Mike                     04-18-1869          S.H. Dailey
  Rebecca J. Hawkins                                 Sam Kelly, JP

MURPHY, Neal A.                  06-14-1849          Dave McCorvey
  Narcissa Leslie                                    H.A. Smith, MG

MURPHY, R.N.                     10-02-1867          J.F. McCorvey
  L.E. Wiggins *      (At home of Mrs E.N. Wiggins) W.G. Curry, MG

MURPHY, Robert N.                10-20-1835          S.D. Parker
  Missouri Hill *                                    _____

MURPHY, Virgil                   04-09-1860          W.B. Hoyt
  Nellie Gindrat                                     _____

MURPHY, William G.               02-08-1849          Edward Hamilton
  Mary J. Hamilton *                                 C. Thames, MG
```

84

MURPHY, William L. Catherine J. Andress	12-28-1872 (At Mr. Andress')	E.J. Andress Benjamin B. Green, JP
MURRAY, John E. Charlotte T. Burton *	11-14-1843	Whitson Pugh T.J. Foster, MG
MURRAY, John E. Nancy A. Stidman *	05-05-1855	J.C. Slade _____
MUSGROVE, Belton Jane Pierce *	04-06-1873 (At Mrs. Pearce's)	S.J. Stanton S.R. Kelly, JP
MUSGROVE, J.S. M.E. Pierce	08-11-1869 (At home of J.A. Kelly)	J.A. Kelly Samuel Kelley, JP
MYRICK, Columbus M.L. Buffington	09-30-1877 (At T.P. Buffington's)	W.H. Robinson Joel Hardee, NP
MYRICK, William N.S.P. Harrison *	03-31-1867 (At Jesse Hays')	John DeLoach Jesse Hays, JP
NASH, S.D. Martha L. Fowler	02-03-1871 (At Mrs. Nancy Fowler's)	H.M. Graham W.G. Curry
NEAL, W.S. Julia L. Morton	11-14-1871 (At Mr. Morton's)	J.W. Davison, Jr. John McWilliams, MG
NEAL, W.S. Sallie B. Slaughter	11-03-1880 (At I.W. Slaughter's)	W.H. McAutry
NELSON, John Sarah Harrison	10-24-1875 (At Joel Hardee's)	J.R. Waite Joel Hardee, NP
NELSON, Watkins L. Hellen Finch	12-01-1875 (At R. Cunningham's)	F.S. Sowell J.L. ___?___ , MG
NETHEAY, E.T. Susan A. Dubose	06-20-1860	John DeLoach T.M. Lynch, Pastor
NETTLES, Andress Susan Andress	06-07-1855 (At Jackson Brown's)	A. Parker Elias Brown
NETTLES, Andrew Mahala Brown *	11-26-1835	Thomas Nettles Cornelius Thames
NETTLES, Andrew Frances Fountain	08-17-1873 (At Mrs. Fountain's)	Nathan Crawford, MG
NETTLES, Andrew J. Sarah J. Andress *	07-24-1861 (At James Andress')	James Andress William L. Gulley, JP
NETTLES, Calvin C. Margaret S. McCants *	01-13-1858	N.S. McColl H.B. Farish, JMP
NETTLES, David Martha Bradley *	11-11-1844	Jackson Bradley Rufus C. Torrey
NETTLES, D.E. C.A. McCants	10-09-1867	John F. McCone _____
NETTLES, George W. Mary Frances Powell	06-26-1858	Joseph B. Parker N. Goodwin, MG
NETTLES, George W. Mary E. Andress *	05-16-1864	James T. Parker M.J. Watson, JP
NETTLES, J.D. M.F. Maxwell	11-30-1876 (At home of Mrs. S. Maxwell)	N.E. Davison L.W. Duke

| NETTLES, Joseph, Jr. | 07-22-1841 | Daniel McColl |
| Ann Johnson | | John Herrington |

| NETTLES, Samuel | 12-17-1835 | William Primm |
| Sarah Finklea * | | Thomas Wilson, JP |

| NETTLES, S.H. | 12-24-1873 | J.A. Dunham |
| M.H. Rikard | (At Mike Rickard's) | Joseph Snell, JP |

| NETTLES, Thomas | 01-14-1836 | N.W. Broughton |
| Nancy Haynes * | | Elias Brown |

| NETTLES, Thomas A. | 08-09-1865 | James L. Smith |
| Mattie A. Robbins * | (At Daniel Robbins') | D.S. McDonald, MG |

| NETTLES, Thomas H. | 02-12-1860 | J.E. Murray |
| Judy A. Rikard | | James M. Davison |

| NETTLES, W.D. | 03-01-1877 | J.D. Smith |
| S.J. Davison | (At Scotland, Ala.) | L.W. Duke |

| NETTLES, William D. | 01-29-1857 | John A. Simmons |
| Catherine McMillan * | | H.A. Smith, MG |

| NETTLES, William T. | 01-26-1848 | Joseph Snell |
| Margaret Dubose * | | L.W. Lindsey, MG |

| NEVILLS, William D. | 12-28-1836 | John W. McClure |
| Lucretia C. Faulk * | | J.J. Roach |

| NEWBERRY, Benjamin F. | 11-30-1855 | John J. Eubanks |
| Josephine Eubanks * | | J.J. Eubanks |

| NEWBERRY, Charles | 12-10-1857 | Benjamin Newberry |
| Elizabeth Thames | (At James Wiggins') | |

| NEWBERRY, Charles H. | 08-28-1859 | J.M. Brown |
| Margaret Carter | | A.J. Lambert, MG |

| NEWBERRY, James | 12-18-1872 | Samuel R. Kelly |
| M.A. McDonald | (At home of N. Thames) | S.R. Kelly, JP |

| NEWBERRY, J.H. | 12-20-1865 | W.T. Newberry |
| E.J. Wiggins | (At the bride's fathers) | George L. Lee, MG |

| NEWBERRY, J.H. | 04-24-1870 | Sam Roberts |
| C.L. Roberts | (At Thomas Roberts') | W.G. Curry, MG |

| NEWBERRY, John | 01-01-1848 | James R. Thames |
| Frances J. Fountain | | Cornelius Thames, MG |

| NEWBERRY, Thomas | 11-16-1859 | James R. Thames |
| Susan Aldridge | | W.W. Simmons, JP |

| NEWBERRY, William | 04-21-1836 | Moses Beard |
| Ann Beard * | | C. Thames |

| NEWBERRY, William J. | 12-20-1867 | John F. McCorvey |
| Caroline James * | (At home of Mrs. James) | A.J. Lambert, MG |

| NEWBERRY, William T. | 12-31-1879 | Eli E. Hendrix |
| Margaret E. Hendrix * | (At Eli Hendris's) | Burney Sawyer, MG |

| NEWBERRY, William T. | 11-26-1866 | W.S. Wiggins |
| Sarah A. Wiggins | (At James Wiggins') | W.G. Curry, MG |

| NICHOLS, J.T. | 12-14-1879 | J.D. Edwards |
| Florence Reed | (At Mrs. Bass') | Burney Sawyer, MG |

NORMAN, Eleazar W. Pantheah A. Womack *	02-29-1855	W.J. Stinger D.C. Fowler
NORMAN, Wesley G. Caroline N. Killam	08-25-1857	J.D. Weatherford W.W. Peavy, Ord. Min.
NORRED, Mullikin Jane Avery	11-22-1836	James H. Bruton ————
NO RIS, Burrel Effy McLeod	07-16-1868	John Norris J.M. Wood
NORRIS, F.J. Imogene Ferrell	05-16-1872 (At Capt. William M. Ferrell's)	J. DeLoach A.J. Lambert, MG
NORRIS, Irvin Memphis L. Ward *	02-27-1878 (At Jim Ward's)	Thomas Ward B. Sawyer, MG
NORRIS, James I. Laura A. Colvin	06-25-1868	T.J. Duke J.M. Hood
NORRIS, John Frances Rolin	06-08-1865 (At home of John Norris)	John Roley M.M. Graham
NORRIS, Samuel L. Emma J. Ogbourne *	11-23-1866 (At N.A. Ogbourne's)	J.E. Whitaker A.J. Lambert, MG
NORTHCUTT, G.R. Lilly Helton *	12-10-1878 (At Pine Orchard)	C.W. McClure L.W. Duke
NORTHCUTT, J.A. Sarah T. Morris *	12-11-1878 (At bride's fathers)	James A. Morris L.W. Duke
NORTHCUTT, James N. Martha R. McClure *	01-01-1852	Sarah McClure N.H. Aldridge, JP
NORTHCUTT, John H. Mrs. Sarah R. Johnson	08-22-1854	W.R. Northcutt John DeLoach, JP
NORTHCUTT, William K. Jane Nettles	01-11-1848	John W. Northcutt John Fore, JP
NORTHRUP, W.H. Sarah E. Lambert *	08-01-1872 (At Martha Lambert's)	John DeLoach A.J. Lambert, MG
NORTHRUP, William H. Mrs. Jane Woodson	06-17-1850	William Pace ————
NORWOOD, John Mary Chunn *	05-08-1851	James McColl H. O'Gwynn, JP
NORWOOD, John, Jr. Effy Biggs	10-30-1866 (At James Rickard's)	R.W. Farish J.J. Bayles, MG
NORWOOD, John W. Margaret C. Hall *	01-05-1859	John J. Rickard J.B. Warren
NORWOOD, W.R. A.J. Andress *	01-21-1867	D.T. McCants ————
NUTT, Joseph E. Susan Daily *	07-24-1839	William Hawkins N.W. Faulkner
NUTT, Washington Ann Eliza James	08-15-1847	James A. Holloway Joel Hardee, JP
NYE, John Ana Bella Hayes	12-06-1838	A.B. Connell ————

O'BANNON, W.H.
  Sallie E. Walker
	03-07-1867
	(At Pineville)
		S.D. Andress
		  E.W. Hare, MG

O'BRINK, John
  Martha Prescoate *
	07-13-1837	Caleb Lindsey
		  Newel Drew

O'CONNELL, Robert
  Mary Ann Eubanks
	07-25-1839	William A. Graham
		  ————

ODOM, William A.
  Nancy McClure *
	11-13-1851	W.W. McClure
		  W.N. Aldridge, JP

ODUM, Jesse F.
  Mrs. R.F. McCants
	09-26-1848	Daniel McColl
		  ————

OFARREL, James
  Mrs. Rebecca Drew
	01-01-1851	John Ofarrel
		  J. Staples

O'GUIN, Hardy
  Martha Bell
	01-27-1869
	(At the bride's fathers)
		Richard Reaves
		  John W. Leslie, Judge

O'GWYNN, Edward B.
  A.E. Heatherington
	01-20-1875
	(At Mrs. R. Heatherington's)
		W.E. Hixon
		  John McWilliams

O'GWYNN, Hardy
  Mary F. Brown *
	11-12-1850	James B. Powell
		  H.B. Farish, MG

O'GWYNN, James
  Mary McColl
	03-08-1840	Edwin Holly
		  ————

O'GWYNN, John
  Sarah Wilson
	08-14-1835	John H. Graham
		  ————

O'GWYNN, John
  A.E. Hancock
	06-12-1868	R. Reaves
		  J.F. Andress, JP

O'GWYNN, John, Jr.
  Sussanah Broughton *
	12-23-1835	Thomas Nettles
		  Elias Brown

O'GWYNN, N.A.
  Roannah Lambert
	12-21-1845	J.J.J. Ferrell
		  ————

O'NEAL, Johnathan A.
  Georgianna Mixon
	11-19-1858
	(At Mr. Mixon's on Friday)
		M.L. Kogers
		  Robert D. Thompson

O'NEAL, John W.
  Aveline V. Larry
	09-23-1835	James A.B. Flinn
		  Asa Parker, JP

ORTH, Jacob
  Mrs. Maria Pearson
	01-02-1860
	(At M. McCorvey's)
		J. DeLoach
		  M. McCorvey, Judge

OSMAND, Andrew
  Rebecka James
	02-20-1838	A. Reed
		  ————

OUSLEY, Thomas
  Polly Ann Hall *
	11-06-1851	H.R. Jo-nson
		  John O'Gwynn, JP

OWEN, David P.
  Josiland E. Nettles *
	10-30-1865	G.C. Nettles
		  ————

OWEN, John
  Mary Hanson
	01-02-1870	Phillip Owens
		  T.E. Feagin, JP

OWEN, John D.
  P. Jane Watts
	12-30-1861
	(In Monroeville)
		John DeLoach
		  M. McCorvey, Judge

OWEN, M.E.
  Mrs. C. Whatley
	09-22-1872
	(At home of the bride)
		J.A. Simmons
		  S.R. Kelly, JP

OWEN, Robert
    Martha E. Thompson
	12-14-1859
	(At Mrs. Ann Thompson's
	on Wednesday evening)
		Andrew Holt
		    R.D. Thompson, JP

OWEN, S.E.
    Ellen V. Hunt *
	07-15-1877
	(At John Hunt's)
		G.A. Hunt
		    L.W. Duke

OWEN, William
    Susan A. Byrd *
	01-11-1875
	(At home of A.P. Byrd)
		John Owen
		    Joel Hardee, NP

OWEN, William C.
    Minerva J. McLeod
	11-01-1866
	(At office in Monroeville)
		William H. Emmett
		    M. McCorvey, Judge

OWEN, William M. Ellen M. Duke	12-28-1854	Daniel Kyser

OWENS, Asberry
    Mallersie Wrighte
	12-05-1880
	(At Robert W. Wright's)
		William Owens
		    Joel Hardee

OWENS, James M.
    Eleanor F. Corley *
	09-23-1842	J.M. Corley
		    Richard Stephens, JP

OWENS, John
    Ora Andrews *
	09-07-1851	William Andrews
		    T.E. Feagin, LP

OWENS, J.R. *
    Nancy J. Kelly
	07-29-1858
	(At Samuel Kelly's)
		J.D. Brown
		    M.M. McCorvey

OWENS, Malachi
    C. Amelia Weeks
	01-10-1853	Walter Owens
		    T.E. Feagin, JP

OWENS, Samuel
    Martha M. Jordan *
	02-21-1850	John Owens
		    J.L. Burson, Minister
		    of M.P. Church

OWENS, Walter
    Elizabeth Aldridge
	02-03-1836	John Hardee
		    D.M. Salter, JP

OWENS, Walter
    Jane H. Weeks
	06-13-1854	John J. Snowden
		    Joel Hardee, JP

PACE, Bryant
    Mary Henderson
	03-22-1842	James G. Butler
		    R.F. Withers, JP

PACE, Bryant *
    Jane Powell
	05-09-1875
	(At home of John Pace)
		John Pace
		    Isiah Talbert, JP

PACE, John
    Martha Ann Rowell
	10-16-1873
	(At Elbert McKinley's)
		Elbert McKinley
		    Isiah Talbert, JP

PACE, John R.
    Martha A. Lewis *
	09-08-1865	W.H. Lewis
		    J.B. Miller, MG

PACKER, David June D. Dubose	12-09-1844	J.W. Foster
PACKER, James T. Elizabeth Leslie *	02-04-1857	L.E. Locklin
PACKER, John Martha Lambert	11-02-1874	
PACKER, Simeon H. Theodora E. Snell	10-24-1859	J.G. Bradley

PADGETT, Elijah
    Mary Jane Grace
	09-18-1856	James McColl
		    Jason Staples, JP

PAGE, Joshua
    Susannah Morris
	02-08-1855	J.D. Gibson
		    J.D. Kendrick, MG

PAINE, A.G. Mrs. Mary Hagaman	11-12-1860 (At Mrs. Hagaman's on Monday evening)	R.D. Thompson Robert D. Thompson, JP
PAINE, John Polly V. Stewart	10-08-1840	Alger Newman, JP
PARBIN, Charles P. Melissa A. Betts *	02-24-1845	E.G. Betts
PARKER, D.T. C.A. Hixon	05-28-1868 (At home of Mr. A. Hixon)	R.T. Kennedy W.G. Curry, MG
PARKER, J.J. Arthurine Foster	11-07-1866 (At Dr. M. Lindsey's)	K.O. Torrey A.J. Lambert, MG
PARKER, John J. Mary A.E. Salter	04-20-1870 (At Abram Salter's)	T.J. Duke W.W. Simmons, JP
PARKER, Lagrunde Henrietta Hudson *	09-24-1839	Richard E. Parker J. Bond, JP
PARKER, James N. Sue Turk	02-09-1879 (At Indian Springs Church)	Seaborne Moore
PARKER, James T. F. Ella McCorvey	10-12-1864 (At M. McCorvey's)	John DeLoach I.H. Salter, MG
PARKER, Othnel Mary E. Henderson *	09-08-1842	J.G. Wallace, JP
PARKER, Pleasant Sarah Daniel *	11-20-1841	James C. Woolworth
PARKER, Richard C. Martha B. Hudson *	04-27-1841	Lagrande Parker T. Bryan, JP
PARKER, Wade A. Mattie Edwards *	10-02-1872 (At Monroeville)	Asa Parker J. Menton Crane
PARKER, William A. Martha A. Foster	04-30-1862 (At Asa Parker's)	J.W. Posey M.M. Graham, MG
PARKER, William T. Manah L. Peebles	11-29-1838	T.P. Marion J.H. Schroebel, MG
PARSON, Joseph Mary R. Griffin *	07-31-1845	Josiah Boyles
PARSONS, Nelson Elizabeth Daily *	04-01-1848	Reddie Rollins
PARTIN, Charles Jones Tempa Riley *	02-12-1836	Richard H. Rumbley Asa Parker, JP
PARTON, John Alley Hamilton	03-23-1837	Abraham Reed E. Brown
PARTRIDGE, Thomas A. Waldrum *	08-07-1834	Henry Mims
PATE, William M. Nancy Owen	02-21-1847	James Byrd Joel Hardee, JP
PATTERSON, Malcom Patsy Green	05-17-1864	F.H. Liddell L.W. Lindsey, MG
PATRICK, Hiram Didana Cotton	06-14-1838	M. Patrick J.G. Wallace, JP

PATRICK, John Elizabeth Booker	11-06-1859	M. Patrick John Hardee, JP
PATRICK, Miligan Jinsey Rumbly	12-26-1847	W.P. Rumbley J.G. Wallace
PATRICK, Milligan Mrs. Martha Emmons	06-22-1854	L. Mayer W.H. Aldridge, JP
PATRICK, Samuel Nancy B. Stacey *	11-12-1872 (At the bride's fathers)	W.H. Patrick John Hardee, JP
PATSON, J.G. H.L. O'Neall	12-21-1870	Thomas J. O'Neal W.G. Curry, MG
PATTERSON, J.A. P.S. Green	08-23-1870 (At Capt. Patterson's)	T.R. Pugh Thomas K. Armstrong, MG
PATTERSON, John Mrs. Martha R. Portis	12-07-1858	H.M. Rumbley Robert Nall, VDM
PATTERSON, Malcom Ann Dukes	06-03-1851	A.J. Aldridge
PATTRICK, William H. Amanda J. Hardee *	09-06-1866 (At Joel Hardee's)	John Hardee Hugh McKenzie
PEARCE, John W. Mary E. Griffin	12-06-1874 (At John W. Griffin's)	D.C. Mims
PEARCE, R.B.F. Juna Cotten	12-03-1874 (At home of Mr. Cotten)	F.C. Fountain, Min.
PEARCE, William H. Henerietta Eham	11-11-1875 (At the bride's mothers)	John Hardee, NP
PEAVY, John W. * M.S. Hales *	12-22-1870 (At home of W. Hayles's)	J.J. Hinson J.T. Bayles
PEAVY, William N. Martha L. Kilium *	08-14-1851	James McColl Rev. J.B. Rabb
PEAVY, William N. A.A. Hayles	10-20-1869 (At the bride's fathers)	M.F. Peavy Thomas K. Armstrong, MG
PELLIE, R.C. M.E. Ingram	12-19-1880 (At T.P. Buffington's)	T.P. Buffington J.W. Joiner, MG
PENNY, Eheophilus Nancy Runnels	04-17-1856 (At home of Miss Nancy Runnels)	D.R. Rankin Uriah Atkinson, JP
PENSIFOY, James H. Mary A. Womack	10-30-1861	J.H. Stokes
PERDUE, William Martha Hales *	01-11-1857 (At nite at Lewis Hales')	William G. Murphy R. O'Connell, JP
PERRIN, J.W. Mattie J. Perrin	06-08-1875 (At Mrs. Mary Perrin's)	J.S. Perrin L.W. Duke
PERRY, Franklin A. Amanda Dixon *	02-14-1865	James L. Perry M.M. Graham, MG
PERRY, James T. Mary E. Riels	07-11-1865	Frank Perry Neil McMillan
PERRY, Rigdon Flora Black	11-10-1842	William Robinson A.S. McMillan

PERRY, Theophilus H. Mary M. McArthy *	11-23-1868	<u>J.M. Wood, MG</u>
PERRYMAN, James W. Evie Simpkins *	03-25-1862 (At J.J. Simpkins')	J.W. Guasoue T.E. Feagin, JP
PERVIS, Benjamin Effy Norris *	02-03-1861 (At Ebeneezer Church)	Burril Norris A.W. Etheridge, MG
PETERS, Elias Cherry Powell *	01-02-1834 (Page now town away)	William Powell John McCorvey
PETTY, I.F. Nancy Fort	10-23-1879 (At William Fort's)	<u>Eld.</u> Thomas Bolton
PETTY, W.J. Eugenia Chavers	10-23-1879 (At R.A. Chavers')	W.R. Chavers Eld. Thomas Bolton
PHILIPS, W.H.H. Elizabeth Newell	10-23-1870 (At Little River Church)	J.S. Jenkins A.J. Lambert, MG
PHILLIPS, Charlie Nancy Jane Smith	04-22-1877 (At Williams Chapel)	R.W. Everett J.L. Skipper, MG
PHILLIPS, James Susan B. Newell *	12-15-1871 (At Charles Corley's)	John A. Simmons A.J. Lambert, MG
PHILLIPS, John Eliza McNeal	03-22-1876 (At Joe Gibson's)	Joe Gibson Joel Hardee, NP
PHILLIPS, John E. Henrietta M.E. Kemp *	09-24-1856	W.B. Kemp ———
PHILLIPS, Ulysses B. Mary J. Gravis *	11-23-1865 (At Mrs. M.E. Ethridge's)	George Wa-son George Watson, MG
PHILLIPS, Zachariah Elizabeth Rikard	12-15-1836	Thomas Speight ———
PIERCE, J.J. D.A. Sellers	03-18-1880 (At home of L.L. Sellers')	D.R. Griffin John E. Parrett, JP
PIGGOT, James M. Sarah D. Mims	02-24-1836	T.H. Coker A.J. Brown, JP
PILLANS, Harry Elizabeth H. Torry	04-28-1875 (At Judge Torry's in Claiborne)	C.J. Torrey J.A. Massey, Rec. of Trinity Church in Mobile
PINER, Wheaton Mary Ann Pritchett	01-02-1851	W.J. Moore J.G. Wallace
PINKERTON, J.W. Josephine Anderson	01-17-1876	——— ———
PITTMAN, Allen Flora A. Rankin	03-01-1870 (At Duncan Rankin's)	H.M. Rumbley W.G. Curry, MG
PITTS, John Sarah Ann Ross*	06-01-1856 (At Herman L. Ross')	R.L. Longmire Joel Hardee, JP
PLEASANT, James W. Jane E. Foster	12-18-1867 (At Dr. J.M. Lindsey's)	J.J. Parker A.J. Lambert, MG
PORTER, Benjamin A. Manerva Vaughn	07-07-1861 (At home of L. Vaughn)	William Morris William L. Gully, JP
PORTER, Benjamin T. Julia C. Liddell	04-04-1861 (On the Ridge Beat)	William Liddell William L. Gully, JP

PORTIS, Benjamin D. Lucy Maiben	08-14-1866	John F. McCorvey C.C. Ellis, MG
PORTIS, David H. Elizabeth Marbin	12-09-1854	J.S. Jenkins Dr. R. Marbin, JP
PORTIS, E.A. Martha Maiben	08-09-1870 (At Dr. R. Maiben's)	I.R. Portis Francis Walker
PORTIS, Samuel G. Martha Gordon	12-04-1838	James Foster John B. Baldwin, NDM
PORTIS, William G. Martha Gordon	12-05-1838	James Foster John B. Baldwin, MDM
POSEY, G.W. Mary A. Blackwell*	04-23-1871 (At Mrs. Blackwell's)	H.M. Rumbley W.W. Simmons, NP
POSEY, J.W. Mary E. Rutledge	06-14-1852	George Clothier R. Graham, MG
POSLEY, S. Jacob Lucy Ann Robert	10-09-1851	Daniel R. Corley J.G. Wallace, JP
POUNCEY, R.B. Elizabeth Harbin	12-26-1847	James McColl Elias Brown
POWE, Calvin S. Mary Bradley	02-08-1854 (At Mrs. Martha Bradley's in the evening)	A.L. Bradley Charles Foster, Judge
POWEL, Elijah Elizabeth Slaughter	10-05-1837	John W. McCaskey Thomas Wilson, JP
POWELL, Ervin Elizabeth Watson *	11-30-1838	George Watson J.G. Wallace, JP
POWELL, Hardy Mary Jane Etheridge *	08-10-1843	Richard Reaves Evant Andress, JP
POWELL, Hardy Missouri Ballard	12-31-1873 (At home of B. Ballard's)	J.C. Homes John W. Leslie, Judge
POWELL, Henry Mary E. Bayles	11-02-1865 (At Jeremiah Bayles')	M.D.L. Bayles John T. Bayles
POWELL, Jasper Sarah E. Kearley *	04-06-1870 (At John Kearley's)	John Kearley J.F. White, JP
POWELL, J.D. Eliza E. Andrews	09-01-1878 (At D.F.C. Rhoad's)	T.J. Emmons D.F.C. Rhoad, JP
POWELL, John B. Isabella Johnson	12-20-1842 (On Tuesday evening)	Robert Parker Leroy A. Kidd, JP
POWELL, Joseph Sarah Tuberville *	08-08-1850	Johnson Tuberville Evant Andress, JP
POWELL, Joseph B. Margaret Johnston *	08-04-1836	Francis M. Johnston E.P. McCay, JP
POWELL, Joseph B. Mary E. Bryant	02-15-1855	James Welch C.W. Hare, MG
POWELL, Mark M.F. McKinley	12-10-1874 (At Jackson McKinley's)	J.T. Bayles, MG
POWELL, S.S. Frances E. Bird *	08-12-1880 (At home of Mr. Bird)	Emanuel Cline, MG

POWELL, Theophilus E.   03=20-1854   D.E. Thrash
  Samantha M. Thrash   (At William L. Thrash's)   John W. Leslie

POWELL, William   08-08-1842   John W. Foster
  June Slaughter   _____

POWELL, W.T.   12-15-1869   Richard Reaves
  Nancy Daniel   (At home of Alex Daniel)   A.J. Lambert, MG

POWERS, James W.   01-18-1859   Robert Powers
  Melvina A. Gould *   J.B. Colley, JP

PRESNALL, Joel   04-08-1850   William Sherman
  Rebecca Presnall *   N.A. Agee

PRESTON, J.E.   04-10-1860   Hugh E. Dauson
  Elizabeth Andress   (At Major S.S. Andress')   C.W. Hare, MG

PREWET, John A.   03-09-1840   Hugh L. Rowell
  Mary Curry *   (Returned without endorsement) _____

PRICE, Thomas   12-07-1874
  Mrs. Bettie E. Sills (At T.H. Brewton's)   A.T. Sims

PRIDGEON, N.G.   01-14-1875   Alex B. Lowery
  Jane E. McArthur   J.M. Rothwell, NP

PRIDGEON, William W.   06-02-1850   James G. Butler
  Mrs. Rosa Chapman   James G. Butler, JP

PRIDGEON, W.W.   10-10-1841   Robert Dabney
  Elizabeth Garner   W.R. Agee, JP

PRITCHETT, B.S.   04-05-1876   J.J. Watson
  Elizabeth Boutwell   (At Mrs. Nancy White's)   E. Cline, MG

PRITCHETT, J.J.   01-03-1861   Joseph Daniel
  Nancy Daniel *   (At Joseph Daniel's)   N.J. Lambert, MG

PRITCHETT, Seaborne   01-03-1837   Thomas Pritchett
  Katherine McMillan *   _____

PRITCHETT, Thomas   03-26-1837   D.W. Dunnam
  Jane McMillan   James Jenkins

PRITCHETT, T.J.   03-13-1877   J.W. Holloway
  S.A. Holloway *   (At James ___)   J.P. Peavy

PRITCHETT, William M.   10-16-1849   John E. Cannon
  Margaret Cannon *   J.G. Wallace, JP

PRUIETT, James D.   07-04-1858   J.W. Hokett
  Mary E. Hokett *   T.E. Feagin, JP

PRUITT, Martin H.   03-17-1845   Mr. Eddins
  Josse (Jane?) McDonald   _____

PUGH, Albert   02-08-1875
  Caroline DeLoach   (At home of G. Boyett)   Elder G. Boyett

PUGH, Albert   02-02-1874   G.W. Pugh
  Caroline DeLoach   (See above marriage)   _____

PUGH, George W.   11-14-1868   D.G. Wilkinson
  Temperance E. Wilkinson * (At Asa Wilkinson's)   Eld. G. Boyett

PUGH, John   09-17-1877   T.W. Womack
  A.E. DeLoach   (At A.E. DeLoach's)   Joel Hardee, NP

PUGH, Mark M. Caroline A. Murray *	12-11-1850	G.E. Longmire _____
PUGH, Pleasant H. Sarah Burton *	12-10-1838	Thomas J. Foster T. Bryan, JP
PUGH, Robert J. Permelia E. Hawkins *	04-25-1852	A.A. Autrey _____
PUGH, T.R. Jinnie Thompson	12-08-1870 (At S. Thompson's)	J.H. Duke L.W. Duke
PUGH, Whitson Susan Murray	11-30-1843	John E. Murray J.G. Holcomb, MG
PUGH, Whitson Sarah Raines	02-19-1845	Duncan McCall _____
PUGH, William L.K. Helton *	01-05-1875 (At William Helton's)	Kyle Cloud W.G. Curry, MG
PUREFOY, Henry Maranda Watts	12-27-1877 (At John Gurps')	_____ James Mason, JP
PUTNALL, Peter Stacy Day *	04-16-1845	Joseph Day _____
QUALL, A.J. Mrs. Mary Murphy	10-07-1880 (At Judge Sowell's office)	_____ W.C. Sowell, Judge
QUALLS, A.J. Mary J. Dees	09-29-1869	William Dees A.J. Lambert, MG
QUALLS, Benton Frances Bradford	05-30-1843	N.S. Graham _____
QUEN, James Sarah East *	10-14-1847	Omen Tatum Joel Hardee, JP
RABB, Daniel F. Mary W. Anders *	10-18-1848	John Harden N. Goodwin, MG
RABB, James A. Mrs. Mary Holoway	11-18-1879 (At minister's home)	W.H. Stacey L.H. Trawick, MG
RABB, James B. Elizabeth Rouland *	01-11-1845	D.P. Baldwin S.J. Hicks
RABY, William A. J.A. Justice *	09-25-1867 (At Samuel S. Cornwall's)	S.S. Cornwall W.B. Dennis, MG
RACHEL, Bryant Sarah Hall	12-05-1854 (At William Chunn's)	W.L. Wiggins John S. Bayles
RACHELS, Bryant Susan E. Wiggins	10-11-1843	Henry Kyser _____
RACHELS, George W. Ann Mariah Wiggins	10-02-1870 (At Wilson Wiggins')	W.S. Wiggins J.T. Bayles, MG
RACHELS, Hiram Isabella A. Wiggins	12-01-1868 (At Thompson Wiggins')	W.S. Wiggins J.T. Bayles, MG
RACHELS, Taylor Nancy J. Chunn	01-05-1879 (At Bryant Rachels')	A. Wiggins J.T. Bayles, MG
RACHELS, Thomas J. Fanny Wiggins *	12-27-1866 (At Wilson Wiggins')	Wilson Wiggins J.T. Bayles, MG

RACHELS, T.J.
  Eliza A. Sellars
	01-09-1879
	(At Joseph Sellers')
		H.B. Wiggins
		  J.T. Bayles, MG

RAIFORD, Robert
  Bettie McCoy
	12-31-1878
	(At Sarah McCoy's)
		C.C. Holder
		  Joseph T. Dailey, GM

RAINES, James H.
  Elizabeth East
	03-04-1865
	(At Owen Tatum's)
		P.H. Davis
		  Nathan Coker, JP

RAINES, T.H.
  Mrs. Cilphy Day
	12-23-1868	J.S. Simmons
		  M.B. East

RAINES, Warren
  M.A. Faulkenbury
	11-13-1876	J.E. Parrett
		  J.H. Raines, JP

RAINES, Willis G.
  Winnie Sanderson
	01-19-1872
	(At Tom Wiggins')
		F.A. Sezmore
		  W.G. Curry, MG

RAINES, Wright R.
  Lenorah P. Andress *
	10-31-1872
	(At Mrs. M. Andress')
		F.M. Wiggins
		  John McWilliams

RAINES, Middleton W.
  Narcissa Curry *
	10-28-1852	E.E. Rains
		  W.M. Longmire, JP

RAISER, Wesley
  M.A.F. Yaw
	04-20-1848	Reuben Craps
		  B.A. Sigler, JP

RALL, Joel Catherine Emmons	12-28-1843	Jacob Rall, Judge

RALL, Noah A.
  Ann E. Hestle *
	01-22-1847	E.G. Betts
		  John McWilliams, MG

RAMEY, S.E.
  E.J. Whisenhunt
	01-24-1878
	(At H.L. Whisenhunt's)
		W.T. Hale
		  P.J. Creek, OMG

RAMSEY, William
  Lucy Paul
	05-28-1871
	(At home of M. Boyles')
		Dixon Hestle
		  J.F. Boyles, JP

RANKIN, D.W.
  Mary V. Leslie
	04-06-1869	J.F. McCorvey
		  W.W. Spence

RANKIN, Hugh Martha P. Cottun	08-30-1860	W. Kilpatrick

RANKIN, R.B.
  A.J. Cotton
	12-05-1868	S.H. Dailey
		  C.W. Hare, MG

RANKIN, Robert B. Susan J. Mims	12-25-1859 (At Baptist Church, Pineville)	James Burgess C.W. Hare, MG

RANKIN, William
  Mary Atkinson
	12-21-1847	James H. Wiggins
		  Hugh Rankin

RASEBERRY, W.
  Susan J.M. Liddell *
	09-17-1870
	(At Mrs. Porter's)
		J.A. Simmons
		  H.J. Hunter, MG

RAULS, Lamech A. Martha F. Flinn	10-20-1867	A.B. Connell

RAWLS, Henry S.
  M.D. Martin *
	11-18-1835	Lemech Rawls
		  F.F. Harris

RAWLS, Joel
  Catherine Kelly
	02-21-1867
	(At Samuel Kelly's)
		C.R. Broughton
		  M.M. Graham, MG

RAWLS, Noah A.
  Mrs. Margaret Newberry
	12-29-1869
	(At Mrs. Newberry's)
		B.N. Walker
		  W.W. Simmons

RAWLS, W.P. Malisa Hendrix	10-10-1877 (At Eli Hendrix's)	John Hendrix J.S. Peavy
RAY, Benjamin F. Nancy A. Wiggins	12-19-1872 (At Joe Wiggins')	George James W.W. Spence, MG
RAY, C.S. Margaret A. Kervin	06-29-1865 (At Daniel McNeil's)	D.M. McNeil M.M. Graham
RAY, H.G.B. Eliza Colson	07-16-1865	J.W. Posey J.W. Posey, JP
RAY, James J. Louisa Medlock	09-05-1850	James T. Partin J.B. Rabb
REAVES, James D. V.J. Brown	12-06-1871 (At Bell's Landing)	Jesse T. Reaves D.T. McCants, JP
REAVES, James L. Sarah S. Vinson	12-25-1833	John W. Vinson ————
REAVES, J.C. D.E. Countryman	04-25-1877 (At G.W. Countryman's)	W.R. Countryman J.T. Bayles
REAVES, Jesse J. M.J. Burgaines *	12-03-1845	Daniel McColl J.G. Holcombe
REAVES, John E. Frances F. Pollard	12-14-1854	Richard Pollard ————
REAVES, J.T. R.J. Reaves	08-28-1873 (At home of W.T. Reaves)	John Azuym Joe Farell, JP
REAVES, Loveless Frances Gibbson	12-21-1870 (At Mary Gibson's)	J.M. Helton Hugh McKenzie, JP
REAVES, Thomas W. Mrs. Elizabeth Jolliff	08-12-1844	Verdel Sawyer Josep S. Vaughn
REAVES, William T. Elizabeth Hendrix *	01-28-1855	W.H. Aldridge C.H. Foster, Judge
REAVES, W.T. Bettie Bell	01-15-1879 (At home of Nathan Bell)	H. OGwynn W.A. Sowell, Judge
REED, Abram ————	10-11-1839	———— ————
REED, Radolphus E. Barton	09-26-1871 (At judge's office)	John DeLoach John W. Leslie, Judge
REED, Robert Florence Baas *	01-26-1876 (At home of Mrs. Baas')	Nick Blackwell J.S. Peavy, MG
REED, Samuel N. Matilda Roberts	06-03-1841	John W. Foster Travis Bryan, JP
REED, Thomas J. Cynthia Robinson	09-15-1841	M.A. Gaston Alger Newman
REGAN, D.J. S.T. Hinson	06-04-1871 (At home of Mrs. E. Hinson)	L. Watson Emanuel Cline, MG
REMLEY, James H. Margaret Wright	09-26-1880 (At C.H. Wright's)	A.B. Owens Joel Hardee, NP
REYNOLDS, A.L. Martha E. McDonald *	12-22-1852	J.H. McDonald D.C. Fowler

REYNOLDS, Thomas G. Mary S. Ballard	01-09-1865	James O'Neil M. McCorvey, Judge
RHOAD, D.T.C. Margaret M. Rikard *	03-07-1857	Lemuel Bowden —————
RHODES, D.B. Eliza Hayles *	12-11-1835	Lewis Hayles William Burps
RICHARDSON, Francis Martha Beard	11-12-1835	S.S. Andress Cornelius Thames
RICHARDSON, John A. Susannah Reaves *	01-23-1847	A.T. Burgess John McWilliams
RICHARDSON, John A. Allice McKenzie (At Hugh McKenzie's)	12-24-1866	A.K. McKenzie Hugh McKenzie
RICHARDSON, John A. Mollie A. Mims	12-10-1868	A.A. McMillan C.W. Hare
RICHARDSON, John W. Mary L. Moore	04-10-1867	S.C. Richardson J.F. Andress, JP
RICHARDSON, R.J. Mary A. Gallaspy	07-13-1854	Jackson Bell L.M. Wilson
RICHARDSON, T.E. Ann Maria Robinson *	05-23-1848	Samuel James Cumming A.W. Jones, OMG
RICHARDSON, William H. Lizzie R. Wood * (At Mr. Henderson's)	01-31-1866	W.S. Wiggins M. McCorvey
RICKARD, Charles G. Caroline Steele	07-21-1841	William Beard Blanton J. Box
RICKARD, Jacob Mrs. Elizabeth Snell	12-05-1838	William B. Rickard William Herrington
RICKARD, John Missouri Hall *	03-02-1855	Thomas Owsley —————
RIGBY, G.W. Isabella Wiggins (At Mrs. Elizabeth Wiggins')	12-16-1879	E.C. Metts John McWilliams
RIGBY, J.L. Irena E. Hendrix * (At Mrs. Hendrix's)	07-17-1873	J.F. Rigby Robert Smith, Min.
RIGBY, Stephen J. Nancy A. Miller *	09-13-1860	Jesse Rigby —————
RIGBY, Stephen T. Jane Griffis *	11-22-1859	George C. Burns —————
RIKARD, Benjamin Malinda Johnson *	02-09-1844	Henry R. Johnson J.G. Holcombe, JP
RIKARD, F.W. Vivian Odom * (At Tukeetchee Church)	09-13-1877	D.F.C. Rhoad J.L. Skipper
RIKARD, George M. Caroline E. Brown *	01-13-1853	W.D. Brown John O'Gwynn, JP
RIKARD, Henry E. Sina E. Haynes *	04-05-1860	L.S. Rikard W.W. Simmons, JP
RIKARD, John A. Elizabeth M. Rikard	12-24-1854	C.H. Rikard H.B. Farrish

RIKARD, Lawrence Juliann Baryanier *	05-30-1840	Jacob Rikard Thomas Wilson, JP
RIKARD, S.T. P.J. Stanton	12-28-1870 (At Mrs. B.J. Stanton's)	H.C. Rikard Archibald McFayden
RIKARD, William Lydia Talbert *	12-12-1867 (At Rawling Talbert's)	L.G. Rikard J.E. Knighten, MG
RILEY, Fred Sophey Ross	10-28-1875 (At Willis Dubeny's)	Joel Hardee
RILEY, Eliphus Mary A. Williams	10-01-1854 (At H.H. Williams')	W. Langham T.E. Feagin, JP
RILEY, James N. Cynthia A. Shannon *	05-26-1855	W.P. East
RILEY, L.R. Ella G. Avant	04-07-1875 (At Burnt Corn)	J.I. Watson B.F. Riley, Min.
RILEY, P.C. C. Northcutt	10-10-1844	W.K. Northcutt James Andress, JP
RILEY, Thomas M. Mrs. Eliza Bradford	12-26-1847	S.W. Lindsey
RILEY, W.G. N.J. Davison	12-22-1870 (At James Davison's)	T. Will Cunningham W.G. Curry, MG
RILEY, Wick W. Ellen L. Stanley	02-15-1870 (At Mrs. Stanley's)	H.M. Rumbley Thomas H. Armstrong, MG
RILEY, William M. Mrs. Anna Nettles	01-17-1852	Will Blace
RILEY, William M. Elizabeth Henderson	12-19-1872 (At James Henderson's)	Arthur Byrd James L. Eddins, MG
RILEY, W.W. Mary A. Shannon	07-11-1869	John DeLoach C.W. Hare, MG
RILEY, W.W. Beck Bayles	12-15-1878 (At home of J.T. Bayles)	J.D. Bayles J.D. Weatherford, NP
RING, William Barbry Ann Lowery Moore	12-19-1856	E.W. Roberts R.O'Connell, JP
RITCHIE, H.J. Julia A. Reaves	11-11-1874 (At John Reaves)	John O'Gwynn Peter J. Cree, MG
RIVERS, George Catherine Jones	04-15-1849	Ephiram Ellis G.D. Foster, JP
RIVES, R.C. F.E. Agee	11-15-1866 (At home of W.R. Agee)	William R. Agee, Jr. A.J. Lambert
ROACH, John J. Martha F. Hill *	12-30-1834	Jesse O. Rawls Thomas S. Witherspoon
ROACH, Oliver Sarah J. Fore *	01-03-1860	Eliphaz Fore A.D. Anderson, JP
ROBBINS, F.R. Jane H. English	05-08-1847	George Robbins T. Burpe
ROBBINS, Francis R. Matilda H. Turner	01-12-1854	William Tomlinson William C. Smith

```
ROBBINS, George B.              11-14-1871          W.J. Curry
   Eliza A. Riley        (At Col. T.M. Riley's)      W.G. Curry, MG

ROBBINS, T.J.                   01-05-1861          H.M. Andress
   Mary E. Hestle                                   ‾‾‾‾‾‾‾‾

ROBERSON, A.B.                  12-21-1873          T.P. Buffington
   Allice Wright         (At John Wright's)          Joel Hardee, NP

ROBERTS, Charley                08-25-1842          William Cook
   Mary Ann Wright                                   William R. Agee, JP

ROBERTS, Charly                 11-02-1874          Leonardo Williams
   Mary F. Williams

ROBERTS, Edmund                 04-25-1835          John W. Hyde
   Christiana McCall                                ‾‾‾‾‾‾‾‾

ROBERTS, Green                  09-01-1843          Warren Allen
   Mary Brooks                                      ‾‾‾‾‾‾‾‾

ROBERTS, Green                  03-26-1851          Wiley Sawyer
   Martha Ann Booker                                ‾‾‾‾‾‾‾‾

ROBERTS, Green                  01-11-1852          T.H. Coker
   Eliza Thames *                                    William Longmire, JP

ROBERTS, Henry                  07-22-1852          William Riley, Jr.
   Ann J. Riley *                                    C.P. Salter, MG

ROBERTS, Jackson                01-19-1841          James Andress
   Nancy Riley *                                     T. Bryan, JP

ROBERTS, James J.               05-03-1858          W.C. Cater
   Sarah J. Daniel                                   James Daniel, MG

ROBERTS, James W.               12-22-1868          J.E. Henderson
   Margaret E. Preston  (At Mrs. Preston's)          E.S. Smith

ROBERTS, John                   02-17-1838          Warren Allen
   Nancy Ann Avery *                                ‾‾‾‾‾‾‾‾

ROBERTS, John M.                09-22-1857
   Abigail A. Thompson                              ‾‾‾‾‾ James Daniel, MG

ROBERTS, L.C.                   06-25-1856          W.J. Robison
   Margaret B. McMillan                              H.S. Smith, MG

ROBERTS, S.M.                   11-25-1869          J.H. Newberry
   M.A. Newberry         (At Isaac Newberry's)       W.G. Curry, MG

ROBERTS, Thomas Lamar           11-28-1833          Sam McCall
   Catherine McCall *                               ‾‾‾‾‾‾‾‾

ROBERTS, William                09-02-1835          B.N. Walker
   Elizabeth Pearce                                 ‾‾‾‾‾‾‾‾

ROBINSON, J.W.                  12-13-1870          G.W. Northcut
   Anna Carter           (At home of Mr. Carter)     W.G. Curry, MG

ROBINSON, J.W.                  11-11-1875
   S.E. Middleton *                                 ‾‾‾‾‾ Joel Hardee, NP

ROBINSON, J.W.                  09-20-1880          S.W. Robinson
   Francis Langham       (At T.S. Langham's)         Joel Hardee, NP

ROBINSON, Richard               11-25-1874          H.H. Hybert
   Emma Bell             (At bride's fathers)        H.H. Hybert, NP & JP
```

ROBINSON, Robert Martha Salter *	11-23-1848	John Salter Hugh Rankin, JP
ROBINSON, Thomas Victoria Reaves	05-31-1874 (At Mary Bird's)	George Boyell
ROBINSON, W.H. S.E. Buffington	11-24-1875 (At T.P. Buffington's)	Joel Hardee, NP
ROBINSON, W.J. E.J. Marshall	07-05-1865	T.J. Stevens W.N. Peavy, MG
ROBINSON, W.R. Matilda Crawford	01-13-1875 (At Henry Crawford's)	N.R. Crawford J.H. Raines, JP
ROBINSON, Wyat Sophronia M. Riley *	10-24-1857	John Owens T.E. Feagin, JP
ROBISON, Cornelius Mary M. Abbey *	10-22-1857 (At J.S.E. Abbey's)	Hudson Hines J.B. Colley, JP
RODGERS, Kinnion Mary Clark	04-01-1845	William C. Ross
ROGERS, Ebenezer Anne Williams	02-20-1855	J.M. Cook William C. Smith
ROGERS, Madison L. Mrs. Mary A. Faulk	01-14-1855 (At F.A. Leynour's)	S.J. Cumming R.D. Thompson, JP
ROGERS, Mills B. Martha E. Preston	03-28-1865	J.E. Fetts (or Letts?) W.W. Spence
ROGERS, William B. Susan Andress	10-25-1865	W.C. Ross, Jr. W.W. Spence
ROGERS, William R. Mary M. Lambert	11-06-1867	John S. Chandron E. Andress, JP
ROGERS, Willis Caroline Andress	01-08-1843	William J. Dubose John McWilliams, MG
ROLEY, Thomas H. Moselle Hendrix	01-29-1880 (At Mrs. Ellen Hendrix's)	John Roley Burney Sawyer, MG
ROLLANS, Redden Mary Rikard	07-04-1847	James C. Rollans J.G. Holcomb
ROLLAR, Harry Margaret Callahan	01-23-1855	L.C. Chamberlain
ROLLINS, James C. Sophia Cornwall	05-14-1843	James Colley J.G. Holcomb
ROLLINS, Rease Frances Rikard *	12-30-1852	John Rikard John O'Gwynn, JP
RONE, Sundy E. Emily Hearing	08-30-1842	William G. Colvin William R. Agee
ROSE, William B. Clarissa Ann Saunders	09-10-1840	Thomas Taylor A.S. Dickinson
ROSS, Alex Elizabeth Boatwright *	06-14-1863	W.W. Simmons Nathan Coker, JP
ROSS, Hugh Martha Griffin *	04-16-1850	George Stainton

```
ROSS, John                              12-16-1841          Nelson Fore
   Mary M. Thames *                                            Daniel Fore, JP

ROSS, Wesley                            12-22-1870          Dr. R. Griffin
   Delia E. McClammy    (At bride's fathers)                 John Hardee, JP

ROSS, William C.                        04-21-1841          J.R. Watson
   Parthena E.T.A. Autrey *                                  Hickman Fowler

ROSS, William C.                        09-04-1818          George B. Walker
   Sarah E. Raines *                                         J.G. Holcomb, JP

ROSS, William                           02-08-1855          Alex Ross
   Elizabeth Griffin *                                       T.F. Feagin, JP

ROTHSCHILD, S.                          08-21-1844          S.R. Watts
   Catherine Adams                                           _____

ROWELL, George W.                       01-16-1862          William Rowell
   Elizabeth Cobb *                                          W.N. Peavy, MG

ROWELL, Johnathan L.                    07-10-1848          Thomas Dean
   Nancy Dean                                                Joel Hardee, JP

ROWELL, J.W.                            06-04-1875          H.W. McKinley
   Nancy Jane McKenzie  (At Ann McKenzie's)                  Isiah Talbert, JP

ROWELL, Stephen                                             Arthur Brown
   Epsey McKinley *                                          _____

ROWELL, William                         02-25-1862          George McKinley
   Catherine J. McKinley                                     W.N. Peavy, MG

ROWELL, William H.                      10-11-1839          Henry L. Rowell
   Eliza Bolton *                                            _____

ROWLEY, George H.                       12-30-1874          J.J. Roley
   Annie Biggs          (At Winfrey Biggs')                  L.W. Duke

ROWLEY, J.J.                            12-31-1876          Asa Parker
   M.E. Fore       (At Mrs. Harriett Ann Fore's)  J.F. White

ROWLS, George E.                        09-16-1858          H.M. Graham
   Missouri E. Lewis *  (At Mrs. Eliza Ann Lewis')  M. McCorvey, Judge

ROYSTER, T.F.                           02-18-1864          D.C. Stanford
   Mary J. Stanford                                          M.M. Graham, MG

RUMBLEY, H.M.                           06-02-1868          W.S. Wiggins
   Emma S. Sowell       (At Mrs. Sowell's)                   M. McCorvey, Judge

RUMBLEY, John                              1838             _____
   Eliza Man (o)                                             _____

RUMBLEY, Wingate P.                     11-13-1834          Milikin Patrick
   Nancy Emmons                                              Joshua Peavy

RUMBLEY, T.A.                           12-21-1870          H.H. Hybert
   Alabama Crook        (At Major W.B. Crook's)              Archibald Fadgen, VDM

RUMBLY, J.W.                            09-04-1867          H.M. Graham
   W.F. Faulke          (At William Faulk, Esq.)             Wesley B. Dennis, MG

RUMLEY, James H.                        01-26-1866          John DeLoach
   Kesiah J. Gregg *                                         J.J. Simpkins, JP

RUMLEY, John D.F.                       07-06-1859          George W. Collins
   Mary A. Wilkinson *  (At T.E. Feagin's office)            T.E. Feagin, JP
```

RUTHERFORD, John J. Jane Smith *	01-12-1854	J.W. Smith H.A. Smith, MG
RYALS, Robert W. Frances Davison	01-16-1873 (At R.T. Porter's)	C.F. Porter D.S. Nall, MG
RYLAND, Richard L. Martha J. Smith	05-27-1869 (At C.W. Smith's)	H.P. Smith John McWilliams, MG
RYLAND, Thomas J. Mary A. Mosley	11-03-1854	Edward Lett —————
RYLE, George Hannah Graham *	02-18-1847	Joseph Graham W.C. Morsett
SADDLER, William A. Emily Waits	01-23-1862	J.H. Flowers —————
SAGER, William Vicey Harris	07-23-1838	Jessie Hill —————
SAGER, William Mrs. Sara L. Harris	04-03-1862 (At W. Sager's)	J.R. Lowery James M. Green, JP
SALTER, A.J. Sarah Helton	06-13-1867 (At William Helton, Sr.'s)	S.H. Daily W.G. Curry, MG
SALTER, Andrew J. Beatrice Grace *	12-05-1850	E. Salter Charles Salter, MG
SALTER, A.W. Emily S. Daily	10-20-1864 (At home of Mrs. B.N. Walker)	Israel Garner M. McCorvey, Judge
SALTER, B.F. Reney Mason *	01-11-1878 (At Midway)	W.H. Woldrup James L. Eddins, MG
SALTER, D.F. Lucy C. Benson	12-14-1873 (At William Coleman's)	J.M. Chapman J.F. Bonner
SALTER, Enoch Eliza Booker *	11-22-1849	Daniel Booker Charles P. Salter, MG
SALTER, George W. Eleander M. Frye	12-18-1859 (At James Hendrix's)	George W. Dixon R.O. Connel
SALTER, Hiram Jane McGinnis	09-26-1839	James McDaniel William C. Faulk, JP
SALTER, James Mary J. Grace *	12-27-1855	J.W. Cobb M.B. East, JP
SALTER, James A. Sarah White *	01-13-1853	W.P. East Hugh Rankin, JP
SALTER, James D. Margaret L. Mixon	12-08-1880 (At Joel E. Mixon's)	J.E. Mixon Joel Hardee, NP
SALTER, John Nancy Booker	12-18-1879 (At home of W.B. Booker)	————— S.L. Ellis
SALTER, John Ann Robinson *	11-16-1851	Chatham Danget H. Rankin, JP
SALTER, John H. Susannah Northcut *	12-16-1852	J.W. Northcut A.J. Brown, JP
SALTER, M.B. June A. Pullen	04-25-1880 (At Mrs. M.M. Pullen's)	D.J. Wrighte D.J. Wrighte

```
SALTER, S.H.                11-20-1876          W.A. Patrick
    Lou Lee             (At Mrs. Mary Henderson's) James S. Rencher

SALTER, William             11-30-1871          T.J. Duke
    Mollie Thompson     (At the bride's home)       James A. Dunham, JP

SAMPEY, Francis M.           03-30-1870          E.A. Henderson
    Sue W. Stallworth   (At home of Mr. Turk)       D.M. Hudson, MG

SAMPSON, W.H.A.              02-22-1841          D.C. Smith
    Caroline Moore                                  J.H. Schroebel, MG

SANDERS, John                07-05-1849          S. Mims
    Mrs. Frances McAllister                         Garrett Longmire, MG

SANDERS, John M.             06-16-1856          Dennis Cosby
    Rebecca F. Watts *                              _____

SANDERS, W.B.                12-22-1869          J.C. Watts
    Nannie Crosley                                  W.W. Simmons

SANDERS, William B.          12-23-1834          Samuel Thames
    Clarissa Powell                                 Thomas Wilson

SANDERSON, C.C.              01-31-1866          Issrael Garner
    P.J. Garner         (At home of I. Garner)      M.M. Graham, MG

SANDFORD, Joel T.            03-24-1841          John B. Sandiford
    Martha Stringer *                               T. Bryan, JP

SAVAGE, J.A.                 09-04-1878          J.C. Savage
    Amelia Locklin      (At Perdue Hill)            L.W. Duke

SAVAGE, Joseph C.            11-28-1876          J.S. Hines
    Anna I. Daniel                                  Thomas J. Beard, Rector
                                                of St. John's Ch. Mobile

SAWYER, Ansil                06-09-1834          William Prewett
    Elizabeth Reaves *                              _____

SAWYER, Burney               10-24-1867          D. Sawyer
    S.A. Holt *         (At home of Mrs. Holt)      M.M. Graham, MG

SAWYER, Drury A.             01-28-1846          James Northcutt
    Sarah Jane Rankin                               J.G. Wallace

SAWYER, J.R.                 11-17-1875          W.C. Dees
    M.M. Dees           (At home of E.T. Dees)      W.G. Curry

SAWYER, Leantim              11-09-1870          W.W. Simmons
    Isabella Pridgeon   (At her father's home)      W.W. Simmons, NP & JP

SAWYER, Lee                  11-27-1877          J.B. Jones
    Mollie Jones        (At home of Thomas Jones)   S.R. Kelly, JP

SAWYER, Wiley                11-24-1875          B. Sawyer
    Sarah Fountain      (At Mrs. Galsy Fountain's)  S.R. Kelly, JP

SAWYER, Wiley                02-22-1857          Bartley Kennedy
    Elizabeth Warrick   (At Mrs. Warrick's)         R.O. Connell, JP

SAWYER, William              07-05-1876          Thomas Ward
    J.L. Blanton *      (At O.J. Snider's)          S.R. Kelly, JP

SCHWAB, A.                   04-28-1859          G.S. Jackson
    Jetty Jacobson      (At M. Jacobson's on        Robert D. Thompson
                        Thursday evening)

SCHWARZ, John                09-23-1853          H. Miller
    Mary L. Miller *                                J.L. Densler, MG
```

SCOGGINS, William J. Alia Grimes *	03-01-1848	William Laughan
SCOGIN, Wright N.E. McClammy *	02-06-1859	John McClammy Elias Brown
SCOTT, Robert G. Mary W. Dellet	07-27-1854	E.L. Smith William C. Smith
SCOTT, Thomas Rebecca Powell	12-05-1833	Johnathan Yeldell Kedar Havis (Page torn)
SCRUGGS, John A. M.E. Jones	12-23-1875 (At the bride's fathers)	John M. Langham Joel Hardee
SEIGLER, C.J. Caroline C. Williamson	09-25-1845	Sartt Williamson ————
SEIGLER, Jacob S. Emma Liddell *	10-05-1848	H.M. Seigler B.A. Sigler, JP
SELF, Thomas Malinda Heankins	01-08-1852	Ned Salter J.G. Wallace, JP
SELLERS, W.H.S. M.E. Holley	10-25-1876 (At Mrs. Hollies', the bride's mother)	J.W. Sellers J.L. Skipper, MG
SERMON, Dave T. Elizabeth McKinney *	02-04-1847	Joel Fore J.H. Sessions
SERMON, E.A. Frances Fore	02-01-1868	N.S. Sermon ————
SESSIONS, G.W. M.A.E. Mathews	12-12-1875	———— H.T. Sims, Minister
SESSIONS, G.W. A.E. Solomon *	07-25-1868 (At Mrs. Elizabeth Solomon's)	T.B. Bailey James L. Eddins, MG
SESSIONS, Johnathan Elizabeth Jones *	08-25-1849	M. Dailey ————
SEWALL, F.L. A.M. Finch	08-02-1875	W.L. Stallworth ————
SEYMOUR, F.A. Sarah N. Gully	07-06-1870 (At S.N. Gully's)	C.F. Seymore John McWilliams, MG
SHAMFIELD, Charles Sarah McCall	05-21-1857	Herman Gans A.J. Lambert, MG
SHANNON, Edward Margaret Rikard	03-05-1843	James Andress James Andress, JP
SHAUNFIELD, Charles Leah F. Carter	02-12-1860 (At home of E. Carter)	George W. Carter A.J. Lambert
SHEARLEY, Joseph J. Missouri Morris *	10-05-1876 (At Enoch Morris')	James A. Mims James S. Rencher
SHEILDS, John Mattie V. Lee	10-27-1870 (At Mrs. E.B. Lett's)	John Watkins W.G. Curry, MG
SHELTON, Thomas Sarah A. Branton *	02-03-1859	Joseph Jinks T.E. Feagin, JP
SHIELDS, C.C. Minnie L. Watkins	12-14-1877 (At Burnt Corn)	J.P. Watkins L.W. Duke

SHIP, James D. Eliza Newell *	08-22-1865	Thomas Hawkins
SHIP, John E. Mary E. Nolan	01-21-1877 (At W. Northrup's)	S.J. Gentry J.D. Weatherford, JP
SHIRE, John Jane Myrick	04-03-1851	Martin Byrd T.E. Frazier, JP
SHIRES, J.A. Florence Wright	01-02-1876	A.B. Roberson Joel Hardee, NP
SHIRLEY, W.R. C.L. Giddins	10-15-1879 (At Mrs. E. Diggins')	S.J. McWilliams Samuel I. Nash, JP
SHOEMAKER, J.W. Martha Gentry	09-03-1875 (At Martha Gentry's)	J.D. Weatherford, JP
SIGLER, Barton A. Elizabeth Hixon *	02-28-2836	Jacob Strocks C. Thames
SIGLER, Ellis B. Rebecca Williamson	01-10-1848	James M. Sigler C. Thames, MG
SIGLER, Henry M. Sarah E. Stevens	01-08-1852	Jacob Sigler N. Goodwin, MG
SIGLER, Jacob S. Elizabeth Hamilton *	09-08-1844	Kelley Hamilton Samuel Kelly, JP
SIGLER, John D. Martha J. Brent	10-19-1865	B.G. Hamilton W.N. Peavy
SIGNOR, Charles W. Mrs. Flora Montgomery	10-10-1850	E.H.J. Mobley J.G. Wallace, JP
SILLS, J.N. A.E. Branton	12-24-1867 (At home of T.H. Branton)	William F. Soloman J.S. Eddins, MG
SIMMONS, C. Travis Martha A. Weston	05-20-1869 (At M.J. Weston's)	W.W. Simmons Joel McWilliams, MG
SIMMONS, C. Travis Elizabeth Smith *	01-20-1853	John Smith John McWilliams, MG
SIMMONS, Edward Elizabeth Peebles *	12-19-1847	H. Fowler A. Travis
SIMMONS, E.M. Kate Busey	12-03-1879 (Near Claiborne)	R. Cunningham L.W. Duke
SIMMONS, James E. Mary A. Rumley	07-19-1866	Elder G. Boyett
SIMMONS, John A. Sarah Fore *	02-26-1843	David McCorvey John McWilliams
SIMMONS, John A. Amanda Stainton	11-09-1865 (At Mrs. Sallie Graham's in Monroeville)	Neil McCorvey M. McCorvey, Judge
SIMMONS, John H. Susan Thompson	11-22-1838	Gideon Davis C. Thames
SIMMONS, Rufus R. Mary J. Wiggins *	09-30-1845	Cooper Wiggins
SIMMONS, William W. Julianna Talbert *	01-27-1847	Silas Talbert W.C. Rose, JP

SIMMONS, W.J. Mary J. Sawyer	12-14-1870 (At her father's home)	G.T. Crapp W.W. Simmons, NP
SIMPKINS, Charles Molly Byrd	11-11-1875 (At Andrew George's)	───── T.F. Williams, Min.
SIMPKINS, William Sarah M. DeVane *	03-11-1850	Joel Hardee Joel Hardee, JP
SIMPSON, Emmanuel Mary McNeil	10-09-1869 (At home of Dr. M. McNeil)	J.M. Brown John McWilliams
SIMPSON, J.H. Martha Jane Brown *	01-02-1867	J.M. Brown J.E. Knighten
SIMPSON, J.J. S.E. Newbery *	12-26-1866	J.M. Brown Eld. J.E. Knighten
SIMS, G.W. Martha N. Bird *	03-01-1867 (At Joseph Bird's)	Joseph Bird Jesse Hays, JP
SINGUEFIELD, S.M. Mary E. Price *	04-12-1841	Daniel Kelley Hickman Fowler, JP
SINKFIELD, William Sarah Burkett	02-26-2874 (At Sarah Burkett's)	───── F.C. Johnson, Min.
SIRMON, Asberry D. Cynthia Susan Hardee *	09-15-1857	Nathan Hardee T.E. Feagin, JP
SIRMON, D.T. Mary E. McKinney	03-11-1860	S.W. McKinney A.C. Ramsey, MG
SIRMON, J.R., Jr. A.M. Byrd	10-10-1880 (At A.P. Byrd's home)	J.I. Thompson Joel Hardee, NP
SKINNER, Rev. B.J. Elizabeth Lett	09-22-1875 (At Mrs. E.B. Lett's)	W.G. Curry W.G. Curry, MG
SKIPPER, J.B. Susan A. Deen	11-13-1879 (At Joel Hardee's)	N.J. Skipper Joel Hardee, NP
SLADE, Thomas J. Mary E. Murphy *	01-15-1855	John Rikard ─────
SLOCOMB, S.N. Margaret L. Hutton *	02-19-1852	J.D. Weatherford N. Goodwin, MG
SLANTON, John S. Elizabeth Ann Daniel	07-26-1843	Silas Jernigan ─────
SLAUGHTER, John W. Sarah C. Fryer *	05-03-1844	Isaac Fryer ─────
SLAUGHTER, Lewis Sarah A. Young *	10-11-1835	Jesse T. Odum Thomas Barfield
SLAUGHTER, S.H. Ella Powell	12-19-1877 (At Packer's Bend)	E.D. King S.M. Nelson, MG
SLAUGHTER, W.H. Harriett P. Hays *	12-14-1846 (At Claiborne)	John Nye William McRee
SLAUGHTER, William R. Elizabeth Bonner *	04-01-1849	S.G. Portis T. Burps, Minister
SMITH, A.J. Mary C. Morris	07-01-1858	P. Straughn William C. Faulk, JP

SMITH, Arthur Amanda Bryant	05-12-1842	Jackson McKinley ————
SMITH, Arthur Alvarry Bowden *	09-16-1844	H.C. Middleton Joel Hardee, JP
SMITH, Calvin W. Charity Johnson	09-23-1835 (Daughter of Mrs. Eliza Johnson)	Murphy McWilliams ————
SMITH, Danson Mary S. Anderson *	09-24-1865 (At Mrs Perry Anderson's)	A.H. Chappell D.S. McDonald, MG
SMITH, Edmund Cecilia Kelly *	11-30-1848	David Salter J.G. Wallace
SMITH, Elley Susan Butler	03-13-1866	John DeLoach William Hill, MG
SMITH, George W. Allie Stainton *	11-14-1872 (At S.P. Rickard's)	J.J. Stanton H.H. Hybert, JP
SMITH, Henry Ann Bohannan *	01-22-1852	Abner Bohannan R.O. Connell, JP
SMITH, Henry Paul Sarah America Henderson (At Capt. Stephen Wiggins') J. McWilliams (Son of Calvin W. & Charity (Johnson) Smith) (Dau. of James G. & Mary Jane (Wiggins) Henderson)	12-22-1869	Neil McMillian
SMITH, Hugh Abigail Soloman	03-22-1877	J.T. Nall J. Talbert, JP
SMITH, Hyram Matilda Bohannon	09-05-1850	Abner Bohannon J.G. Wallace, JP
SMITH, Isaac Caroline Coker *	08-14-1842	W.H.S. Pearce William Holloway, JP
SMITH, James Caerinna Fore *	02-08-1873 (At bride's home)	A.W. Wallis John Hardee, JP
SMITH, John Kitty Anderson	02-15-1834	Richard R. Riley John McWilliams
SMITH, John Hearthy T. Dailey *	05-11-1843	Harmon Smith Joshua Peavy
SMITH, John P. Cary E. Fore	10-09-1874 (At bride's mothers)	J.M. Smith John Hardee, JP
SMITH, Randolph Sylvaney Mills	08-15-1880	———— John Burney, JP
SMITH, Samuel J. Mary J. Linton	12-09-1873	William Linton T.M. Riley, JP
SMITH, Stephen H. Elizabeth Atkinson	02-24-1867 (At Mrs. Atkinson's)	Bryant Crawford N. McMillan, JP
SMITH, Thomas C. Mary C.R. Williams	12-02-1875 (At Mrs. Mary C.R. Williamson's in Scotland, Ala.)	B.F. Wood J.M. Crane, MG
SMITH, W.H. Laura Simmons *	11-08-1868 (At Baptist Church in Monroeville)	J.A. Simmons W.G. Curry, MG
SMITH, W.H. Martha S. Hicks *	08-11-1872 (At Willis Hicks')	W.S. Wiggins James L. Eddins

SMITH, Wiley J. Frances McLaine	12-12-1872 (At Aley McLaines')	W.J. Downs J.F. White, JP
SMITH, William C. Rebecca D. Colburn	04-05-1853	L.J. Cumming Robert Nall
SMITH, William H. Margaret Sessions	11-17-1870 (At Sarah Sessions')	James Sessions Joseph T. Dailey
SMITH, William W. Elizabeth Talbert *	12-22-1859	John DeLoach Elias Brown, MG
SMITH, Willis Rita Crawford	11-24-1853	John N. Atkinson David W. Kelly
SMITH, W.J. Mary F.A. Gibbons	05-08-1867	William Griffin J.B. Colley, JP
SMITH, W.L. Nancy B. Salter *	04-25-1866 (At C.W. Smith's)	W.B. Green M.M. Graham, MG
SMITH, Young S. Mary Winden	08-03-1837	William B. Rikard J.H. Schrobel, MG
SNART, George Elizabeth Taylor	10-06-1869	R. Reed John W. Leslie, Judge
SNEAD, C.D.H. Frances E. Shaw *	07-19-1871 (At Dr. J.L. Shaw's)	J.A. Simmons W.G. Curry, MG
SNELL, James W. Isabella R.N. Nettles *	01-06-1852	Enos Finklea L.W. Lindsey, MG
SNELL, John H. F.S. McCants	08-14-1863	W.R. Norwood ————
SNELL, John W. Berneter Green	10-24-1860	C.R. Broughton L.W. Lindsey, MG
SNIDER, Jacob Mary Knowles	01-12-1845	Benjamin H. Dinson ————
SNIDER, Obangan J. Catharine Daniel	12-01-1859 (At William Daniel's)	D. Sawyer R.O. Connell, JP
SNOWDEN, J.E. Mary C. Childers *	05-02-1858	George Salter Joel Hardee, JP
SNOWDEN, John Emily Brasell	09-03-1843	W.G. Curry W.C. Marrow, MG
SNOWDEN, John J. Catherine Roberts	06-15-1854	Walter Owens Joel Hardee, JP
SNOWDEN, Joseph Sussannah Johnson	04-01-1860 (At Clortville)	John DeLoach T.E. Feagin, JP
SNOWDEN, J.W. E.A. Stifflemire	12-21-1869	M.B. Stillemire T.E. Feagin, JP
SNOWDEN, Oscar S. Mary O. Wright *	02-13-1880 (At Samuel Wright's)	D.G. Wilkins Elder Thomas Bolton
SNOWDEN, R.S. Billie McClammy	12-01-1876 (At John McClammy's)	———— J.L. Eddins, MG
SNOWDEN, Thomas Nancy Thames *	07-28-1836	William Thames ————

SNOWDEN, William Martha E. Coker	07-09-1855	J.B. Dennis Joel Hardee, JP
SNOWDEN, William Catherine McClammy *	07-06-1861	John N. Snowden ————
SNOWDEN, William J. Louisa McClammy *	11-19-1876 (At John McClammy's)	———— Joel Hardee, NP
SNYDER, Jacob Mrs. Nancy Stewart	04-18-1839	David Foster J.G. Wallace, JP
SOCKE, James J. Francis Sampey	12-22-1850	Daniel McColl J.P. Robbins
SOLOMAN, Bice G. Jean Mineroa Goodwin *	11-16-1843	Dr. Owens Daniel P. Wright, JP
SOLOMAN, R.T. E.A. Frye *	02-14-1878 (At Mrs. Mary Fry's)	Charley Frye Barney Sawyer, MG
SOLOMAN, William T. Allice E. Mooney	10-22-1865	W.W. Simmons Elder G. Boyett
SOLOMON, F.W. D.A. Grant	12-31-1878 (At home of J.W. Grant)	I.H. Williamson Joel Hardee
SOLOMON, James B. Sarah J. Grimes *	11-04-1855 (At William Grimes')	William Grimes S.A. Farmer, MOG
SOLOMON, John A. Elizabeth Myrick	12-01-1850	John W. Williamson T.E. Feagin, JP
SOLOMON, Leonard J. Virginia Stifflemire *	03-14-1858	Duncan Wright T.E. Feagin, JP
SOWELL, Samuel M.C. Isabella Duke *	01-22-1857 (At home of Mrs. Duke)	John A. Simmons M. McCorvey, Judge
SOWELL, Thomas F. Fannie A. Goodloe	05-11-1875 (At home of F.F. Sowell)	A.J. Sowell J.M. Rothwell, NP
SOWELL, Thomas F. Jane Henderson *	11-10-1858 (At Othneal Parker's)	McDuffie Morris Robert D. Thompson, JP
SOWELL, T. Sump N.I. Rankin	04-29-1867 (At Mr. D. Rankin's)	J.F. McCorvey John McWilliams
SOWELL, William C. Isabella Roberts *	03-26-1857 (At Thomas Roberts')	W.J. Grissett M. McCorvey, Judge
SPEIGHT, Thomas Jane Galaspy	07-15-1834	William Bell ————
SPENCER, George W. R.J. McCants	10-19-1866	John R. McCants ————
SPENCER, Oliver H. Mary E. Liddell	12-01-1865	T.J. Duke ————
SPENCER, Samuel H. Elizabeth W. McCants	08-18-1859	Oliver H. Spencer ————
SPENCER, William J. Eliza J. Medaris *	12-22-1852	Malachi Mederis Joel F. _____, JP
SPOTTSWOOD, Thomas E. Callie E. Mann	05-27-1869 (At P.E. Church)	W.R. Henderson J.H. Ticknor

SPURLING, Levi Mrs. Zada Avery	10-14-1849	A. Parker D. Hestle, JP
STABLER, C.C. S.F. McKinley	07-13-1867	Elbert McKinley J.F. Andress, JP
STABLER, Daniel J. Isabella Rogers	08-24-1860 (At Mrs. Stabler's)	W.C. Tuberville W.N. Peavy, MG
STABLER, Enos Lucy Anderson	03-20-1853	Benjamin Chapman Evant Andress, JP
STABLER, John Mary J. Anderson	10-03-1863	Joseph Powell William W. Peavy, MG
STABLER, Malachia Jane Haynes *	12-22-1836	Hardy Powell Elias Brown
STABLER, Samuel J. Olivia L. Moore	12-14-1859 (At William Moore's)	William Tomlinson A.J. Lambert, MG
STACEY, Andrew J. Mary J. Grimes *	01-31-1869	A.B. Lowery, JP
STACEY, Edward Hannah H. Hendrix *	09-04-1856	David Hendrix R.O. Connell, JP
STACEY, Edward Frances Lampy	03-06-1858	N. Blackwell M. McCorvey, Judge
STACEY, George W. Matilda Wright *	09-08-1850	Stephen Wright Joel Hardee, JP
STACEY, George W. Mary J. Grimes	09-08-1864 (At Robertson's & Agee's store in Claiborne, Ala.)	James Lowremoure Robert D. Thompson, JP
STACEY, Harrison Anna J. Hendrix	07-10-1866 (At Judge's office in Monroeville)	Edward Stacey M. McCorvey, Judge
STACEY, Harvey Malinda Alice Ross	05-18-1867	John DeLoach Z.D. Cothsell, MG
STACEY, James Caroline Hughes	07-12-1880 (At Judge Sowell's office)	F.M. Jones W.C. Sowell, Judge
STACEY, J.M. Mary Hales	02-16-1860	John Jay James Daniel, MG
STACEY, Manning Sarah Thames	11-15-1857 (At home of John White)	A.J. Brown A.J. Brown, JP
STACEY, Manning Nancy E. Russell	05-08-1865	Ollen Bratcher J.W. Posey, JP
STACEY, Milton L. Frances J.T. Childress	11-16-1860	John DeLoach
STACEY, Monroe Octavia Wagoner *	05-27-1866	Benjamin A. Tussell B.A. Sigler
STACEY, Monroe Sarah Wilkinson	08-03-1879 (At Andrew Stacey's)	A.J. Stacey J.L. Eddins, MG
STACEY, Thomas Mrs. Mary Higdon	12-08-1864 (At Edward Taylor's)	Franklin Taylor N.W. Sugden, JP
STACEY, Wesley Manda Stabler *	12-05-1878 (At Manda Stabler's)	Aaron McKinley R.M. Tuberville, JP

STACEY, William H.   05-14-1863   Mathew Lambert
  Sophronia A. Ross *   (At John Ross')   John M. Greene, JP

STACEY, William Harvey   12-01-1852   Joel White
  Nellie Jeanetta Riley * (Son of William & Sarah   J. McWilliams, MG
                              Stacey)

STACEY, William J.   04-06-1863   Neill Salter
  Mrs. Victoria F. Bandy   (At Dr. Spottswood's   M. McCorvey
                              in Monroeville)

STACEY, William W.   04-19-1857   James Lovitt
  Nancy Andrews *   (At George W. Stacey's   R.D. Thompson, JP
                              on Sunday evening)

STACEY, Willis   12-26-1877
  Mary A. Fore   (At C.R. Broughton's)   G.W. Salter, JP

STACIA, John   11-26-1833   J.A. Draughn
  Caroline Stabler   _____

STAIMTON, George   11-01-1871   J.A. Simmons
  Laura Dees *   (At home of Mr. A. Dees)   John McWilliams, MG

STAINTON, Chalmus   S.P. Rikard
  I.L. Rikard *   (At Henry Rikard's)   John McWilliams, MG

STAINTON, John A.   03-19-1862   D.L. Stainton
  Mrs. Ellen Gully   M.J. Weston, JP

STAINTON, William W.   12-19-1867   H.T. Craps
  Catherine G. Craps   (At home of Mrs. Bethea)   W.B. Dennis, MG

STALLWORTH, Benjamin F.   09-06-1855   J.G. Stallworth
  Mrs. Mary J. Stallworth   H.B. Farrish

STALLWORTH, F.M.   12-16-1875   Thomas I. Kimball
  Rebecca S. Boroughs   (At Dr. Boroughs')   W.G. Curry, MG

STALLWORTH, M.P.   01-22-1879   W.L. Stallworth
  Belle McDuffie   (At the McDuffies')   T.Y. Abernathy, Clergy

STALLWORTH, N.C.   12-21-1858   W.H. Kroger
  P.J. Riley *   (At home of T.M. Riley)   J.B. Colley, JP

STALLWORTH, Nicholas   11-14-1872   O.A. Barnett
  Dovey Stallworth   (At Pineville)   Neil Gibbs, MG

STALLWORTH, N.J.   05-17-1866   John Dickinson
  M.R. Burgess   (At Mr. J.W. Burgess'   D.S. McDonald, MG
                              at Pineville)

STALLWORTH, Robert L.   11-14-1869   G.B. Robbins
  Sue O. Stallworth   (At Mrs. Eliza Stallworth's) D.M. Hudson, Min.

STALLWORTH, William A.   11-10-1849   James M. Travis
  Celina McCants   _____

STALLWORTH, W.L.   11-02-1879   H.H. Hybert
  Lillian Finklea *   (At Bell's Landing)   E.E. Owen

STANDEMIRE, Henry   04-27-1848   John L. Daily
  Harriett E. Daniel   _____

STANLEY, Green   04-05-1865   Issac Hicks
  Emily Brown *   (At Donald Brown's)   D.S. McDonald, MG

STANLEY, William H.   10-01-1865   J.L. Thompson
  Missouri F. Hayle   John A. Henry, JP

STANTON, David T. Cebry Ann Rumbley	07-17-1857	John Stanton R.O. Connell, JP
STANTON, E.E. A.S. Harreson	01-04-1877 (At John Hendrix's)	John Hendrix Burney Sawyer, MG
STANTON, George Jefferson Mary Fore *	05-25-1838	Daniel Fore John M. Williams
STANTON, Samuel Clarissa Williamson	04-02-1835	Emanuel Cline Elias Brown, Ord. Min.
STANTON, S.J. E.S. O'Gwynn	02-12-1873 (At home of Henry O'Gwynn)	J.H. Ryland John McWilliams, MG
STANTON, William B. Mary A. Williamson	01-15-1842	John A. Stanton ————
STANTON, William B. Sarah Ann Berry *	08-14-1836	Osburn Coleman C. Thames
STAPLES, J.J. Elizabeth Daniel	05-10-1838	David Cannon T. Burps
STAPLES, John L. Azilia C. Williams	02-24-1853	Robert Wilson T.E. Feagin, JP
STARKE, James C. Gabriella G. Johnston	12-20-1855	S.P. Gray N. Goodwin
STAUNTON, Joseph Priscilla Jane Talbert	03-23-1848	Richard Talbert ————
STEELE, Andrew J. Sarah P. Daniel	10-18-1854	John Steele H. Standemire
STEELE, James Matilda Brown	06-20-1866 (At home of H. O'Gwynn)	John D. Weatherford A.J. Lambert, MG
STEELE, L.D. A.L. English	12-10-1868	J.C. Arthur W.W. Spence
STEPHENS, Ozamus A. Nancy Marintha Andress	12-22-1842 (Daughter of Isaac and Mary (Nettles) Andress)	Daniell McColl Daniel Fore
STEVENS, Ozamus Jane Boatwright	05-12-1834	Joseph O. Rowls ————
STEVENS, Thomas J. Lydia A. McCorvey	10-18-1860 (At M. McCorvey's)	J.F. McCorvey A.J. Lambert, MG
STIDMAN, Jesse Martha A. Middleton	05-05-1855	L. Bowden ————
STIFFLEMIRE, E.D. Mary J. Boyd *	12-05-1869	J.G. Evers Robert Wilson, MG
STIFFLEMIRE, John P. Martha E. Dailey	12-01-1865	L.P. Soloman J.W. Feagin, JP
STINSON, George Caroline Byrd	11-28-1858	Joseph Stinson Joel Hardee, JP
STINSON, Henry Lewey English	12-21-1876 (At home of Mrs. English)	Joel Hardee, NP
STOKES, John H. Elizabeth Ward	09-28-1851	George W. Wright Joel Hardee, JP

STRAMLER, Samuel C. Ann Bethea	12-26-1843	Jacob Rall Thomas D. Lea, Pastor
STRAUGHN, P. Frances W. Watson	12-05-1866 (At J.R. Watson, Sr.'s)	R. Fowler E. Cline, MG
STRIDER, Philip Caroline Stine	03-02-1847	L. Mayer G.P. Foster, JP
STRINGER, James Rebecca Ann Jackson	12-06-1849	Garrett E. Longmire William M. Longmire, JP
STRINGER, W.H. S.A. Dunn	10-14-1868 (At home of Dennis Crosby)	J.N. Wates J.B. Colley, JP
STRNGER, William E.A. Watts *	07-22-1841	James B. Watts T. Bryan, JP
STRINGFELLOW, J.W. Martha A. Byrd *	03-29-1854	A.P. Byrd D.C. Fowler, MG
STROCK, James B. S.L. Daily *	03-05-1868 (At John Sigler's)	John D. Sigler M.M. Graham, MG
STROCK, J.B. Mary Kearly	02-10-1869 (At home of M. Kearly)	J.A. Simmons John McWilliams, MG
STROCK, Thomas R. M.E. Newberry	02-24-1867 (At Mrs. A. Newberry's)	T.J. Duke M.M. Graham, MG
STRODE, C.E.R. Virginia P. Womley	10-15-1849 (At Presbyterian P.E. Church)	L. Gibbons J.H. Kiknor
STRODE, William R. Mary Goin	10-06-1870 (At Mrs. R.G. Scott's)	C.L. Scott W.W. Spence, MG
STUCKEY, Erastus L. Caroline E. Wainwright *	02-21-1850	Burrell James J.R. Rabb
STUCKEY, George W. Mattie Brooks	12-12-1880 (At Samuel Brook's)	William Booker, MG
STUCKEY, James H. Martha E. Fields	10-30-1879 (At John Hardee's)	H. Kile John Hardee, JP
STUCKEY, John Sarah Monroe	02-25-1876	T.M. Riley, Jr.
SULLIVAN, Michael Mary Ann Rachels *	09-10-1850	John McCorvey H. O'Gwynn, JP
TABERT, John Hester Davison	10-09-1838	John Brown Daniel Fore, JP
TALBERT, Arthur Elizabeth Andress *	03-05-1846	James Andress
TALBERT, Isiah Margaret M. Etheridge	09-04-1860 (At Mrs. Etheridge's)	William S. Etheridge W.N. Peavy
TALBERT, John W. America M. Watson	08-09-1866	Joseph E. Watson Joseph E. Knighton, LMG
TALBERT, Richard Elvira A. Simmons *	04-06-1848	Travis Simmons John McWilliams, MG
TALBERT, Silas Henrietta Bryant	04-05-1866	David Salter J.E. Knighten, MG

TALBUT, Joseph Sarah Nettles *	04-22-1851	E.T. Andress Elias Brown
TALLE, William Mary L.C. Edwards *	04-13-1848	John H. Justice T. Burps
TATUM, Hugh Caty Harp	10-04-1876 (At home of John Whiteson)	Chris Waters J.H. Raines, JP
TATUM, J.H. Lydia Falkenberry *	01-31-1867 (At the home of Lizzi Falkenberry, before a large congregation)	Charles Simmons M.B. East, JP
TATUM, Monroe Mary E. Lewis *	10-08-1876 (At Thomas F. Lewis')	Hugh Tatum J.H. Rains, JP
TATUM, Owen Jane Ross	01-15-1835	Willis Middleton Daniel P. Wright
TATUM, R.T. Mossouri Salter	04-07-1870 (At Mrs. Salter's)	J.H. Raines T.S. Wiggins
TAYLOR, Andrew Elizabeth Ross *	02-05-1865 (At John Ross')	Franklin Taylor N.W. Sugdeb, JP
TAYLOR, Andrew J. Mary P. Holland *	03-24-1838	D.M. Holland ————
TAYLOR, Armstead Sarah Harbin	09-05-1839	Nelson Fore Daniel Fore, JP
TAYLOR, David Caroline Lowery *	11-17-1853	S.P. Taylor W.H. Aldridge, JP
TAYLOR, Edmund Abagail Lambert	06-18-1841	A.J. Stephens Alger Newman
TAYLOR, Elias Martha Taylor	01-17-1866 (At office in Monroeville)	Franklin Taylor M. McCorvey, Judge
TAYLOR, Elijah Mary Lambert *	02-11-1836	Hugh Davison Elias Brown
TAYLOR, Franklin Caroline Lambert	12-22-1845	James Taylor ————
TAYLOR, G.R. Winnaford Taylor *	09-07-1865 (At Mrs. Taylor's)	A. Taylor M.M. Graham
TAYLOR, Henry Rosannah Kelly *	09-26-1848	Samuel Kelly John S. Dailey
TAYLOR, Henry R. Mary Jane Chubby *	01-07-1847	H.J. Watkins G.L. Foster, JP
TAYLOR, H.J. Mary Weaver	08-09-1880 (At home of John Hardee)	S. Murlin John Hardee, JP
TAYLOR, James Winny Lambert *	09-27-1837	Hardy Powell Elias Brown
TAYLOR, John Sabina S. Crapps	02-28-1839	Lemuel Crapps Dixon Heath, JP
TAYLOR, Sandford Frances Harbin *	10-22-1834	S.S. Andress ————
TAYLOR, Simon P. Martha M. Craps	01-11-1845	William Taylor J.G. Wallace, JP

```
TAYLOR, S.P.                    03-27-1856          Neil Salter
  Mary L. Roberts           (At M. Rutherford's)      R.O. Connell, JP

TAYLOR, Thomas                  04-01-1841          Robert Packer
  Harriett Powell *           (In the evening)        Leroy A. Kidd, JP

TAYLOR, Washington              10-05-1846          T.R. Watts
  Matilda Colbert *                                   _____

TAYLOR, Wilbur                  10-11-1839          Richard Taylor
  Elizabeth Johnson *     (Son of Richard Taylor)     _____

TAYLOR, William                 04-09-1841          Daniel McColl
  Elizabeth Roberts                                   _____

TAYLOR, William                 03-15-1842          O.P. Shephard
  Rebecca McCoy                                       W.H. Peebles

TAYLOR, William J.              09-15-1864          Alex King
  Louisa J. King            (At John King's)          M.M. Graham, MG

TAYLOR, William J.              12-16-1874          William Craps
  Ada V. Bethea            (Near Monroeville)         W.R. Lowery
                                                      H.H. Hybert, JP

TEMPLIN, Charles                10-18-1866          John W. Butler
  Nancy J. Curry           (At Mr. E. Curry's)        S.A. Pilley, MG

TEMPLIN, R.H.                   12-06-1871
  M.E. Curry              (At home of Ed Curry)       Hugh McKenzie, JP

THAMES, A.P.                    12-10-1868          William East
  Aceneth Holloway                                    C.W. Hare, MG

THAMES, C.                      10-19-1871          R.C. Brown
  Amanda Avery *        (At home of John Avery)       John McWilliams, MG

THAMES, Cornelius E.            01-17-1850          W.W. McColl
  Mary E. McCollum                                    N. Goodwin, MG

THAMES, Friendly                05-15-1842          A.B. Olford
  Lurana Sturdevant                                   William Holloway, JP

THAMES, Friendly                01-20-1867          John Roley
  Leah Colley                                         M.M. Graham, MG

THAMES, Harvey                  12-04-1856          Jeremiah Helton
  Martha E. Johnson *                                 A.J. Brown, JP

THAMES, James                   01-15-1860          W.T. Thompson
  Annette Young        (At William Thompson's)        A.J. Lambert, MG

THAMES, James R.                10-10-1839          William Newberry
  Jane Newberry                                       J.H. Schroebel, MG

THAMES, John                    01-13-1867          N.C. Thames
  Mrs. A.A. Roberts      (At Issac Thompson's         Z.D. Cottrel, LE
                           on Sunday)

THAMES, Johnathan               04-07-1834          James Wiggins
  A.S. Creighton *                                    _____

THAMES, John W.                 12-13-1872          H. Stacey
  Abagail Ward *           (Near Claiborne)           John Thames

THAMES, N.C.                    01-11-1868          M.J. Weston
  M.E.O. Stephens                                     J. McWilliams, MG

THAMES, Stephen                 01-13-1854          Terrence Conner
  Mrs. Margianna Conner                               David W. Kelly, JP
```

THAMES, Thomas Nancy Norris *	10-16-1868	Burrell Norris J.M. Wood, MG
THAMES, Travis R. Mrs. Margaret A. Wilson	12-07-1852	C.J. McDonald C. Thames, MG
THAMES, William Mrs. Elizabeth J. Torry	12-31-1848	Travis R. Pope C. Thames, MG
THIGPIN, Thomas L. Miss Smith	12-02-1836	Alfred Finch ————
THOMAS, John C. Louisa Stacey *	07-10-1862	Thomas Langham M. McCorvey, Judge
THOMAS, Nathan H. Emeline Agee	03-12-1854	James Jones William N. Peavy
THOMPSON, A.N. Susan J. Kelley *	11-03-1869 (At Joel Rawls')	A.T. Holt J.E. Knighten
THOMPSON, George Eliza E. Thames	02-22-2877 (At home of F. Thames)	George Johnson J.M. Rothwell, NP
THOMPSON, George R. Permelia R. Crawford* (At Courthouse in Monroeville)	11-12-1868	C.T. Brantley John Leslie, Judge
THOMPSON, George W. Frances J. Newbery * (At James Newberry's on Sunday evening)	11-29-1864	E.H. Atkinson Robert D. Thompson, JP
THOMPSON, George W. Mary Ann Middleton	11-05-1857	Malachi Holley Joel Hardee
THOMPSON, James B. M.A.R. Lowrey *	08-02-1845	A.B. Lowery ————
THOMPSON, Jacob Nancy Kibler	09-01-1863	Joseph Powell W.N. Peavy, MG
THOMPSON, Jessie Elizabeth Holley	05-05-1850	T.R. Thompson H. O'Gwynn, JP
THOMPSON, Jesse Sussannah Daniel	01-01-1852	Thomas Thompson R.O. Connell, JP
THOMPSON, J.H. M.F. Courtney	03-08-1871 (At the bride's home)	H.E. Courtney L.W. Duke, MG
THOMPSON, J.M. Mrs. O.C. Thompson	03-14-1874 (At J. Thompson's)	W.T. Thompson A.J. Lamber
THOMPSON, John L. Anna W. Lambert *	05-19-1850	William Lambert T. Burps
THOMPSON, John W. Lavina Vincent *	01-22-1840	Samuel R. Thompson W.W. Broughton, JP
THOMPSON, Joseph Catherine Miles	11-16-1847	William Murphy C. Thames, MG
THOMPSON, N. Rebecca Ailstock	10-14-1867	H.M. Lambert ————
THOMPSON, Nathaniel Ann Williamson	01-10-1837	Thomas Thompson John S. Roach, JCCMcCTY
THOMPSON, Robert F. Amanda C. Roberts *	12-16-1858	Thomas Thompson Elias Brown, MG

THOMPSON, S.R.	02-13-1878	J.T. Wiggins
Mittie Wiggins *	(At J.T. Wiggins')	J.T. Bayles
THOMPSON, Thomas	09-14-1873	W.S. Wiggins
Olivia Hammon	(At T. Thompson's)	C.J. Torrey, JP
THOMPSON, William E.	09-19-1858	Thomas Thompson
Susan A. Cotton *	(At Pine Grove Church)	R. O'Connel, JP
THOMPSON, William T.	07-25-1850	John D. Lambert
Martha A. Young	(At Claiborne)	James Daniel
THOMPSON, Z.D.	09-17-1861	_____
Mary E. Young *		_____
THOMPSON, John L.	04-06-1869	S.J. Stevens
N.R. Stevens		W.W. Spence
THORNTON, Jay M.	12-17-1851	Bennett McMillan
Minerva McMillan		J.G. Wallace, JP
TIMOTHY, Tom	12-23-1880	A.W. Davis
Emeline Deese	(At J.D. Weatherford's)	J.D. Weatherford, NP
TOBIN, Cornelius D.	01-27-1835	John L. Gill
Margaret Jenkins *		Thomas S. Witherspoon
TOLBERT, William	06-07-1838	Elbert McKinley
Eliza McKinley *		J.H. Graham, JP
TOMLINSON, William	09-07-1854	Gavin G. Watson
Sarah J. Moore *		N. Goodwin
TOMLINSON, William	04-21-1870	W.S. Wiggins
Lydia V. Kennedy	(At James Fountain's)	W.G. Curry, MG
TORRY, David A.	04-09-1835	Samuel G. Portis
E.S. Marshall *		J.H. Schroebel, MG
TORRY, John A.	03-29-1859	L.E. Torrey
Evaline F. Burn *	(At William Thames)	J.H. Ewing, MG
TORRY, R.C.	02-03-1869	John DeLoach
Mary A. Henshaw		G.B. Lee, MG
TOULMAN, Harry T.	05-04-1869	N.A. Agee
Mary M. Henshaw	(At Judge Torry's in Claiborne)	Richard H. Wilmore, Bishop
TRAVIS, Mark B.	03-02-1854	D. McColl
Louisa S. Bradley		A.W. Jones, OMG
TRAWICK, William H.	09-12-1858	P.P. Park
Sarah Brown		T. Moody, MG
TUBERVILLE, D.M.	12-19-1871	R. Tuberville
Mary E. Ikner	(At home of Jacob Ikner)	J.F. White, JP
TUBERVILLE, James	09-23-1858	Benjamin Chapman
Irena Rebecca Bryant	(At Asa Bryant's)	Elias Brown
TUBERVILLE, James J.	11-22-1866	William C. Tuberville
Annie L. Bryant	(At the bride's home)	J.F. White, JP
TUBERVILLE, Jesse F.	11-07-1865	A.J. Morris
Eliza J. Tuberville	(At James M. McKenzie's)	N.W. Synder, JP
TUBERVILLE, John	03-15-1866	A.J. Morris
Sarah L. Morris		William N. Peavy, MG

```
TUBERVILLE, Johnson          03-17-1875        R.B. Tuberville
   Della Bohannon            (At David Bohannon's)   J.G. Bradley, JP

TUBERVILLE, Joseph S.        10-29-1873        Jesse F. Tuberville
   Matilda Ikner             (At Jacob Ikner's)   J.G. Bradley, JP

TUBERVILLE, Richard M.       07-17-1857        George W. Davison
   Mary J. Walker *                            George Clothier, JP

TUBERVILLE, W.B.             02-02-1870
   Joanah Tuberville         (At Johnson Tuberville's)  Hugh McKenzie, JP

TUBERVILLE, W.C.             04-06-1873        Aaron McKinley
   Mary F. McKinley          (At W.C. Tuberville's)   J.F. White, JP

TUCKER, Archy B.             04-14-1842        James Henderson
   Amanda Henderson                            John McWilliams

TUCKER, Robert              12-29-1878
   Tina Weaver               (At home of Mrs. Nancy Weaver)  S.L. Ellis, JP

TUCKER, Robert              03-10-1853        James H. Ryland
   Catherine McClammy                          _____

TUCKER, Thomas J.            08-02-1845        D.M. McColl
   M.A.M.E.S. Brown *                          _____

TURBERVILLE, Jesse           10-15-1859
   Elizabeth McIntosh        (At judge's office)   M. McCorvey, Judge

TURBERVILLE, Jesse           07-18-1867        J.W. Daily
   Martha A. Morris          (At Johnson Turberville's)  J.G. Bradley, JP

TURBERVILLE, J.M.            12-15-1878        J.L. Turberville
   Missouri Bohanon          (At David Bohanon's)   Peter J. Cree

TURBEVILLE, J.F.             01-22-1880        G.L. McKinley
   Margaret Rikard           (At Travis Bales')   R.M. Turbeville, JP

TURBEVILLE, John             04-24-1842        James Turbeville
   Angelina Bryant *                           Jesse G. Bradley, JP

TURBEVILLE, Johnson          02-15-1841        William Hughes
   Eliza Rhodes                                J.G. Bmoley, JP

TURBEVILLE, R.B.             11-12-1876        H.W. McKinley
   C.J. McKinley             (At Walton McKinley's)   I. Talbert, JP

TURBEVILLE, R.M.             09-22-1856        Elber McKinley
   Sarah E. Stabler          (At Elbert McKinley's)   John S. Bayles, MG

TURBEVILLE, William C.       11-06-1856        Richard Turberville
   Margaret J. Forehand *                      W.W. Simmons, JP

TURNSTALL, Peyton R.         01-22-1852
   Laura L. Slaughter                          A.J. Lambert, MG

UNDERWOOD, Thomas J.         01-21-1869        Bassell Miller
   Susan E. Miller           (At home of B. Miller)   W.J. Curry, MG

VANHOOSEN, W.N.              10-15-1879
   Elizabeth Rachels         (At Bell's Landing)   H.H. Hybert, NP

VAUGHN, William              12-23-1838        John P. Crec (?)
   Margaret Rikard                             J.M. Clark, JP

VAUGHT, J.P.                 06-09-1880
   Lilly L. Bullard *        (At bride's fathers)   W.C. Sowell, Judge
```

119

VICK, J.D. Bettie Slaughter	05-16-1865	John B. Williams W.N. Peavy, MG
VICKERY, A.M. Mary P. Hardee	12-16-1880 (At Midway)	J.G. Vickery Frank P. Scanelyth, Eld.
VICKERY, John D. Sarah Knowles *	12-29-1853	A. Manning David W. Kelly, JP
VICKEY, Thomas W. Nancy Loveless	12-25-1877 (At home of bride)	_____ George R. Scogin, MR
VINSON, Davis Susan Hennington	04-15-1841	Thomas Pritchett Thomas Wilson, JP
WADFORD, G.B. Tempy Blackwell	08-26-1879 (At Mrs. M. Blackwell's)	Moses Byrd Joel Hardee, NP
WAGGONER, George J. Indiana Tucker *	08-04-1872 (At John Booker's)	G.H. McCreary G.R. Scoggins
WAINWRIGHT, H.D. H.L. Baxter	12-26-1865 (At Mr. Harwood's)	Alex Davis N.W. Sugden, JP
WAINWRIGHT, Hustin D. Lovey Davis	02-28-1843	Hugh Rankin A.S. McMillan
WAITE, J.R. A.R. Chappell	09-11-1875 (At the bride's fathers)	Samuel Brooks J.H. Higam, MG
WALKER, Bartlett Rebecca C. Rawls	12-19-1847	R.O. Connell R.O. Connell
WALKER, C.P. M.J. Cruch	05-06-1880 (At Madison Ward's)	M. Ward W.C. Sowell, Judge
WALKER, George Mary M. Rains	02-20-1845	Whitson Pugh S. Ross, JP
WALKER, John Nancy M. Fuller *	11-01-1836	John T. Dees John McWilliams
WALL, J.A. Mary E. McKinley	09-01-1878 (At Walter McKinley's)	Walter McKinley I. Talbert, NP
WALL, John J. S.E. Byrd *	12-28-1876 (At A.P. Byrd's)	Allen Byrd Joel Hardee, NP
WALLACE, A.W. Luarcha Cunningham	08-05-1867	T.J. Duke W.D. Garrett
WALLACE, John H. Jenetta Jones *	12-23-1856	Samuel Langham Joel Hardee, JP
WALLACE, William J. Martha A. Blackwell	05-16-1860	A. Wiggins J.J. Simpkins, JP
WALLIS, Henry D. Mary B. Snowden *	06-15-1869 (At Thomas Snowden's)	A.W. Wallis Joel Hardee, JP
WALLIS, S.D. Sarah Brantley	12-10-1877 (At home of Lucy Brantley)	Phillip Andress Joel Hardee, NP
WALSTON, Samuel C. Catherine A. Robison *	04-29-1863	T.E. Feagin T.E. Feagin, JP
WARD, Henry Millie Tatum	06-15-1865	P.H. Davis _____

WARD, John Elizabeth Bird	01-29-1842	Edwan Blackwell J.G. Foster, MG
WARD, William Martha Ann Chasley *	10-17-1847	John Ward Joel Hardee, JP
WARDROOPER, Francis Mary M. Peebles *	02-13-1845	F.B. Carter E.B. Eastman, MG
WARREN, C.W. Sarah Ann Simmons	06-16-1869	W.J. Sessions Francis Walker
WARREN, J.C. Elizabeth Jane Simmons	04-07-1869	C.W. Warren Francis Walker, MG
WARRICK, James Mary McArthur	06-26-1855	H.H. Asberry ————
WATERS, Bright Louisa Murphy	02-08-1865	James H. Barnett J.R. Watson, JP
WATERS, Charles W. Polly Salter *	06-09-1835	Daniel Hooks ————
WATERS, Charles Milley Ann Tatum	10-05-1876 (At Owen Tatum's)	Hugh Tatum J.H. Raines, JP
WATERS, Needham Eliza A. Harper	10-07-1868 (At bride's fathers)	J.B. Harper John McWilliams, MG
WATERS, Needom Sarah Rabb *	09-23-1858 (At Esq. Coker's)	John DeLoach M.E. East, JP
WATERS, S.D. M.J. Murphy	12-21-1872 (At home of Mr. Watters)	W.L. Murphy Benjamin B. Green, JP
WATERS, W.H. M.J. Day	12-24-1877 (See marriage below)	———— ————
WATERS, William H. M.I. Day	12-26-1877 (At R.T. Tatum's)	S.L. Ellis, JP
WATKINS, Charles W. Minna H. Lett *	04-26-1865 (At Mrs. Lett's)	J.W. Posey Wesley B. Dennis, MG
WATKINS, H.H. Ida P. Chapman	09-07-1877 (At bride's fathers)	John P. Watkins James S. Rencher
WATKINS, Richard L. Margaret R. Draughon	10-16-1833 ("Burned")	J.H. Sebrobel, MG
WATSON, Cary M.F. Hinson	12-11-1872 (At Emer Hinson's)	W.H. Bell E. Cline, MG
WATSON, Daniel G. Sarah T. Atkinson *	11-25-1850	William M. Atkinson J.G. Wallace, JP
WATSON, F.M. Margaret Burson	12-15-1878 (At Mrs. Burson's)	J.I. Watson B.H. Craighton, MG
WATSON, George Nancy Maning	10-21-1837	A.B. Maning Asa Parker
WATSON, George Jr. Ellen Andress *	03-10-1853	Nathaniel Henderson J.P. Robbins, LD
WATSON, George A. Sarah E. Crook	12-20-1871 (At the home of Mr. Crook)	J.M. Watson John W. Leslie, Judge

WATSON, George T.   07-28-1880   G.A. Watson
  Mary F.M. McDonald   (At Thomas McDonald's)   Emmanuel Cline, MG

WATSON, G.W.   04-24-1866   E.C. Lindsey
  Joannah H. Williams

WATSON, Isaac   09-28-1842   Hugh Johnson
  Harriet Crawford *   J.G. Holcomb, JP

WATSON, Jackson   12-25-1853   J.R. Watson
  Henrietta Hinson *   J.P. Robbins

WATSON, Jackson E.   01-14-1839   Ervin Powell
  Elizabeth Powell

WATSON, John J.   07-22-1856   S.J. Cumming
  Missouri A. Nevells * (At William C. Nevell's)   M. McCorvey, Judge

WATSON, John W.   07-29-1880
  Riller Rikard   (At Pineville)   John Burns, JP

WATSON, Joseph F.   12-18-1872   John DeLoach
  Emma J. Rogers   (At Mrs. Rebecca Rogers')   C.W. Hare, MG

WATSON, J.R.   07-15-1858   George Watson, Jr.
  Caroline V. Patrick * (At Wiley Patrick's)   Neil Gillis

WATSON, J.W.   01-24-1878   J.H. Gwynn
  M.C. Womack *   (At Mrs. Womack's)   James A. Mason, JP

WATSON, Leslie   11-15-1871   John Bell
  S.E. Hinson   (At Emmer Hinson's)   Emanuel Cline, MG

WATSON, Samuel   02-03-1870   J.J. Snowden
  Mrs. Mary Robinson   (At Joseph Snowden's)   T.E. Feagin, JP

WATSON, Seaborn   04-18-1836   James Hannah
  Martha Slaughter *   T. Burrps

WATSON, Thomas C.   05-23-1855   D.G. Watson
  Martha J. Atkinson *   Hugh Rankin, JP

WATSON, William   10-22-1846   J.R. Watson
  Ann Jane Lampy *   H. Fowler, JP

WATTERS, Bryant   06-01-1873   F. Metts
  Ellen Smith   (At Mrs. Mosley's)   B.B. Green, JP

WATTS, Benjamin T.   11-15-1842   William Stringer
  Susan Scoggin *   James O'Neal, JP

WATTS, David   01-14-1872   M. Frederick
  Martha Richardson   (At Mrs. Richardson's)   D.T. McCants, JP

WATTS, E.W.   10-13-1870   J.A. Simmons
  Trena N. Morris   (At Monroeville)   W.W. Simmons, NP & JP

WATTS, James C.   01-06-1870   J.N. Northcut
  Mrs. A.M. Victor   (At Pineville)   C.W. Hare

WATTS, John   01-21-1837   O.H. Stallworth
  Nancy Johnston

WATTS, John N.   10-15-1873   S.H. Dailey
  Liddia A. McMillian   (At Mrs. Cotton's)   John W. Leslie, Judge

WATTS, John N.   10-05-1864   John DeLoach
  Caroline V. McMillan (At William McMillan's)   M. McCorvey, Judge

```
WATTS, L.S.                          03-02-1869        H.M. Graham
   M.F. Gould            (At Pineville Baptist Church) C.W. Hare, MG

WATTS, Ludwell P.                    08-29-1857        Vinson S. Watts
   Mary Myrick                                         T.E. Feagin, JP

WATTS, Thomas J.                     03-20-1843        W.G. Godbold
   Elizabeth E. Godbold                                ─────────

WATTS, Thomas J.                     05-25-1865        E.J. Watts
   Susan Hawkins         (At John B. Canton's)         M.M. Graham, MG

WATTS, Thomas R.                     02-07-1838        Jessie O. Rauls
   Mary H. Tiller                                      H. Schrobel, MG

WATTS, Vincent                       01-19-1843        R.S. Watts
   Martha Ann Harris *                                 J.D. Loftin

WATTS, Vinson T.                     10-13-1861        D. Sawyer
   Frances Myrick                                      H.G. Owen, MG

WAY, Joseph D.                       03-15-1838        James Davis
   Mary Ann Bradley                                    J.H. Schroebel, MG

WAYMON, D.A.                         11-13-1878        Lab Covin
   Molly Covin           (At William Guskey's)         Joel Hardee, NP

WAYMON, James C.                     07-20-1879        Lab Covin
   E.V. Covin            (At Mrs. Gaskey's)            Joel Hardee, NP

WEATHERFORD, Charles Jr.             02-28-1861        McDuff Mann
   Martha V. Staples     (At Mt. Pleasant)             R.Y. Reaves, Pastor

WEATHERFORD, John D.                 06-09-1864        Johnathan English
   Elizabeth E. Waller                                 A.J. Lambert, MG

WEAVER, Algenion S.                  08-30-1838        James Sowell
   Nancy Patrick                                       T. Bryan, JP

WEAVER, A.S.                         12-16-1836        Hiram Patrick
   Aggy Patrick *                                      ─────────

WEAVER, G.W.                         10-24-1872        T.H. Raines
   Sallie Raines         (At the bride's home)         George R. Scoggin

WEAVER, Miligan                      07-22-1860        Neill Salter
   Martha E. Branson *                                 W.W. Simmons

WEBB, J.T.                           07-04-1867        William A. Porter
   L.A. Porter                                         E. Andress, JP

WELCH, Francis H.                    09-03-1857        James McColl
   Rebecca Ann Brown *                                 Evant Andress

WELCH, James                         02-04-1857        Joseph B. Powell
   Irene Stabler *                                     ─────────

WELCH, James                         02-04-1864        James Parker
   Martha E. Greene                                    J.G. Bradley, JP

WELCH, John B.                       12-27-1855        Moses Kahn
   Rosanna Beakman                                     John McWilliams, MG

WELCH, William P.                    05-04-1870        J.W. Portis
   C.G. Portis           (At Claiborne)                W.W. Spence, MG

WELLS, H.H.                          07-21-1880        W.W. McMillan
   Susan Johnson         (At J.I. Watson's hotel)      W.C. Sowell, Judge
```

```
WELLS, James                    10-23-1853      B. Blank
   Nancy Roberts *                                 J. DeLoach, JP

WELLS, John H.                  04-30-1850      Milton Powell
   Mary Ann Burps *                               J.W. Laney

WESTON, James Malachi           02-10-1848      Willis Rogert
   Mrs. Nancy Stevens                             James McWilliams, MG
         (She was the widow of Ozamus A. Stevens)

WESTON, W.J.                    12-07-1871      M.J. Weston
   E. Dubose               (At Dr. Herrington's)   John McWilliams, MG

WHATLEY, Benjamin F.            07-12-1860      Franklin Taylor
   Julia J.R. Crocker     (At O. Coley's on Thursday  Robert D. Thompson, JP
                           evening)

WHATLEY, Edmund L.              05-23-1868      John Johnson
   Sarah F. Johnson                               M. Hood

WHATLEY, Walter                 08-02-1845      Nathaniel Murphy
   Miss Lambert                                   _____

WHEELER, A.A.                   11-20-1866      John L. Holley
   C.M. Bayles *          (At Jeremiah Bayles')    John T. Bayles, MG

WHISENHANNT, L.M.               07-07-1871      J.F. Ehisenhannt
   A.E. Lyon *            (At John Whisenghant)    J.G. Bridley, JP

WHISENHAUNT, H.L.               08-11-1868      J.L. Holley
   M.M. Thompson                                  J.F. Andress, JP

WHISENHENT, J.H.                12-07-1876      W.T. Hall
   M.A. Burgess           (At Mrs. Ann Burps')     P.J. Cree, MG

WHISENHENT, L.M.                09-23-1880      W.H. Holly
   Annie Holly            (At J.W. Broughton's)    P.J. Cree, MG

WHISENHENT, Nicholas            11-24-1862      Jeremiah W. Bryant
   Susanna L.E. Bryant                            W.N. Peavy, MG

WHISENHENT, William A.          01-14-1847      N.P. Whissenhent
   Mary A. Bryant                                 Evant Andress, JP

WHITAKER, Joseph E.             09-05-1866      F.J. Norris
   J.P. Norris            (At Col. William Morris'   A.J. Lambert, MG
                           in Monroeville)

WHITE, Hugh L.                  12-23-1858      Hugh Talbert
   Susan J. Talbert *     (At Rowlings Talbert's)   Elder Elias Brown

WHITE, John                     10-24-1860      W.W. Simmons
   Missouri Harp          (At Joseph Nettles')     John McWilliams, MG

WHITE, John                     12-06-1838      John Kearley
   Jemimah Kearley                                J.T. Bryan, JP

WHITE, John A.                  07-04-1877      S.B. Nall
   Nancy A. Nall          (At home of S.B. Nall)    Joel Hardee, NP

WHITE, John C.                  12-20-1837      Abijah White
   Mary Ann Fortenberry                           _____

WHITE, Richard A.               01-29-1857      William A. Drew
   Caroline R. Drew *                             Henry Urquhart

WHITE, William A.               03-26-1871      W.W. Giddings
   Nancy Pritchett        (At Thomas Pritchett's)   H.J. Hunter, MG
```

```
WHITE, William M.                12-21-1858          Emanuel Cline
  Hellen M. McMillian  (At Murdock McMillan's)         M. McCorvey

WHITESIDE, John                  09-04-1838          P.C. Andress
  Olive Bond                                           M.D. Hixon, JP

WHITTLE, A.                      07-28-1859          Sol DeLoach
  Mrs. Mary A. Riley   (At Robert Wilson's)            T.E. Feagin, JP

WIGGINS, Adam                    01-07-1847          James Byrd
  Mary Ward *                                          Joel Hardee

WIGGINS, Allen                   03-23-1870          William Dees
  Rebeca Norwood       (At John Norwood's)             John Bayles, MG

WIGGINS, Daniel                  01-10-1877          John DeLoach
  Mattie E. Talbert    (At Mr. Talbert's)              John McWilliams, MG

WIGGINS, Elijah C.               01-09-1867          M. Frederick
  Sarah A. Rigby *     (At Jesse Bayles')              J.T. Bayles, MG

WIGGINS, Elijah D.               04-04-1846          Richard Holly
  Mary A. Barnes                                       Evant Andress

WIGGINS, F.M.                    12-24-1872          Drewry Massey
  Mary Holley *        (At home of John Holley)        John McWilliams, MG

WIGGINS, H.B.                    01-27-1879          J.T. Ousley
  H.E. Gates           (At Dumety Gunn's)              J.T. Bayles, MG

WIGGINS, H.S.                    12-20-1879          W.R. Wiggins
  M.L. Lee             (At home of William Lee)        J.L. Eddins, MG

WIGGINS, J.A.                    10-28-1870          J.H. Bayles
  S.D. Andress         (At J.T. Bayles')               J.T. Bayles

WIGGINS, James                   08-21-1834          Thomas Wiggins
  Maria Thames *                                       James Newberry, JP

WIGGINS, James                   09-07-1837          Allen Hixon
  Abigail Thames                                       ‾‾‾‾‾‾‾

WIGGINS, James T.                03-16-1843          Henry O'Gwynn
  Abagail Etheridge                                    Joseph C. Wiggins
                                                       J.G. Bradley, JP

WIGGINS, J.L.                    02-14-1880          C.E. Broughton
  Laura J. Broughton   (At C.R. Broughton's)           W.C. Sowell, Judge

WIGGINS, John                    01-14-1836          Richard Hurry
  Mary "Polly" Hurry                                   C. Thames
                (Son of Elijah and Marian (Locke) Wiggins)
                (Daughter of Richard Hurry)

WIGGINS, John J.                 11-02-1856          J.M. Byrd
  Catherine Wallace *                                  Joel Hardee, JP

WIGGINS, John T.                 10-10-1059          W.S. Wiggins
  Elizabeth Black                                      ‾‾‾‾‾‾‾

WIGGINS, Joseph                  01-13-1850          J.Y. Fountain
  Harriet A. Fountain *                                John McWilliams, MG

WIGGINS, Joseph                  11-20-1873          A. King
  Martha Atkinson      (At home of Eli Hendrix)        Samuel R. Kelly, JP

WIGGINS, Joseph                  12-08-1876          T.P. Buffington
  M.O. Burgamine       (At C.G. Brantley's)            Joel Hardee, JP
```

WIGGINS, Joseph Cooper   03-04-1844   John Wiggins
  Elizabeth Hurry   ─────────

WIGGINS, Leonard L.   01-26-1840   W.R. Whatley
  Missy Whatley *   Elias Brown, MG

WIGGINS, L.R.   04-10-1861   W.S. Wiggins
  Frances McMillan   (At A.S. McMillan's)   M. Mccorvey, Judge

WIGGINS, Nathan   10-08-1840   John Wiggins
  Libby E. Creighton *   C. Thames

WIGGINS, O.J.   12-21-1878   E.D. Wiggins
  Emma Roley *   (At John Roley's)   B. Sawyer, MG

WIGGINS, Robert   05-02-1838   Wilson Wiggins
  Mahaled Hamilton *   Elias Brown

WIGGINS, Robert D.   02-09-1835   William M. Huntington
  Permelia E. Sprawl *   J.H. Schroebel, MG

WIGGINS, Stephen   05-28-1846   William H. Fountain
  Elizabeth C. Marion *   John M. Williams, MG

WIGGINS, S.W.   12-09-1868   ─────────
  Mary J. Rawls *   (At the bride's fathers)   John McWilliams

WIGGINS, Thomas   12-05-1858   E.D. Wiggins
  Lurana Rachels   (At William Chunn's)   John T. Bayles, MG

WIGGINS, Thomas D.   12-17-1857   W.S. Wiggins
  Sarah A. Lindsey *   (On Thursday)   C.W. Hare

WIGGINS, Thomas S.   04-10-1867   J.F. McCorvey
  H.B. McCorvey   W.W. Spence, MG

WIGGINS, William Calloway   02-10-1851   James T. Wiggins
  Rutha Barnes   Evant Andress, JP

WIGGINS, Wilson J. (S?)   08-30-1834   John Biggs
  Mary Biggs *   (At Methodist Episcopal Church) H.B. Travis

WIGGINS, W.N.   11-11-1874   D. Massey
  L.A. Bowden   (At Mrs. L. Bowden's)   Isaih Talbert, JP

WIGGINS, William Richard   08-26-1867   Abner Dees
  Susan Ellen Weston   (At M.J. Weston's)   John McWilliams, MG
         (Son of John & Mary (Hurry) Wiggins)
         (Dau. of James Malachi and Nancy (Andress) Weston)

WIGGINS, W.S.   11-20-1879   Joseph Wiggins
  J.T. Adkinson *   (At Joseph Wiggins')   J.M. Rothwell, NP

WILKINSON, David G.   01-16-1855   Asa Wilkinson
  Sarah Byrd   (At home of Moses Byrd)   T.E. Feagin, JP

WILKINSON, George   06-12-1872   J.A. Simmons
  Sarah E. Burtram   (At Judge's office)   John W. Leslie, Judge

WILKINSON, Henry A.J.   08-27-1865   D.J. Wilkinson
  Jincy J. Feaster *   J.J. Simpkins

WILKINSON, J.P.   11-10-1880   J.D. Mathews
  Cora Snowden *   (At Joseph Snowden's)   Elder Thomas Bolton

WILLIAMS, C.M.   10-12-1876   J.C. Williams
  Bettie Sermon   (At Joel Hardee's)   F. Jetter, Minister

WILLIAMS, George   05-24-1868   H.W. McKinley
  L.A. Schoffeild   J.F. Andress, JP

WILLIAMS, Hosen Lucinda Gatlin	12-19-1850	<u>T.E. Feagin</u>
WILLIAMS, I.S. Mary C. Robison	10-04-1865	A. Foster W.N. Peavy, MG
WILLIAMS, James A. Cornelia R. Morrissett	12-23-1863	W.J. Robison William N. Peavy
WILLIAMS, John Melinda Powell	06-01-1843	John S. Dailey J.G. Bradley, JP
WILLIAMS, John B. Catherine G. Moore *	07-15-1856	Arthur Foster N. Goodwin, MG
WILLIAMS, John B. Kitty Maibin	08-30-1865	William A. Parker W.N. Peavy, MG
WILLIAMS, Seaborn Winney Loyd	04-06-1876 (At J.D. Weatherford's)	E.P. Morris J.D. Weatherford
WILLIAMS, Washington Edie Ann Harris	10-10-1876 (At office in Monroeville)	Charles McCarthey W.C. Sowell, Judge
WILLIAMSON, James S. Martha W. Roach *	09-21-1837	John J. Roach J.H. Schroebel, MG
WILLIAMSON, J.E. M.A. Sirmon	12-04-1879 (At Joel Hardee's)	D.C. Curry Robert Smiley, MG
WILLIAMSON, John M. Elizabeth Thompson *	12-03-1835	Samuel Stanton Cornelius Thames
WILLIAMSON, John M. Harriett P. Owens *	10-11-1838	Robert Williamson C. Thames
WILLIAMSON, John W. Maria Soloman *	01-25-1852	F.B. Robbins T.E. Feagin, JP
WILLIAMSON, Richard Sarah Gaston	08-28-1838	Michael Durr J.H. Schroebel, MG
WILLIAMSON, Robert Elizabeth R. Barry	01-22-1838	William Staunton C. Thames, MG
WILLIAMSON, Samuel D. Ann Cato *	01-17-1850	Abner Aldridge C. Thames, MG
WILLIAMSON, Sarke Mary Ann Reed	05-11-1845	_____ _____
WILLIAMSON, S.D. Louisa McNeill	03-07-1867 (At James McNeill's)	C.R. Broughton John McWilliams, MG
WILSON, Augustus Josephine Langham	12-05-1878 (At Phillip Owens')	Wilbur Hems Joel Hardee, JP
WILSON, Green E.A. Collins *	12-02-1860 (At G.W. Collins')	G.W. Collins T.E. Feagin, JP
WILSON, Hiniant S. Nancy Jane Daniel	04-12-1838	Dixon Hestle James Andress
WILSON, Jack R. Sallie A. Marshall *	04-07-1851	John Marshall _____
WILSON, William J. Martha Williams	01-07-1858 (At Elyphas Riley's)	James McColl T.E. Feagin, JP

```
WINSLETT, Randall            12-31-1835          Allen Petters
  Harriett Harp                                    Thomas Wilson, JP

WITHERS, Richard H.          12-07-1839          Cypean Lambert
  Dorry Ann Lambert                                T. Burrps

WOLF, Adolph                 01-04-1851          Lazamus Mayes
  Nancy Jacobson                                   N.A. Agee

WOMACK, Lewis                01-24-1867          Willis Chiles
  Emma Chiles                                      W.D. Garrett, JP

WOOD, A.J.                   12-28-1867          William Porter
  N.A. Bryant                                      M. McCorvey, Judge

WOOD, Benjamin F.            01-07-1839          R.O. Connell
  Jane Robison *                                   _____

WOOD, Calvin R.              08-06-1850          W.W. McColl
  Eliza Marshall *                                 _____

WOOD, J.M.                   10-10-1867          T.J. Duke
  M.A. Wright       (At John Massingale's)         M.M. Graham, MG

WOODAM, J.N.                 02-25-1858          Adam Wiggins
  Mary Y. Wiggins * (J?)                           Joel Hardee, JP

WOOD, John                   01-04-1870          A. Wiggins
  Mary Fisher       (At Jordan Fisher's)           Joel Hardee, JP

WOOD, John W.                12-28-1867          W.S. Wiggins
  Perlena Rikard                                   _____

WOODHAM, J.N.                12-10-1859          John Wiggins
  Eliza Wiggins *                                  J.J. Simpkins

WOODSON, A.G.                03-23-1843          Hugh Jones
  Jane Henderson                                   _____

WOOLWORTH, James C.          04-30-1840          Thomas Mason
  Winneyford Perkins   (At the M.E. Church)        Peter Haskins, Elder

WRENN, William J.            11-02-1876          J.A. Fore
  Eugenia E. Busey    (At R.A. Lambert's)          L.W. Duke

WRIGHT, Charles T.           01-05-1873          J.H. Wright
  Henrietta Stifflemire * (At Mrs. E.J. Stifflemire's)  Joel Hardee

WRIGHT, Duncan               03-30-1861          J.J. Simpkins
  Frances Stifflemire  (At Jane Stifflemire's)     T.E. Feagin, JP

WRIGHT, George               02-10-1850          J.H. Stikes
  Mary J.M. Stokes *                               Joel Hardee, JP

WRIGHT, George W.            01-09-1868          S. Middleton
  M.E. McLendon *   (At William Hopkins')          James L. Eddins, MG

WRIGHT, Jefferson            01-04-1857          L.J. Soloman
  Sarah Jane Soloman * (At John Soloman's)         S.A. Farmer, MG

WRIGHT, Jeptha               12-11-1866          J.T. Davis
  Sarah E. Robbins                                 _____

WRIGHT, John                 03-15-1846          Stephen Wright
  Eliza Ann Soloman                                Joel Hardee, JP

WRIGHT, John W.              11-03-1872          W.B. Kemp
  Mary Ingraham     (At William Ingram's)          Joel Hardee
```

WRIGHT, L.C.
  T.E. Stinsin
	01-09-1878
	(At D.G. Wilkinson's)
		D.G. Wilkinson
		  Joel Hardee, NP

WRIGHT, Rob
  Narcissa Andrews
	05-12-1874
	(At Groom's residence)
		_____
		  Joel Hardee, NP

WRIGHT, Samuel
  Mary Caroline Soloman *
	11-02-1842	Stephen Wright
		  _____

WRIGHT, Stephen
  Mary Johnston
	08-20-1840	W.B. Alfred
		  M.D. Dixon, JP

WRIGHT, Wade
  Drucilla Grimes
	08-09-1857	John DeLoach
		  T.A. Farmer

YOUNG, Benjamin H.
  Mary Knowles *
	07-28-1853	Green Brown
		  W.H. Aldridge, JP

YOUNG, Jacob J.
  Mary A. Middleton *
	10-16-1854	H.W. Dailey
		  L.W. Lindsey

YOUNG, Jacob J.
  Malinda E. David
	12-09-1841	John Young
		  J.G. Holcomb, JP

YOUNG, John
  Elizabeth Hussa (?)
	04-23-1840
	("Bond Mislaid")
		_____
		  Thomas Wilson, JP

YOUNG, John
  Elizabeth Henson
	04-17-1841	James Hardaway
		  _____

YOUNG, William
  Rebecca Hussey
	01-07-1844	John Young
		  J.G. Holcombe, JP

YOUNG, William
  Julia Ann Dailey *
	01-04-1849	L.O. Dailey
		  J.G. Wallace, JP

YOUNGBLOOD, A.J.
  Katie Harper
	10-21-1874
	(At the bride's home)
		W.T. Joiner
		  J.B.F. Watts, Minister

YOUNGBLOOD, David
  Anna Mason *
	01-09-1873
	(At Richard Mims')
		William Hicks
		  James L. Eddins, MG

YOUNGBLOOD, J.R.
  Nancy Hicks
	08-08-1851
	(See marriage below)
		Jesse Hicks
		  _____

YOUNGBLOOD, J.R.
  Nancy Hicks
	08-15-1857	Jesse Hicks
		  W.M. Longmire

CONECUH COUNTY MARRIAGES

COUNTY SEAT: EVERGREEN, ALABAMA

(1866-1876)

NOTE: This addendum contains approximately 600 marriages from Conecuh
County, Alabama.   It spans the years of the Reconstruction Period in
the south from 1866 to 1876.   This section has been included in this
volume since Conecuh County was formed from and adjoins Monroe County.
Many of the same families settled in both counties.   These marriage
records are the earliest on file in Conecuh County due to a courthouse
fire in Evergreen that destroyed all records through 1865.

A reverse index for brides is provided separate from the Monroe
County reverse index.   No attempt was made to change any spellings;
they are transcribed here just as they were originally recorded.   An
asterick following the bride's name indicates that the marriage was
performed by consent.   A marriage by consent showing that one or both
parties were not of age may be of value to the researcher in approximating ages.

Conecuh County was created on February 13, 1818 by the terri-
torial legislature.   The county included all of south Alabama east of
its present western boundary and south from the present Lowndes County
line extending to the Chattahoochee River.   The first white settler in
Conecuh County, Samuel Buchanan, arrived in 1815.

1. GROOM 2. BRIDE	DATE	SERVICE BY
ADAMS, John Q. Carolyn Horton	04-28-1867 (At George Robinson's)	Jesse Thames
ADAMS, W. Nancy Barlow	04-21-1872	Thomas Ansley, MG
ALBREAST, Charles G. D. Benten	10-25-1874	J.M. Wood, MG
ALDRIDGE, Linus Sukey Willis	06-11-1872 (At Bemis' Store)	Franklin Yates, Min.
ALEXANDER, George Margaret Brown *	12-23-1874	Ingram Spence, MG
ALEXANDER, James Mary A. Brown	02-18-1869	William Sheffield, MG
AMERSON, Thomas Sarah Carter	03-24-1871	A.W. Jones, Judge
ANDERSON, D.J. Elizabeth White	07-05-1868	J.F. Lee, JP
ANDERSON, William T. Susan Chavers *	08-16-1868	Emanuel Cline, MG
ANDREWS, James Mary L. Gulley *	11-27-1867 (At Henry Gulley's)	J.W. Sampey, Minister
ANGLE, J.J. Sarah E. Brown *	03-26-1871	A.W. Jones, Judge
ANGLE, W.J. Virginia Windham	04-29-1875 (At her father's residence)	L.M. Piggott
ASHLEY, W.T. S.A. Anderson *	01-17-1871 (At Mrs. Anderson's)	Andrew Jay, MG
ATKINSON, J.C. Louisa Harold	11-17-1868	T.S. Sowell, JP
ATKINSON, Captain James W. Sarah C. Morrow	07-16-1867	————
BAGGETT, J.G. M.C. Mason	10-13-1873	————
BAGGETT, Richard T. Mrs. Sophia Hobbs	04-09-1867	Andrew Jay, MG
BAIN, W.S. Carolyn S. Johnson * (Dau. of John Johnson and Nancy Garlington Salter Johnson)	01-01-1868	J.R. Jones, MG
BAKER, W.S. Martha Butler *	01-16-1868 (At Daniel Butler's)	A.W. Jones, MG
BALLARD, James C. Phebe E. Gulley *	12-24-1872 (At Harry Gulley's)	E. Cline, MG
BANFIELD, H.H. S.A. Howell *	12-19-1872	Rev. Thomas Ansley

BARFIELD, John R.   02-28-1867   W.W. Graham, MG
  Martha Tisdale   (At Mrs. Tisdale's)

BARLOW, Elias, Jr.   01-03-1869   William Sheffield, MG
  Susann Daniels   (At Harper School House)

BARLOW, Theodocius   02-20-1867   J.R. Jones, MG
  Mary Ann Etharage

BARNCASTLE, William Henry   10-20-1867   Charles Bankstin, JP
  Mary Fuquae *

BARRON, Thomas T.   11-12-1873   Wm. Beard, JP
  L.D. McCall   (At Residence of Asa Johnston)

BEARD, Blake   02-12-1871   Wm. Beard, JP
  Laura Bruton *   (At Wm. J. Bruton's)

BECK, J.W.   01-06-1868   F.S. Sowell, JP
  M.E. Moore

BECK, Wilson   06-19-1868   Henry Urgerbrub, MG
  Lou M. Lamm   (At Capt. J.F. Bonifay's at Mobile, Ala.)

BEDDINGFIELD, Charles A.   10-22-1873   Robert Smilie, MG
  Drucilla Watson *

BEDDINGFIELD, John S.   06-28-1874   D.L. Carter, JP
  Sarah Dixon

BEDGOOD, S.A.   03-04-1872   J.M. Matthews, JP
  Frances Pearson   (Res. of James F. Ingram)

BELL, C.A.   12-17-1867   Francis Walker, MG
  F.A. Thompson   (At bride's mothers home)

BELL, M.H.   08-01-1873   _____
  Scitha A. Ball *

BELL, T.S.   12-24-1872   William Watson, JP
  Media Thompson   (At C.W. Bell's)

BENSON, William   02-04-1869   H.J. Hunter, MG
  Nancy C. Reed *   (At J. Reed's)

BETHIS, Goodman   12-19-1872   J.E. McIver, MG
  Vida Raburn *   (At Brooklyn)

BETTS, James R.   12-11-1873   D.L. Carter, JP
  Victoria Salter *   (She was descended from Eli & Susan
                          Lasseter Salter)

BIGGS, Charles M.   12-25-1874   L.W. Duhe
  M.C. Helton *

BIRD, Andrew   01-13-1872   _____
  Victoria Milligan *

BLACK, E.L.   11-22-1866   James T. Higdon, JP
  Elizabeth Lee *   (At Res. of Mrs. Adilla Lee)

BLACK, James   08-22-1867   B.L. Anderson, JP
  Mary E. Ellis

BLACK, James   09-23-1871   A.M. Thomaston, MG
  Misuri Garrett

BLACKBURN, Joseph M.   12-16-1869   W.J. Overstreet, OMG
  Mary A. Householder

BLACKSHER, William Christa Lankford	10-22-1868	John S. Moore, OMG
BLACKWELL, W.J. Laura J. Cooper *	04-23-1874	A.W. Jones, Judge
BLEVINS, James C. Alice C. Salter *	12-19-1866	Georga Christian, JP
BLEW, Elbert J. Eliza A. McGowan	12-04-1868	F. Cook, MG
BOND, Fisher Clara Nicholson	10-06-1868 (At Evergreen)	G.W. Boggs, Bishop
BOOKER, Franklin Texana Salter *	09-16-1869 (At A.J. Salter's)	J.M. Wood, MG
BRANCH, Monroe Nancy Diamond *	12-26-1872 (At Mr. Diamond's)	Rev. Ingram Spence
BRANCH, William G. S.A. Moore *	05-09-1867 (At Mary Moore's, mother of the bride)	John M. Henderson, Judge
BRANTLEY, E.A. M.J. Thomas	01-19-1870 (At Res. of Alfred Thomas)	Jesse Thames
BRANTLEY, Harris H. Susan R. Page	12-16-1868	William Beard, JP
BRANTON, C.F. M.M. Smith	11-23-1868	_____
BROOKS, M.G. M.A. McIntyre *	10-24-1873	_____
BROOKS, Nathaniel Martha A. Brooks *	02-04-1875	W.D. Hidgon, JP
BROOKS, Samuel Susannah Harrell	03-04-1870	William Beard, JP
BROOKS, Samuel Narcissa Hammonds	03-28-1872	A.W. Jones, Judge
BROWN, David J. Mary E. Aarons *	02-15-1871 (At J.C. Travis's)	Alfred J. Miller, MG
BROWN, J.H.L. Sarah A. Reid	01-02-1868	J.M. Piggott, JP
BROWN, James B. Susannah Davis *	06-21-186?	_____
BROWN, James S. Susan Davis	01-26-1872 (At Mrs. Davis')	James E. Brown, JP
BROWN, W.E. Ollie Stinson	11-20-1873	A.W. Jones, Judge
BROWN, Zach E.M. Joiner	04-27-1871	A.W. Jones, Judge
BRYANT, Thomas Elizabeth Warren	12-05-1867	Charles Backstin, JP
BRYER, P.M. Margaret C. Hawthorn	10-12-1869	William Beard, JP

BULLOCK, Isaac Martha Jane Morgan	02-20-1868	J.M. Piggott, JP
BURKETT, James Epsey Weaver	01-03-1871	Wm. Sheffield, MG
BURKETT, James M. Francis L. Burkett	11-11-1868	Wm. Beard, JP
BURT, B.F. A.B. Thompson	08-28-1873	Robert Smith, MG
BUTLER, James M. Fannie Holliman	———	———
CALLAHAN, A.G. Mary Garrett	09-06-1868	Parson Lowery
CALLOWAY, Origin E. Eliza Ann Dunn *	11-12-1870	———
CAMPBELL, Abner Mrs. Rebecca Moneyhan	10-05-1867 (At Res. of Andrew Jay)	Andrew Jay, MG
CAMPBELL, Davis Nancy Bryant *	01-21-1869 (At C. Bachiten's)	J.F. Cook, MG
CAMPBELL, Wiley Mary Hawsey	03-17-1867	John S. Martin, JP
CARDWELL, Tilman T. Emily Johnson	03-08-1868	J.R. Jones, OMG
CARIGE, Charles Mary E. Joiner *	07-03-1867	———
CARTER, David L. Martha J. Bell *	03-12-1872	———
CARTER, L.W. Sophronia McKee	11-16-1870	Archibald McFadyen, FDM
CARTWRIGHT, Nathaniel Sarah J. Bohanan	04-05-1869	William Beard, JP
CATHAN, Thomas H. A.C. Knighton	10-15-1868	J.R. Jones, OMG
CHAPMAN, Charles E. S.E. Thomas *	05-11-1873 (At Res. of L.B. Chapman)	A.W. Jones, Judge
CHASTAIN, George Martha L. Chapman	10-27-1847	Rev. Alexander Travis
CHITTY, G.A. C. Reid *	02-09-1871	R.H. Varner, JP
CHITTY, J.S. Harriett Reeves *	07-07-1874	R.H. Varner, JP
CHUTE, George T. Sarah Mays *	12-19-1866	T.S. Sowell, JP
CLARK, W.D. Amanda Davis	03-09-1870 (At Mrs. Davis's)	W.A. Walker, JP
COALMAN, Allen V. Mary Davis	12-01-1873	J.E. Brown, JP

COBB, James   09-07-1865   J.J. Jarnegin, JP
  Mary Pearson

COBB, Samuel D.   06-22-1866   W.C. Morrow, MG
  Sarah A. Holloman

COBB,S.P.   03-30-1874   Ingram Spence, MG
  Mrs. E. Harague

COKER, J.H.   07-17-1871   _____
  H.R.S. Troutman *

COKER, William H.   02-21-1867   J.R. Jones
  Mrs. Elizabeth Patterson

COLEMAN, P.S.   05-17-1871   A.J. Miller, MG
  Susan Wiggins   (At Kay Wiggins' Residence)

COLLINS, H.F.   11-28-1872   William D. Tomlinson, NP
  M. Jane Heniu?   (At Evergreen)

COOK, James J.   10-10-1867   J.M. Piggott, JP
  Emily C. Higdon

COOPER, A.J.   10-07-1868   _____
  Tabitha E. Blair

COOPER, J.J.   01-13-1867   R.H. Varner, JP
  E.J. Wellis *   (At R.H. Varner's)

COOPER, J.J.   11-25-1873   S.L. Lowery, MG
  Susannah L. Hammons *

COOPER, John B.   08-26-1872   A.W. Jones, Judge
  A. Mosley   (At Mrs. A. Thomas's)

COOPER, Monroe E.   08-25-1874   John W. Morgan, JP
  Elizabeth Creamer

COVIN, William   10-25-1874   John W. Morgan, JP
  Elena Durden

COWART, Thomas J.   01-23-1873   R.H. Varner, JP
  Mary _____

COWART, W.Y.   02-01-1870   R.H. Varner, JP
  Nancy C. Piggott

COX, David H.   10-14-1869   William Beard, JP
  S.F. Moore

CRAWFORD, John S.   05-17-1869   J. M. Wood
  Sarah C. Thompson   (At Rural Hill, Conecuh Co.)

CREAMER, P.C.   10-24-1874   R.H. Varner, JP
  Aelpha Powell   (At Cooper's Store)

CROSBY, James M.   02-22-1867   S. Maxwell, OMG
  Nannie Stallworth

CUNNINGHAM, James   04-14-1858   Ithiel Lee, JP
  Susan J. McCrearey * (Records substituted on proof Apr. 11, 1870)

DANIEL, G.B.   03-21-1869   William Sheffield, MG
  Ann H. Mason

DANIEL, James   01-10-1867   R.H. Varner, JP
  Phereba Etharage *   (At Abel Etharage's)

DANIEL, Thomas Henrietta Haddow *	12-20-1868	J.L. Skipper
DANIELS, A.L. Alice A. Baggett *	11-08-1869 (At R.T. Baggett's Res.)	Rev. Jacob Smith
David, Wilson A. Martha Burton	11-14-1867	J.J. Cooper, MG
DAVIS, M.A. Mary E. Thomas	11-25-1873	Rev. A. Lunsford
DAVIS, William Eliza Lee	04-13-1873 (At Res. of Mrs. Lee)	Rev. Ingram Spence
DAW, James S. Mary B. Atkinson	02-09-1872	_____
DAW, John S. Annie J. Davidson *	12-24-1874	John N. Sowell, JP
DAW, Z.T. M.E. Johnson *	01-12-1874	_____
DEAN, James D. Anna Mixon	12-09-1874 (At Mixon's)	W.W. Walker
DEAN, Stephen Frances Watt	08-25-1867 (At Res. of Thomas Dunn)	J.T. Higdon
DEEN, F.M. Matilda Joiner *	11-29-1866	J.S. Martin, JP
DEEN, John S. S. Page *	12-04-1871	_____
DEER, J.H. Lydia Hart	05-01-1871	_____
DEWBERRY, John Harriett Higdon	02-10-1874 (At Mr. Blackwell's)	David S. Nall, MG
DIAMOND, James Margaret McDavid	02-02-1872	A.W. Jones, Judge
DIAMOND, John Matilda Johnson	07-24-1873	L.D. Carter, JP
DIXON, James Susan H. Sheffield	08-21-1867	Elias Barlow, JP
DOBBS, William H. Lucinda Etheridge	01-26-1868	R.H. Varner, JP
DOLLYHITE, William H. M.E. Pew *	09-15-1869 (At home)	Jacob Smith
DONALD, John C. Swina Stanley *	07-15-1872	_____
DOUGLAS, Henry H. Permelia Lee *	05-28-1868	R.H. Varner, JP
DOWNING, John Jane Mancell	07-25-1866	C. Backstein, JP
DOWNING, W.C. Elizabeth Bozeman *	11-14-1866	_____
DREADEN, John F. Caroline Ward *	12-30-1872	_____

DREW, James Mary E. Giddins	04-27-1870 (By affidavit)	S.G. Forbes, JP
DRURY, John F. Salina Ann Sizer	02-11-1868	John F. Lee, JP
DUKE, William A. Sophronia A. Brown	10-01-1868 (At Russell Brown's)	S.W. Postell, MPC
DUNN, Stephen A. Sucludia Calloway *	06-08-1868	_____
DURDEN, Peter M. Elizabeth Langham	06-19-1870 (At S.H. Langham's)	E. Cline, MG
ELLIS, A.J. S.I. Witherington *	12-17-1866	_____
ELLIS, Samuel L. Sarah O. Salter	02-16-1860	J.M. Wood, MG
ELLIS, William J. M.I. Castlebury	10-13-1868 (At A.C. Tippins)	F.S. Sowell, JP
ETHAREDGE, S. Alitha Brown	10-18-1873	A.W. Jones, Judge
ETHERIDGE, A.F. Safronia Curry *	12-19-1872	R.H. Varner, JP
ETHERIDGE, J.L. M.A. Sirmon	12-22-1870	R.H. Varner, JP
ETHERIDGE, Malachi W. Sarah A. Darby *	12-29-1868	Andrew Jay, Gospel Min.
ETHERIDGE, W.T. Nannie Bradley *	10-12-1871	_____
EVANS, Russell L.R. King *	08-04-1869	J.M. Wood
FEAGAN, D.A.J. Jennie A. Riley *	09-19-1869	Andrew Jay, MG
FEW, John L. Rachel Whiteside	04-10-1873	_____
FIELDS, Green B. Nancy M. Dredin	01-09-1868	J.S. Martin, JP
FINCH, Lewis Carrie H. Martin *	12-23-1874 (At E.W. Martin's)	W.G. Cary
FINCH, Lewis Mary Cunningham *	09-18-1872 (At Mrs. S. Cunningham's)	M.G. Curry, MG
FORTNER, Nathan M. Sarah E. Sheffield *	11-28-1869	Thomas Ansley, OMG
FOSTER, John Martha A. Fleming	09-01-1867	B.L. Anderson, JP
FOWLER, Elly J. Mary A. Floyd *	10-29-1871	_____
FRANKLIN, Benjamin D. Eliza Jordan *	12-25-1866	Benjamin G. Fleming, MG

FULLER, James L. Martha Rives	12-03-1874 (At Sepulga)	R.H. Varner
GARNER, James Sarah C. Ward *	01-08-1874	R.H. Varner, JP
GARRETT, O.W. R.J. Bell *'	01-29-1872	_____
GASKEY, J.W. Clementine Johnson	01-08-1868 (Dau. of John Johnson & Nancy Garlington)	J.R. Jones, MG
GASTON, James M.E. Andrews *	10-12-1869 (At Belleville, Conecuh Co.)	S.G. Forbes, JP
GIBSON, M.M. Martha Smith	08-01-1867	J.R. Lowery, MG
GILLISON, John W. P.J. Spence	10-03-1872	W.J. Hamm, JP
GILMORE, Jacob Frances Kendrick	01-11-1872	Jacob L. Skipper, MG
GILMORE, John Sarah Hunter	08-19-1873	_____
GILMORE, Stephen Helen L. Wright *	06-20-1868	_____
GLOVER, Phillip Rebecca Harris *	05-12-1875	F.M. Walker, Judge
GODWIN, Samuel Lavina Padgett *	12-26-1867	S.F. Pilly, MG
GOLDSBY, Robert Susanne E. Pressley	10-31-1867	William Beard, JP
GOODSON, J.C. Mrs. M.J. Bullard	11-12-1872 (At Evergreen)	W.A. Walker, JP
GOODWIN, L.J. Carrie Watts	01-13-1873	George Christian, NP
GRANBURY, John M. Sallie McIver	10-03-1870	J.E. McIver, Licensed Minister
GREEN, Robert M. Vince Jane Cooper	07-22-1867	C. Backstin, JP
GREEN, William J. Matilda M. Murphy	05-26-1870	William Watson, JP
GRICE, F.M. Nancy S. Downing *	01-15-1867	Charles Backtin, JP
GRIFFIN, John R. Serena Ivey	11-20-1867	P.O. Postell, MPC
GRIFFIN, W.J. Frances Mooney *	09-19-1872	W.D. Tomlinson
GRIFFITH, James M. Nancy J. Sullivan	05-19-1867	Emanuel Cline, MG
GRIMES, John T. E.S. Waters *	07-24-1860	J.M. Smith, MG

GULLEY, Henry Ginnie Burt	11-27-1867	Emanuel Cline, MG
GULLY, J.M. M.J. Ivy	12-17-1873	Emanuel Cline, MG
HALL, George W. Sarah Joiner	05-01-1873 (At Residence of Mr. King)	Rev. Ingram Spence
HALL, James P. Amelia F. Long *	04-24-1874	_____
HALL, Ransom Martha M. Mitchell	02-18-1872	A.G. Smith, MG
HAMMOCK, R.A. Fanny Simmons	12-30-1868	Jesse George, JP
HAMMOCK, S.W. Carolyn Manning	01-06-1869	William B. Stanton, JP
HAMMONDS, C.G. E.M. Lee *	02-24-1871	_____
HAMMONDS, James Harriett Matthews	10-28-1868 (By Affidavit)	William Beard, JP
HAMMONDS, William W. Delilah Loe	04-18-1867	S.L. Lowery, MG
HANEY, Andrew Sarah Fuller *	12-10-1872	R.H. Varner, JP
HARDIN, John B. Ada Brown	07-27-1872	L.A. Johnson, JP
HARDY, William Martha Pearson	07-05-1874 (In Castleberry)	William Beard
HARE, Martin Sarah Beasley	01-31-1867	J.M. Bryers, MG
HART, Jesse Mary Bowden	08-15-1872 (At Mr. Bowden's)	Rev. Ingram Spence
HART, John W. Martha A. Murphy	12-24-1868	William Sheffield, MG
HARRIS, G.W. Elizabeth Moseley *	08-03-1869	William Beard, JP
HARRIS, L.W. Laura Nored *	02-05-1873	Andrew Jay, MG
HARRISON, James M. Martha C. Thomas	04-26-1868	J.L. Skipper, MG
HART, John W. Martha A. Murphy *	12-24-1868 (At Mrs. Murphy's)	William Sheffield, MG
HASKINS, David J. Rachael Wite	11-03-1867 (At D.J. Haskins)	Rev. Thomas Ansley
HASSELL, John J. Miss Miller Godwin *	01-27-1869	John S. Moore, OMG
HENDRICKS, Nathan Caroline Butler	07-22-1867	William P. Miller, MG

HEROLD, B.H. Emiline Bain	09-27-1866	William Welch, JP
HEROLD, Henry Amanda Atkinson	09-20-1866	Charles Backstein, JP
HIGDON, J.T. A.E. Thompson * (At Mrs. E. Thompson's)	11-04-1869	J.M. Wood
HIGDON, L.L. M.E. Brantley	10-15-1874	Ingram Spence, MG
HIGDON, Samuel Mary M. Etheridge	12-26-1867	R.H. Varner, JP
HIGDON, Thomas D. Elizabeth L. Hines	07-15-1869	Emanuel Cline, MG
HILBORN, William Nettie Johnson * (At Pollard)	12-03-1867	J.F. Lee, JP
HINES, J.A. F.S. Higdon * (At Mrs. Higdon's)	07-15-1874	Ingram Spence, MG
HINES, J.P. Mary E. Broughton	12-18-1866	Andrew Jay, MG
HIXON, W.H. Josephine Coker	03-20-1872	Franklin Jeter, MG
HIXON, W.S. Lory L. Coker (At Residence of Dr. Coker)	04-11-1871	Franklin Mason, MG
HODGES, R.E. C.A. McCreary *	01-18-1870	Andrew Jay
HOLLAND, W.J. Ann J. Bruton	04-13-1871	Rev. A. Jacob Smith
HOOKS, James Ann Kelley *	10-31-1872	Rev. J.P. Lunsford
HOOKS, John M. Josephine Bolton * (At Mrs. Elizabeth Bolton's)	01-05-1871	A. Lunsford, MG
HORTON, A.W. Mary E. Lee *	01-09-1867	_____
HOWARD, Calvin Netta Henderson	07-04-1874	Daniel Shephard
HOWARD, L.E. Permelia A. Young * (At Sarah Young's)	11-03-1869	Elder G. Boyett
HOWELL, D.W. Florence M. Cunard *	01-02-1868	Thomas Ansley, MG
HOUSE, Augustus Mary Powell *	02-20-1873	John M. Wood, MG
HUGGINS, William H. S.A.E.F. Smith * (At Res. of Samuel Padgett)	01-06-1875	John D. Platt, MG
HUGGINS, William H. S.E. Young	01-04-1872	_____
HYDE, A.J. Rebecca J. Hyde *	06-28-1873	_____

HYDE, Fell M.J. Ivey *	09-24-1873	J.L. Burson, MG
HYDE, J.A. Joanah Tolbert	01-15-1872	W.P. Miller, Elder
IELAND, James A. Theodosia A. Miller (At Rev. W.P. Miller's)	12-21-1869	Rev. Thomas Ansley (See Island)
INGAHAM, Jacob Harriett Franklin	09-05-1868	Robert Beddingfield, Licensed Minister
ISLAND, James A. Theodicia U. Miller (At Rev. W.P. Miller's)	12-21-1868	Thomas Ansley, MG (See Ieland)
IVY, Charles * Ida M. Burnett	10-27-1873	_____
JACKSON, Duncan Martha McKee *	01-08-1874	William P. Miller Elder, M.E. Church
JACKSON, E.P. Mary Holland	01-29-1868	Jacob Smith, MG
JAMES, Zachory T. Margaret E. Beasley *	05-28-1873	_____
JOHNSON, Andrew J. Nancy C. Windham	10-05-1871	A.J. Miller, Elder
JOHNSON, James S.A. Brown	12-03-1871	A.W. Jones, Judge
JOHNSON, James Margaret Kelly *	11-06-1873	J.M. Wood, MG
JOHNSON, James C. Mary E. Sowell	04-23-1871	A.J. Miller, MG
JOHNSON, James G. Sarah Garner *	10-05-1870	_____
JOHNSON, James Jefferson Mrs. S.C. Lumpkin	04-05-1872	R.S. Rabb, MG
JOHNSON, James R. A. Upton	04-18-1871	A.W. Jones, Judge
JOHNSON, J.S. Martha S. Daw *	12-24-1874	John N. Sowell, JP
JOHNSON, R.L. F.U. Roberson *	07-07-1873	_____
JOHNSON, Noah Matilda Dixon	08-21-1867	Jacob McGowan, JP
JOHNSON, S.D. P.F. Wiggins (At Residence of J.G. Johnson)	05-28-1871	A.J. Miller, MG
JOHNSON, Thomas Susan Paggett	08-13-1869	A.W. Jones, Judge
JOHNSTON, John B. 05-12-1867	05-12-1867 (At Sepulga)	R.H. Varner
JOHNSTON, Monroe Tempey Johnston *	05-09-1870	A.W. Jones, Judge

```
JOINER, John A.                    01-14-1869        J.R. Jones, OMG
   Suthia Dobbs

JOINER, Jefferson                  08-17-1871        A.W. Jones, Judge
   Susan Etheridge

JOINER, L.F.                       04-09-1868        J.F. Piggott, JP
   Nancy Jane Reeves *

JOINER, L.W.                       05-21-1869        A.W. Jones, Judge
   Nancy E. Etheridge

JOINER, Madison                    12-11-1871        A.W. Jones, Judge
   F.B. Etheridge

JOINER, W.F.                       07-13-1868        J.S. Martin, JP
   Mrs. Rebecca Salter

JONES, Adam J.                     12-08-1867        Rev. J. Thames
   Mrs. Harriett Jane Price  (At Mrs. H.J. Price's)

JONES, Charles A.                  04-01-1869        William Sheffield, MG
   Susan Evans            (At Res. of John Evans)

JONES, D.S.                        12-15-1872        James E. Brown, JP
   Amanda Hall *             (At Mrs. Hall's)

JONES, George W.                   12-24-1868        William Beard, JP
   Lucinda P. Johnson * (Son of A.W. Jones, Judge)

JONES, J.A.                        01-09-1867        _____
   Nancy Sledge

JONES, James L.                    07-10-1867        Rev. J. Thames
   A.C. Adams               (At Mrs. Shavers)

JONES, J.P.                        06-11-1874        Ingram Spence, JP
   L.A. Varner *

JONES, J.S.                        09-02-1874        A.W. Jones
   Elnora Chancey

JONES, Menton                      12-02-1868        _____
   Jane Kendrick

JONES, Noel B.                     08-18-1868        Andrew Jay, Gospel Min.
   Mary A. Shipp           (At Mr. R. Shipp's)

JONES, Thomas A.                   12-13-1866        S. Maxwell, MG
   Serena A. Wright

JONES, William P.                  11-02-1870        W.C. Morrow, MG
   Sophronia A. Faulk    (At R.A. Callahan's)

JONES, W.W.                        10-09-1871        J.L Skipper, MG
   Sarah Dean

JOURNAGAN, William A.              01-09-1866        Jacob Smith, MG
   Mary Gay *

KELLY, Gabriel                     12-08-1868        _____
   Nancy Dean *

KELLY, John H.                     02-27-1873        J.M. Wood, MG
   Adaline Joiner *  (Son of James M. & Sarah C. (Sims) Kelly)

KELLY, J.H.                        10-08-1874        Ingram Spence, MG
   M.C. Mason
```

```
KEMP, D.                          01-18-1870      William Sheffield, MG
  S.A. Grigers           (At Res. of James Grigers)

KENDALL, Thompson                 01-26-1870      W.C. Morrow, MG
  Mary Chandler

KENDRICK, A.S.                    01-05-1870      D.J. Wright
  Louisa F. Gilmore *

KENDRICK, Green R.                02-19-1874      R.H. Varner, JP
  A.C. Joiner *

KIRKLAND, John J.                 12-19-1869      I. McDonald, OMG
  Charity E. Hamm *

KNOWLES, James L.                 10-29-1874      R.H. Varner, JP
  M.A. Joyner

LAMPKIN, Z.T.                     01-20-1869      A.W. Jones, Judge
  Sarah Salter *          (At Z.W. Salter's)

LANE, William M.                  04-05-1868      J.L. Skipper, MG
  Elizabeth C. Haskins (At Mrs. E.C. Haskins)

LASHLEY, Jacob                    03-29-1871      R.H. Varner, JP
  Mary Reid *

LAUGHLIN, W.E.                    12-26-1870      W.A. Walker, JP
  A.C. Brown               (At Evergreen)

LEE, A.L.                         12-09-1871      _____
  M.L. Amos *

LEE, George                       02-28-1867      J.S. Martin, JP
  Joycy S. Hawsey

LEE, George                       11-10-1874      D.L. Carter, JP
  I. Higdon             (At Mrs. Nancy Higdon's)

LEE, J.D.                         10-24-1869      S.L. Lowery, MG
  Elizabeth McLelland        (At Mr. Lee's)

LEE, Jesse                        03-22-1867      J.L. Bryers, MG
  Sarah L. Burton *         (At A.C. Burton's)

LEE, Johnathan                    02-07-1873      _____
  Georgia Sessions

LEE, Richard                      02-13-1872      _____
  Nancy Morris

LETSON, William H.                02-04-1869      C.L. Thornton, MG
  Susan E. Stewart *         (At Sparta)

LINARN, (Leman?) S.J.             01-28-1875      F.M. Walker, Judge
  Elizabeth Dimond *

LINK, John                        05-15-1873      Ingram Spence, MG
  M.J. Presly

LONG, Henry B.                    12-23-1874      Andrew Jay, MG
  Fannie E. Autrey *

LOVELESS, E.P.                    08-13-1868      Elias Barlow, JP
  Lilly Cochran *

LOVETT, Henry                     10-16-1870      Emanuel Cline, MG
  Levey Jones *
```

LOWREY, Andrew B. Susan E. Salter *	06-23-1872	D.J. Sampey, MG
LOWERY, W.A. Mary Nalls *	05-21-1872	David S. Nalls, MG
LUNSFORD, George M. S.F. Harrison	11-04-1874 (At Res. of E. Hardens)	J.P. Lunsford, MG
LYNCH, Chandler Nancy M. Gilburn	10-26-1868	A.J. Miller, JP
LYON, George W. O.C. Powell	03-09-1870 (By Affidavit)	A.W. Jones, Judge
MADDOX, Silas Lizzie Snowden	11-26-1868	T.S. Sowell, JP
MANCILL, J.F. R.A. Hardin	08-18-1872	J.M. Travis, MG
MASON, J.A. Sophronia Northcutt	11-17-1870	A. Jay, MG
MASON, James Amanda McGowan	04-03-1867 (At James McGowan's)	John F. Cook, MG
MARTIN, Edward Mary S. Jones	01-16-1871	J.E. Bell, MG
MARTIN, I.J. Cecilia Knowles	01-14-1869	Jesse George, JP
MATHEWS, George G. Sophronia Perdue	12-10-1872 (At Edmund Mathews)	Rev. Thomas Ansley
MATHEWS, J.M.F. M.E. Adams *	01-19-1871	William Sheffield, MG
MAULDIN, Elias Nancy Journigan	10-22-1867 (By Affidavit)	Jacob Smith, MG
MAYO, J.L. Melissa J. Lee	12-22-1868 (At Pollard)	F.S. Sowell, JP
MAYO, Mark Nancy C. Peevy	05-28-1868 (At Evening Star Church)	S.G. Mayo, Presiding Elder
MAYSON, F.R. Anna Baxter Sizer	02-11-1868	John F. Lee, JP
McCLAMMY, John Amanda Douglass *	09-26-1869	J.M. Wood, Minister
McCONNOC, W.D. Mrs. Martha Smith	01-24-1871	A.W. Jones, Judge
McCORKEL, Madison Sevia Miller	09-26-1869	_____
McCORMACK, W.D. Martha Smith	01-24-1871	_____
McCREARY, Robert J. Emily E. Stanley	08-03-1869	W.J. Curry, MG
McCREARY, R.J. Mary H. Stanley *	12-22-1872	W.G. Currey, MG

McGOWAN, Alexander Mrs. Nancy McGowan	11-07-1866	J.L. McGowan, JP
McGOWAN, James E. Laura H. Kennedy	12-20-1870	A. Jay, MG
McGOWAN, Taylor M.A. Stinson *	02-02-1871	A.W. Jones, Judge
McQUEEN, Clay Francis M. White	01-20-1867	T.S. Sowell, JP
MEYERS, J.R. E.M. Yates	11-25-1873	A.W. Jones, Judge
MILES, J.W. Mrs. Sarah H. Williamson	09-22-1870	A.I. Miller, MG
MILLER, John B. Nancy J. Pressley	08-04-1870 (By Affidavit)	Thomas Ansley, MG
MILLER, Isaac H. Victoria Bonds	10-28-1874	R.S. Rabb, MG
MILLER, Thomas R. Elizabeth Foshee	09-15-1868	_____
MITCHELL, C.J. H.C. Stearnes	05-14-1873 (At Evergreen)	William Brittains, Rector, St. Mary's
MITCHELL, Charles I. Hortence C. Sternes	05-14-1873 (At St. Mary's Church)	William Brittain, Rector
MIXON, John A. Josephine S. Wright *	12-13-1866	S. Maxwell, MG
MIXON, J.F. Sarah Kyser	04-24-1867	A.W. Jones, OMG
MIXON, Richard Julia Middleton	08-11-1872 (At Peter Middleton's)	Thomas H. Williams
MONROE, Frank A. N.A. Autry *	11-20-1873 (At St. Mary's Church)	William Brittian, Rector
MORGAN, J.E. Mary J. Hyde	01-07-1874	A. Lunsford, MG
MORGAN, Millard F. Elizabeth Kenderick	01-02-1870 (By Affidavit)	R.H. Varner
MOSELEY, George M. Mary Pressley	10-30-1870	A.W. Jones, Judge
MUDGE, Warcham S. Susannah Smith	10-24-1867 (At A.J. Smith's)	Thomas W. Postell, JP
MUMFORD, James Frances Griffin	02-05-1869 (At her father's residence)	J.W. Wood, MG
MURPHY, John A. Mary C. Harper *	12-01-1870	A. Jay, MG
NALL, Daniel W. A.C. Wolf	10-27-1873	_____
NALL, David I. * S.A. Ryals	02-24-1873	_____

NEWBERRY, Ira J. S.I. Shell *	12-28-1866	J.M. Piggot, JP
NIPPER, Silas F. Chiney F. Chira	12-22-1867	John S. Moore, MG
NORRED, Julius M. Susan F. Lee *	05-18-1870	William Beard, JP
NORTHCUTT, G.W. Mary Carter *	12-08-1868	Andrew Jay, MG
NORTHCUTT, William D. Mrs. Ann Miller	12-22-1867	Thomas Ansley, MG
ODOM, Aaron Nettie Brantley	12-18-1871	A.W. Jones, Judge
O'FERRELL, Joseph Elizabeth McGougin *	10-20-1869	J.J. Cooper, MG
OGWYNN, Charles D. Margaret L. Thames	11-02-1871	Allen Thomaston, MG
OWENS, A.B. Isabella Hamock	12-25-1867	S.L. Lowery
OWENS, C.D. Mrs. E.A. Atkinson	08-04-1870	S.G. Forbes, JP
OVERSTREET, J.W. Nancy Dyke	02-07-1868	J.R. Jones, OMG
PAGE, Bennett C.M. Daw *	01-18-1870	William Beard, JP
PAGE, J.F. H. Kyser *	02-12-1873	W.W. Walker
PAGE, J.D. Carlurine Ward *	11-05-1873	J.M. Wood, MG
PAGE, H. Laura Autrey *	07-26-1869 (At Evergreen)	J.H. Tickner, MG
PAGE, Samuel Frances Murphy * (At J.V. Edeker's)	12-24-1872	J.M. Wood, MG
PARKER, John W. Arcipa Peeples *	12-20-1866	G. Williams, MG
PARTIN, Isaah Charlotte Joiner	01-27-1872	_____
PEACOCK, L.L. Caroline Martin	09-26-1867	J.L. Higdon, JP
PEAVY, Mikel Martha E. Estes * (At Residence of William Davis)	12-27-1874	James C. Travis, JP
PERDUE, George Catherine Kent	03-28-1872	W.P. Miller, MG
PIERSE, Thomas J. Martha Jane Blackwell (At the Blackwell's)	11-27-1874	David S. Nall, MG
PINKERTON, A.J. Elizabeth Jones	10-01-1868	J.M. Piggott, JP

PINKERTON, James Lucy Ann Reeves *	01-25-1872	_____
PLATT, Robert B. Lucy Jones *	01-29-1874 (At A.W. Jones Res.)	Robert Smilie, MG
PORTER, Henry Mrs. Jane Pipkin	08-28-1867	Andrew Jay, MG
POSEY, John Nancy Blackwell *	08-01-1871	_____
POWELL, G.W. * Margaret House	03-13-1873	J.M. Wood, MG
PRESSLEY, S.J. S.F. Daniels *	10-16-1871	_____
PRICE, Elizah Emma Stevens	07-22-1869	William Beard, JP
PRINGLE, B.F. M.J. Herrington *	03-11-1868	J.F. Lee, JP
PRITCHETT, C.C. Charlotte E. Henderson *	12-29-1872	Rev. S.L. Lowery
PRITCHETT, William O. Martha E. Hart	02-23-1867 (At Res. of Henry Hart)	A.J. Miller, JP
PURNELL, J.L. S.C. Thomas *	12-08-1870	A.Jay, MG
PURNAL, S.H. S.A. Ray *	09-02-1869	Jesse Thams, MG
PURVIS, John Fannie E. Knowles	10-17-1867	J.L. Bryers, MG
QUALES, Wesley Nancy Hall	09-21-1868	_____
RABB, William Mary Morrow *	12-24-1867 (At Evergreen)	W.C. Morrow, MG
RALLS, John Eletha Barlow	07-16-1874	James P. Lunsford, MG
RAY, John D. Gideon Mary M. Smith	03-25-1875 (At her father's res.)	A.W. Jones, MG
RAY, Thomas J. Fanny J. Daw *	01-01-1874	A.W. Jones, Judge
RAY, William Nancy J. Daw	01-09-1866	W.C. Morrow, MG
REED, A.G. Anna Grace	01-14-1869	E. Cline, MG
REID, A.J. Anna Grace	01-14-1869 (See Above)	E. Cline, MG
REID, J.A. A. Bond *	11-14-1872	W.J. Hamm, JP
RENFROE, M.W. Catherine R. Cook *	01-29-1873	_____

```
RICHBOURG, H.C.                    09-10-1873        J.S. Bryers, MG
   Margaret H. Bell *           (At Bell's House)

RILEY, Thomas Mercer               07-29-1874        Franklin Jeeter, MG
   Sarah Martin

RILEY, W.A.                        12-15-1869        W.C. Morrow, OMG
   F.E. Lee

RITCHIE, L.J.                      07-17-1867        John L. Cook, MG
   M.M. Dunavon

ROBERTS, Levi W.                   12-08-1870        William Beard, JP
   Susan E. Brown         (At the courthouse by affidavit)

ROBERSON, E.L.                     11-29-1866        William Watson, JP
   Kate Bell *

ROBINSON, C.M.                     02-16-1873        Andrew Jay, MG
   Julia Raburn *

ROBINSON, J.M.                     02-06-1870        C.L. Thornton
   Kate F. McIver

ROBERTS, T.                        05-26-1868        J.T. Hogdon, JP
   Mary A. Pritchett

ROWELL, James                      11-16-1870        Archibald McFadyen, VDM
   Sarah Carter *

RUDIN, O.O.                        03-20-1875        Andrew Jay, MG
   Loula C. Irwin         (At Baptist Church in Evergreen)

RUSSELL, Abram                     10-17-1867        William Beard
   Matilda Kendrick            (At Courthouse)

SALTER, Cuyler                     11-27-1866        Emanuel Cline, MG
   Catharet Burt *         (At Mr. J.H. Burt's)

SALTER, Jesse C.                   08-01-1867        J.M. Wood, Minister
   Mary Ann Taylor *

SALTER, John H.                    09-02-1869        J.W. Wood, MG
   Sarah Salter *         (At Widow Salter's)

SALTER, John S.                    01-05-1872        _____
   J.E. Chitty *

SALTER, Thomas H.                  09-24-1874        E. Cline, MG
   Serena E. Ivy

SALTER, T.M.                       12-18-1872        J.M. Wood, MG
   Susan Langley          (At Mr. Langley's Res.)

SALTER, Watkins A.                 12-25-1870        J.M. Wood, Minister
   Nicey E. Salter *      (At Breckenridge Church)

SALTER, William                    01-11-1872        J.M. Wood, MG
   Julia House

SALTER, Zodoc W.                   02-27-1866        John Knighton, MG
   Holly W. Salter

SAMPEY, A.D.                       02-28-1869        J.W. Jourdan, Pastor
   E.A. Robins            (At Belleville in M.E. Church South)

SAMPEY, Greenbury G.               09-05-1867        W.B. Dennis, MG
   Hattie Burnett         (At Res. of Mrs. M. Burnett)
```

SAMPEY, E.R. Alice Finch	04-22-1872	_____
SAMPEY, John W. H.S. Houghton *	04-22-1872	_____
SANDFORD, J.J. Mary Mitchell	04-15-1875	George Lee, MG
SANFORD, R. M.J. Howell	01-05-1871 (At Mr. Howell's)	_____
SAVAGE, L.W. Cora Matthews	11-15-1870 (At Sparta)	T. Lewis, Rector St. Mary's, Evergreen
SCOGIN, A.S. Lucy S. Witter	10-01-1873	A. McSeaman Douglas, MG
SCOGGIN, A.T. Martha A. Pilly *	09-01-1867 (At S.F. Pilly's Home)	S.F. Pilly, MG
SCOGGIN, G.B. Eliza G. Pilly	01-01-1868	S.F. Pilly
SHAMBO, Peter Georiana Chamberlain *	11-27-1866	_____
SHAVERS, Dyasper Marth A. Creamer	03-31-1872	W.J. Hamm, JP
SHAVER, P.C. Mary G. Grigers	02-23-1870 (At James Grigers)	William Sheffield, MG
SHAW, D.D. M.A. Hanson	01-07-1872	Jesse Thames
SHEFFIELD, Coleman Mary S. Hooks *	02-02-1871 (At Residence of John Lunsford)	Robert Smilie, MG
SHEFFIELD, Evan Sarah E. Miller	11-12-1868	William P. Miller, PE
SHEFFIELD, William H. Nancy J. Miller *	03-04-1869 (At Bride's fathers)	W.B. Miller
SHELL, G.H. J.D. Still	02-27-2868 (At E. Still's)	Jacob Smith
SIMMONS, Levi S. Evelyn Landon	06-23-1867	C. Backstin, JP
SIMS, James A. Hazelton Dean	11-18-1869 (At Mrs. M. Dean's Res. by affidavit)	Rev. Franklin Yates
SKINNER, William L. F.A. Martin	01-29-1872	_____
SMITH, A.G. Flora Sheffield	06-16-1867	John F. Lee
SMITH, Chesley C. Martha R. James	06-08-1870	F.W. Postell, MPC
SMITH, E.C. Mary A. Ivey	02-17-1867	A.W. Jones, MG
SMITH, Hesekiah Loverett Pierce *	08-01-1875 (At Mrs. Pierce's House)	David S. Nall, MG

SMITH, Jacob Lucinda York *	06-05-1868	————
SMITH, Lemuel Sallie Jones	10-01-1868	J.M. Piggott, JP
SMITH, R.J. M.A. Ray *	04-22-1869	F.W. Postell, MG
SMITH, W.E. M.M. Callahan	04-29-1872	————
SMITH, Uriah M.L. Floyd	08-04-1870	M. Watson, JP
SNOWDEN, C.J. E.B. Strange	10-22-1874	L.A. Johnston, JP
SNOWDEN, Jeff Octavia E. Waugh	07-04-1869 (At her father's Res.)	R.H. Varner, JP
SORRELL, D.S. A.A. Johnson *	01-25-1866	T.S. Sowell, JP
SPENCE, David A.E. McGraw *	09-04-1872	Ingaham Spence, MG
SPENCE, Ingraham Sarah F. Mason *	12-13-1866 (At Res. of S.P. Mason)	Andrew Jay, MG
STALLWORTH, W.L. Betty Saltsman	06-10-1868 (At W.D. Saltsman's)	Andrew Jay, Gospel Min.
STEARNS, John S. Kate A. Autry	10-06-1868	William Beard, JP
STEEL, David C. Emily A. McCormick	05-17-1868 (Sunday)	J.M. Henderson, Judge
STEELY, James B. Ann Thomas *	06-20-1868	Elder Jesse Thames
STEWARD, M.P. Susan Cox *	09-30-1869 (At Bride's mothers)	William P. Miller, P.E.
STONE, Perry Susan E. Finley	06-07-1874	L.A. Johnston, JP
STUCKEY, Joshua C. Sarah J. Gilmore *	12-19-1867 (At John Gilmore's)	J.M. Piggott, JP
STUCKEY, William Frances Salter	09-12-1869	J.M. Wood, MG
SUDDITH, George E. Fannie Bradley	01-03-1871 (At Miss Bradley's)	————
SUNDY, F.W. Martha A. Jones	08-31-1865	I.J. Jarnigan, JP
SUTHERLAND, Hugh R. Mary McRay	12-24-1866	————
SUTHERLAND, James W. Sarah Ann Moorer	09-16-1874	R.S. Rabb, MG
TAYLOR, James Nancy Journigan	11-14-1866	————

TAYLOR, J.L. Sarah Evans	10-14-1869	R.H. Varner, JP
THAMES, C.R. Mary Kelley *	02-21-1871 (At W.J. Kelley's)	L.M. Thomason, MG
THOMAS, H.C. Sarah C. Harper *	01-05-1871	Andrew Jay, MG
THOMAS, J.A. F.E. Hodge	09-13-1871	J.E. McIver, MG
THOMAS, Joseph A. Susan E. James	11-26-1868	Elder Jesse Thames
THOMAS, L.J. Anna Chapman	11-30-1869	J.W. Postell, OMG
THOMAS, Robert P. Sarah A. Ray	08-01-1872 (At Mr. Ray's)	Rev. Ingram Spence
THOMAS, William Louisa House	01-11-1869	A.W. Jones, Judge
THOMPSON, B. M. Pollard *	10-28-1869	William Beard, JP
THOMPSON, James A. Catherine Witherington	12-15-1869	E. Cline, OMG
THOMPSON, John A. Anna Laura Witter	11-20-1867 (At Mrs. C. Thompson's)	Emanuel Cline, MG
THOMPSON, John M. M.A. Cannon	10-14-1874 (At Sarah Thompson's)	E. Cline, MG
THOMPSON, G.I. Mary Salter	01-04-1871	A.G. Duke, JP
THORNTON, William I. Rachael Thompson *	11-13-1867 (At Mr. E. Thompson's)	Emanuel Cline, MG
TIPPINS, George M. Susannah Thompson *	01-31-1867	C. Backstin, JP
TIPPINS, P.H.M. Julia E. Castlebury *	01-01-1867	T.S. Sowell, JP
TOLBERT, J.H. Ida Perdue	09-10-1874	Rev. A. Lunsford
TOLBERT, Neall Ably Barlow	03-08-1872	_____
TOMLINSON, J.A. N.A. Overstreet	03-27-1872	_____
TOMLINSON, William J. Emily D. Bain	02-02-1870	J.W. Overstreet, LMG
TRAWICK, L.A. Grimsey Partin	11-19-1870 (At Gravella)	A.W. Jones, Judge
TRAWICK, T.G. M.A. Ward *	11-09-1873	J.M. Wood, MG
VARNER, J.A. Cynthia Dobbs *	01-14-1869	J.R. Jones, OMG

VICKIE, J.G. Dora J. McClure *	12-30-1868	_____
WADE, Elijah T. Mrs. Mary E. Wilkerson	01-22-1867 (At Dr. Harper's)	Elias Barber, JP
WALLER, William Sarah Botts	05-20-1867 (At Pollard, Ala.)	John F. Lee, JP
WAR, James Malinda Wheeler	02-25-1867	J.M. Henderson, Judge
WARD, James A. Eliza Joiner *	11-24-1870	R.H. Varner, JP
WARD, S.R. Nancy S. Page *	11-05-1873	J.M. Wood, MG
WARD, William A. Francis C. Wagner	11-09-1874 (At Mt. Zion Methodist Church South)	Joseph M. Scott, MG
WARD, William H. Margaret Chitty	03-01-1868	J.R. Jones, OMG
WARTON, A.W. J.A. Irwin	12-08-1874 (At Res. of Dossy Huston)	John D. Plate, Minister
WATHE, Samuel Delaney A. Miller	11-03-1867	J.L. McGowan, JP
WATSON, John S. Alice Bradley *	12-16-1874 (At Res. of Sam Bradley)	Robert Smiley, MG
WATTS, J.B.F. G.A. Williams	05-28-1871	J.M. Wood, MG
WATTS, James R. Mrs. Sarah E. Douglass	08-08-1867 (At Bride's residence)	J.T. Higdon, JP
WEAVER, Franklin, G. Becca A. Hawsey	08-04-1873	R.H. Varner, JP
WEAVER, Richard Emily Martin	03-22-1870 (At Singleton Martin's by affidavit)	E. Cline, MG
WEBB, James M. S.F. Collins *	02-07-1871 (At Residence of W.D.J. Collins)	Robert Smilie, MG
WE_B, John Nancy M. Ingraham	12-21-1868 (At Mrs. Ingram's)	John F. Cook
WHITMAN, W.A. Sarah Elizabeth McWilliams	10-18-1871	A.W. Jones, Judge
WIGGINS, J.A. Eliza Haskins *	01-02-1867	A.F. Miller, JP
WIGGINS, Kennard Mary E. Coleman	11-24-1874	F.M. Walker, Probate Judge
WILLIAMS, A.P. Malinda Eram * (widow)	03-23-1875	G.W. Lee, MG
WILLIAMS, John G. Margaret S. Mixon *	09-05-1867	W.W. Graham, MG
WILLIAMS, William W. Emma Mixon	01-24-1875	Joseph M. Scott, MG

152

WILLIAMS, Zachariah Mrs. Arabella Godbold	07-27-1870 (At William Beard's)	F.W. Postell, MPC
WILLIAMSON, John L. Henrietta Sanks	05-25-1868	_____
WILLIAMSON, Isiah P. Sallie Thomas	07-07-1868	_____
WILSON, Anderson Sarah A. Goodson	10-21-1868	Elias Barlow, JP
WILSON, Stephen Susan Deen	07-17-1868	R.H. Varner, JP
WINDHAM, Aaron Sarah E. Hall	08-21-1870	J.F. McDonald, MG
WISHAM, H.F. Martha A. Windahan	10-05-1871	A.J. Miller, Elder
WINDHAM, James T. M.E. Smith *	10-16-1871	_____
WITHERINGTON, S.L. S.I. Daw *	12-26-1871	_____
WOOD, R.M. H.M. Daw *	02-19-1875	J.W. Sowell, Actg. JP
WRIGHT, Christopher Nancy E. Pinkerton	11-03-1872	W.J. Hamm, JP
WRIGHT, James Elizabeth Branch *	04-02-1867	R.T. Baggett, JP
WRIGHT, W.C. Maggie I. Jones	12-24-1867	S. Maxwell, OMG
WRIGHT, James H. Catherine R. Cook *	12-18-1874	_____
WRIGHT, Samuel Nancy J. Gilmore *	02-04-1869	H.H. Sturgis, MG
YATES, W.J. M.A.T. Myers *	04-05-1875	A.W. Jones, MG

****
BRIDES OF MONROE COUNTY
****

Godwin, Florence C. 64
Goin, Mary 114
Godbold, Elizabeth E. 123
Goodloe, Fannie A. 110
  Mary A. 5
Goodwin, Jean Mineroa 110
Gordan, Caroline R. 43
  M.E. 4
Gordon, Martha 93(2)
  M.F. 79
Gordy, Mary J.E. 58
Gospfin, Pamelia 5
Gould, Melvina A. 94
  M.F. 123
Gouldsby, Emma 8
Grace, Alabama 38
  Amanda M. 54
  Beatrice 103
  Caroline 82
  Epsey Ann 22
  Margaret F. 22
  Mary J. 103
  Mary Jane 89
  Nannie J. 44
  Tabitha 42
Graham, Eliza E. 69
  Hannah 103
  Mariam 51
  Mary 22
Gramling, Hugine V. 77
  Martha M.E.M. 77
  Willa E. 77
Grant, Augusta A. 50
  D.A. 110
Gravis, Mary J. 92
Gray, Fannie J. 19
  Leah R. 50
Green, Berneter 109
  Eliza 84
  Lizzie 66
  Patsy 90
  P.S. 91
Greene, Martha 123
  Nancy 34
  Sarah A. 13
  S.C. 26
Gregg, Kesiah J. 102
Grey, Seala R. 19
Griffin, Almeda R. 83
  Bettie 77
  E.F. 41
  Elizabeth 102
  Martha 101
  Mary E. 91
  Mary J. 44(2)
  Mary R. 90
  Melissa A. 77
  Sarah R. 44
  Susan R. 60
  Virginia J. 29
Griffis, Jane 98
Griffith, Sarah 27
Grimes, Adaline 76
  Alia 105
  Amanda 53,67
  Ann 60
  Apenath 53
  Catherine D. 54
  Drucilla 129
  Eliza 55
  Elizabeth 14,34
  Elizabeth Mrs. 46
  Margaret 42
  Mary 76
  Mary C. 21
  Mary J. 111(2)
  Sarah J. 110
  Susan 50
Grissett, Flora 81
Grooms, Tabitha A.E.
Gulley, Sarah N. 105
Gully, Mrs. Ellen 112

Guned, Mattie A. 44
Gunn, Hulda A. 13
  Ida 67
  M.M. 13
Guthery, Samantha E. 52
Gwatney, Frances E. 72
Haddox, Almira A. 36
  N.E. 60
Hagaman, Mrs. Mary 90
Hale, Martha 59
  Mary J. 47
Hales, Martha 91
  Mary 111
  M.S. 91
Hall, Katherine N. 42
  Margaret C. 87
  Mary S. 13
  Missouri 98
  Polly Ann 88
  Sarah 95
Hamilton, Alley 90
  Elizabeth 106
  Leanor Mrs. 60
  Lucinda 84
  Mahaled 126
  Mary J. 84
Hammon, Martha C. 15
  Olivia 118
Hammond, Sarah 82
Hancock, A.E. 88
Hannah, Nancy 64
Hanson, Mary 88
Harbin, Eliza 15
  Elizabeth 93
  Frances 115
  Sarah 115
Hardee, Amanda J. 91
  Cynthia Susan 107
  Margaret E. 53
  Mary P. 120
Harp, Caty 115
  Harriett 128
  Missouri 124
  Phebe 26
Harper, Eliza A. 121
  Katie 129
  Mary C. 56
Harreson, A.S. 113
Harris, Edie Ann 127
  Martha 13
  Martha Ann 123
  Sara L. Mrs. 103
  Vicey 103
Harrison, Ann H. 28
  Mary J. 9
  N.S.P. 85
  Sarah 85
  Sarah Ann 83
Hastin, Amanda 45
Hassy, Mrs. Mary 80
Hathcock, Mrs. Julia 69
Hawkins, Elizabeth 28
  Elizabeth Mrs. 31
  Frances 21
  Malinda 105
  Prudence 36
  Permelia E. 95
  Rebecca J. 84
  Sarah 28
  Susan 123
Hawthorne, Adaline 78
  Susan C. 60
Hausey, Sarah 60
Hayle, Missouri F. 112
  Susan M. 69
Hayles, A.A. 91
  Eliza 98
  Mary 42
  Mary J. 65
  Sarah 42
  Sarah A. 49
Hayes, Ana Bella 87

Haynes, Ellander 83
  Jane 111
  Nancy 86
  Sina E. 98
Hays, Harriett P. 107
Heankins, Malinda 105
Hearing, Emily 101
Heathcock, Maria 52
Heatherington, A.E. 88
Helton, Billie 37
  Lilly 87
  L.K. 95
  M.S. 74
  Mary M. 25
  Maryan 12
  M.R. 37
  Rebecca 73
  Sarah 103
Hemmington, Mary J. 43
Henberger, Emelie L. 70
Henderson, America 108
  Amanda 119
  Catherine 44
  Elizabeth 26,63,99
  Margaret A. 54
  Jane 110,128
  Mary 89
  Mary A. 79
  Mary A. Demanas 71
  Mary E. 90
  Missouri 66
  Nancy C. 66
  Nannie Mrs. 33
  Rebecca 33
  Sarah A. 80,108
Hendrick, Lucy Ann 62
Hendrix, Anna J. 111
  Artimesia 42
  Catherine 67
  Elizabeth 97
  Elizabeth Ann 28
  Hannah H. 111
  Irena E. 98
  Isabell 63
  Jo Anna 50
  Julia 2
  June 69
  Leah 24
  Louisa C. 9
  Malisa 97
  Margaret 52(2)
  Margaret E. 86
  Mary 41
  Moselle 101
  Orra Ann 69
  Rosanah 19
Hennington, Susan 120
Henry, Mrs. M.D. 1
Henshaw, Mary A. 118
  Mary M. 118
Henson, Elizabeth 129
  Rebecca A. 6
Herbert, Mary E. 62
Herrin, Catherine 47
Hestle, Ann E. 96
  Mary E. 7,100
  Margaret J. 6
  Mollie E. 17
Hicks, Martha S. 108
  Matilda 66
  Nancy 129(2)
  Nicey 29
  Susan F. 51
Higdon, Amanda Demarias
  64
  Mary Mrs. 111
  Sarah L. 26
Hightower, Martha L. 14
Hill, Martha F. 99
  Missouri 84
Hiller, Henrietta 43
Himmington, Martha 17

BRIDES OF MONROE COUNTY

Hines, Elizabeth A. 61
  Lula 27
  Nancy E. 11
Hinson, C.L. 7
  Henrietta 122
  Martha 7
  M.A. 7
  M.F. 121
  N.J. 7
  S.E. 122
  S.T. 97
Hirst, Matilda 12
Hixon, C.A. 90
  Elizabeth 106
  Maria 38
  M.M. 11
  M.V. 51
  Mary 52
  S.E. 39
Hobbs, Kesiah 13
Hokett, Mary E. 94
Holden, Eliza 9
Holder, Amanda 4
  Martha 66
  Mary 62
Holland, Mary P. 115
Holley, Dorcus 6
  Elizabeth 117
  Martha 61
  Mary 125
  M.E. 105
Hollerwy, M.A. 27
Hollinger, Levitice H. 49
  Mary 82
Hollingsworth, Emily 21
  Fidelia 26
  Frances 26
Holloway, Aceneth 116
  Eliza 37
  Fannie 71
  Martha A. 66
  Martha J. 80
  Mary 80
  S.A. 94
Holly, Ann 16
  Annie 124
  Margaret 71
  Mary Ann 3
Holman, M.C. 36
  O.E. 72
Holoway, Mrs. Mary 95
Holt, Addie 69
  Henrietta 73
  S.A. 104
Hooks, Martha 32
Hopkins, Catherine 47
Horton, Susan C. 48
Houghman, Elizabeth 15
House, Levitia 22
  Mary J. 53
Howe, Elizabeth L.M. 33
  Mary J. 53
Hoyle, Carole 56
Hudson, Henrietta 90
  Martha B. 90
Hughes, Caroline 111
Humphrey, Sarah J. 58
Hundley, Sarah A.M. 50
Hunt, E.A. 57
  E.S. 75
  Ellen V. 89
  Susan 72
Hunter, Elizabeth B. 67
  Nancy 23
Hurry, Elizabeth 126
  Fannie E. 56
  Frances 31
  Mollie E. 17
  Nancy 81
  Polly 125
Hurt, Elizer 83
Hussa, Elizabeth 129

Hussey, Rebecca 129
  Mrs. 25
  Nancy 34
Hussy, Angelina 15
Hutto, L.V. 21
Hutton, Margaret L. 107
Hutts, Elifora 39
Huzzey, Ann 13
Hybert, Maria A. 75
  Sarah J. 73
Hylert, Mary 38
Ikner, Martha A. 24
  Matilda 119
  Mary E. 118
  Tabatha Ann 2
Ingraham, Mary 128
Ingram, E.C. 11
  M.E. 91
Ivey, Eliza 75
  Nancy 53
  Sarah 8
Jackson, Mary C. 64
  Rebecca Ann 114
Jacobs, Frances 28
Jacobson, Jetty 104
  Nancy 128
James, Ann Eliza 87
  Caroline 86
  Maria 35
  Rebecka 88
Jay, Dicey 48
  Irena 53
  Mary A. 31
  May N. 34
Jenkins, Billie 70
  Laura 11
  Margaret 118
  Naney D. 6
Jennings, Mary E. 81
Johnson, Ann 86
  Charity 108
  Elizabeth 40,116
  Isabella 93
  Jane E. 29
  Malinda 98
  Martha E. 74,116
  Mary J. 29
  Mary L. 26
  Nancy 76
  Nancy J. 5
  Rosie 66
  Sarah F. 124
  Sarah F. 124
  Sarah R. Mrs. 87
  Sophia Ann 43
  Susan 123
  Sussannah 109
Johnston, Adaline H. 45
  Emily 24
  Gabriella G. 113
  Margaret 93
  Mary 129
  Nancy 122
Jolliff, Mrs. Elizabeth 97
Jones, Catherine A. 28
  Catherine 99
  Elizabeth 105
  Elo 48
  Frances 5
  Frances E. 47
  Jenetta 120
  Margaret 65
  Martha 81
  Mary A.J. 2
  Mary I. 18
  M.E. 2,105
  Mollie 104
  Narcissa 46
  Sallie 18
  Susan 54
Jordan, Elizabeth 79
  Martha E. 27

Jordan, Martha M. 89
  Mary June 32
Justice, Bettie 5
  J.A. 95
  Mary E. 58
Kahn, Jeanetta 9
Kearley, Jemimah 124
  Sarah E. 93
  Tabitha 14
Kearly, June 63
  Mary 114
Kelley, Susan J. 117
Kelly, Catherine 96
  Cecilia 108
  Delilah E. 49
  Julia Ann 24
  Mary M. 62
  Nancy J. 89
  Rosannah 115
Kemp, Henrietta Maria 32
  Henrietta M.E. 92
  Junietta M. 32
  Martha 35
  M.J. 17
Kendall, Miss 3
Kennedy, A.E. 68
  Catherine 42
  Henrietta 56
  Lydia V. 118
  Mary Mrs. 38
  Mary J. 69
  Matilda 22
  Saber Ann 19
Kervin, Margaret A. 97
Kibler, Nancy 117
Kidd, Eastha 22
  Frances 4
Kile, Elizabeth 32
  Matilda 43
Killam, Adella 56
  Alabama 15
  Charoline N. 87
  Sarah R. 23
Killium, Martha L. 91
Kimbel, Josephine 1
  M.J. 56
King, Annie A. 84
  Goode 67
  Louisa J. 116
  Nancy E. 41
  Rebecca S. 65
Kinsey, Olivia 46
Kirby, Sarah 48
Kirley, Missoria 51
Knoles, Georgia Ann 34
Knowles, Amanda A. 57
  Jane 33
  Mary 109,129
  M.F. 24
  Sarah Mrs. 9
  Sarah 120
Kolb, Fannie 73
Kreighton, Cynthia M. 7
Kyle, Rebecca J. 50
Lacy, Elizabeth A. 61
  Jennie 70
Ladd, Henrietta 17
Lambert, Miss 124
  Abigail 69,115
  Anna 1
  Anna W. 117
  B.E. 31
  Bathena 19
  Caroline 115
  Christianna 12
  Ciney C. 68
  Dorry Ann 128
  Drucilla 34,43
  E.M. 34
  Emily 50
  Jane 32
  Ida L. 58

Lambert, M.A. 72
  Margaret 6
  Martha 64,65,89
  Martha E. 56
  Mary 11,131
  Mary L. 34
  Mary M. 101
  M.J. 34
  Permelia A. 46
  Roannah 86
  S.A. 20
  Sarah E. 87
  Sarah 47
  Sarah Ann 37
  Winny 115
Lampy, Ann Jane 122
  Frances 110
  Margaret 9
Langham, Amy E. 36
  Frances 100
  Josephine 127
  Mary L. 83
  L.G. 65
Laris, Mary A.M. 79
Larry, Aveline V. 88
Latham, Laura 7
Lawrence, S.A.E. 18
Leason, Lucinda 82
Ledkins, Amanda M. 59
  Frances Emma 60
Lee, Adaline 65
  Bettie 47
  Lou 104
  Lucinda 31
  Maggie 59
  Martha 55
  Mattie V. 105
  M.L. 125
  Sarah A. 47
  Sarah Ann 13
  Susan Eliza 57
Leo, Sarah 3
Leoftin, Serena 28
  Sina 66
Leslie, Elizabeth 30,89
  Jane 30
  Margaret 19
  Mary Ann 41
  Mary V. 96
  Narcissa E. 84
  Sallie B.V. 53
  Sallie J. 74
Lett, Elizabeth 107
  Martha P. 10
  Minna H. 121
  Sarah W. 33
Lewis, Martha A. 89
  Mary E. 115
  Missouri E. 102
Liddell, Emma 105
  Julia C. 92
  Mary E. 110
  Susan J.M. 96
Lindsey, Cornelia H. 53
  Elizabeth 54
  Emeline A. 8
  Pheaney Caroline 55
  Sarah A. 126
Linton, Mary J. 108
Linum, Amanda 10
Lisinba, Elizabeth 31
Little, M.E. 20(2)
Lloyd, Mary L. 57
  Nancy Caroline 34
Locke, Rebecca Ann 29
Lockland, Amelia 25,104
Loftin, Delila 5
  Edith A. 49
  Elizabeth 50
  Elizabeth Mrs. 7
Longmire, Elizabeth 74
  Henrietta M. 68

Longmire, Mary Mrs. 83
Lot, Martha F. 21
Loveless, Harriette
  Jane 11
  Nancy 120
Lowe, Nancy A. 47
Lowery, Caroline 115
  Flora J. 16
  Josephine 29
  Louise 52
  Missouri M. 73
  Sarah J. 10
Lowremoure, Sarah A.L. 64
Lowry, Christian Elizabeth
  25
  M.A.R. 117
  Mary Jane 41
  Saleanear 56
  Sarah Ann 65
Loveless, Jane 12
Loyd, Williamina Ann 34
  Winny 127
Luccas, Mrs. Frances 38
Lumpkins, Caroline 24
Lynch, Elizabeth 74
  Margaret 22
Lyon, A.E. 124
  Sarah T. 69
Lyphrit Ann A. 74
Magee, Julia 70
Maiben, Lucy 93
  Marriah 25
  Martha 93
Maibin, Kitty 127
Malden, Mary A. 51
Mallett, Hannah 60
Mann, Callie E. 110
  Eliza 16,102
  Julia S. 72
Manning, Nancy 121
Maphee, Rosa 49
Marbin, Elizabeth 93
Marion, Elizabeth C. 126
  Melinda A. 62
Marshall, E.J. 101
  Eliza 128
  Elizabeth L. 26
  E.S. 118
  Martha W.A. 1
  Sallie A. 127
Martin, Deborah G. 40
  Delphia T. 24
  M.D. 96
Mason, Almira 68
  Anna 129
  Frances A. 76
  M.M. 35
  Pennelia P. 27
  Reney 103
Masons, C.V. 81
Massingale, Mrs. Caroline
  81
Massey, Eddy 80
  Elvira 25
  Mary E. 20
Masson, Martha E. 71
Mathews, Catherine 9
  M.A.E. 105
Maxwell, M.F. 85
  Margaret 41
Maynor, Elizabeth 58
McAliston, R.J. 51
McAllister, Mrs. Frances
  104
McArthur, Ellen 38
  Jane E. 94
  Julia 49
  Mary M. Mrs. 24
  Mary 121
McArthy, Mary M. 92
McCall, Catherine 100
  Christiana 100

McCall, Emogene 78
  Sarah 105
McCants, C.A. 85
  Celina 112
  Cora J. 55
  Elizabeth W. 110
  F.S. 109
  Maggie E. 7
  Margaret D. 57
  Margaret S. 85
  Mary J. 23
  R.F. Mrs. 88
  R.J. 110
  Sarah J. 16
McCarty, Martha 61
McCasky, Mary S. 45
McClammy, Allis 3
  Billie 109
  Caroline 49,119
  Catherine 110
  Delia E. 102
  Eliza 14
  Julia 82
  Louisa 110
  Martha Ann 11
  Mary F. 69
  Nancy 14
  N.E. 105
  Sarah 10,42
McClen, Dora 16
McClure, Amanda A. 3
  Arriane 36
  Henrietta 51
  Jennie 47
  Louisa 75
  Mahala 58
  Margaret M. 15
  Martha R. 87
  Nancy 88
  Rebecca E. 8
McColl, A.J. Mrs. 82
  Isabella 33
  Madeline L. 29
  Maria 44
  Mary 88
  Mary Ann 44
  Sarah 2
McCollum, Mary E. 116
McConnell, Sarah E.M.B.M.
  19
McCorkle, Leouisa A. 8
  Rachel 28
McCormick, Mary 78
McCorvey, Annie B. 71
  B.J. 46
  F. Ella 90
  H.B. 126
  Lydia A. 113
  Mary E. 41
  S.H. 50
  Sarah L. 67
McCoy, Bettie 96
  Isabella 33
  Rebecca 116
  R.S. 67
McCraery, Martha A. 84
McCrary, Rebecca 74
  Mary 74
McCurry, Perthanea 82
McDaniel, Rebecca 26
McDonald, Anna 49
  Elizabeth Mrs. 67
  Janne 94
  M.A. 86
  Martha E. 97
  Mary A. 42
  Mary F.M. 122
  Mary J. 54
  Mary W. 70
McDuffie, Belle 112
  Maggie 74
McGee, Virginia 54

McGill, Mary Jane 10
McGinnis, Jane 103
McInnis, Martha J. 37
  Mary 83
McIntosh, Amanda 44
  Ann 44
  Elizabeth 119
McKenzie, Allice 98
  Ann 29
  Louisa P. 30
  Mary D. 82
  Nancy Jane 102
McKinley, Ann E. 83
  Ann E.E.L. 46
  Asenath 76
  Catherine J. 102
  C.J. 119
  Eliza 118
  Elizabeth 14
  Epsey 102
  Julia A. 78
 · Lucinda 10
  Mary 10
  Mary E. 120
  Mary F. 119
  M.F. 93
  S.F. 111
McKinney, Elizabeth 105
  Elmira 76
  Mary 2
  Mary E. 107
  Matilda 39
McLain, Helan 44
  Martha 46
McLaine, Frances 109
McLane, Josephine 78
McLendon, M.E.M. 128
McLeod, Effy 87
  Minerva J. 89
McLeure, Jane 58
McMillan, Caroline V. 122
  Catherine 86
  Frances 126
  Jane 82
  Jennet 17
  Frances A. 46
  Hellen M. 125
  Jane 92
  Jeremiah 22
  Julia 30
  June 29
  Katherine 94
  Liddia A. 122
  Margaret B. 100
  Margaret C. 30
  Martha 8,13,59
  Martha J. 26
  Mary 19
  Mary A. 30
  Mary J. 45
  Minerva 118
  Sarah A. 3
  Susan A. Mrs. 74
  Hellen M. 142
  Sophronia 7
McMuller, Mary E. 13
McNeal, Eliza 92
McNeil, Mary 107
  Mary J. 29
McNeill, Louisa 127
  Margaret E. 67
McPherson, Sarah J. 20
McWilliams, Catherine 30
  June 30
  Margaret 57
  Mary Ann 63
  Mary R. 39
Medaris, Eliza J. 110
Medlock, Louisa 97
  Martha 63
Megginson, Josephine M.
  40

Meigs, Caroline H. 58
Melton, Harriett 11
Melvine, Sarah J. 70
Metts, Mary Ann 15
Metzger, Amelia 54
  Caroline 41
  Henrietta 67
  Theresa 70
Middleton, Ada 2
  Amanda 32
  Caroline L. 32
  Cassinder 82
  Cynthia 65
  Elizabeth 18,79
  Emelia A. 18
  Georgia Anna 3
  Jane 2
  Lucrisia 39
  Lucretia J. 81
  M.A. 81
  Martha A. 113
  Mary 82
  Mary A. 129
  Mary Ann 117
  Mary E. 13
  Nancy 18
  Penny 55
  Sarah 57
  S.E. 100
Miller, Elizabeth 60
  Hannah F. 13
  Martha 44
  Mary L. 104
  Nancy A. 98
  Sarah A. 75
  S.E. 81
  Susan E. 119
Miles, Ardelia 33
  Catherine 117
  Martha Ann 33
  Mary A. 64
  Sarah Ann 65
Mills, Sylvaney 108
Mims, Agunepta 44
  Amanda 53
  Asseneth 46
  Avarilla 46
  Cynthia 76
  Emily 82
  Margaret 13
  Margaret Mrs. 15
  Mary 21,82
  Mary T. 76
  Melinda 13
  Mollie A. 98
  Sarah D. 92
  Sarah J. 53
  Susan J. 96
Mishut, Mary 81
Mitchell, Elizabeth A. 75
Mixon, Georgianna 86
  Margaret L. 103
  Mary A.E. 23
Monroe, Eliza 70
  Sarah 114
Montgomery, Mrs. Flora 106
Moody, M.B. 11
  P.A. 33
  Permelia A. 16
Mooney, Allice E. 110
Moore, Barbry Ann Lowery
  99
  Caroline 104
  Catherine G. 127
  Elizabeth 11
  Hortensia 26
  J.S. 26
  Kathy S. 43
  Martha B. 68
  Mary L. 56,98
  Olivia L. 111
  Pauline 26

Moore, Sarah J. 118
Morgan, Dicy 4
Morris, E.B. 10
  Elvina 79
  Frances 4
  Frances C. 32
  Henrietta 44
  Margaret J. 18
  Marsena 12
  Martha 8,12
  Martha A. 119
  Martha O. 70
  Mary 57
  Mary A. 36
  Mary C. 107
  Mary E. 52
  Mary Jane 36
  Missouri 105
  Nancy A. 80
  Sarah A. 81
  Sarah L. 118
  Sarah T. 87
  Susannah 89
  Trena N. 122
  Vicy 22
Morrisette, Caroline 5
Morrissett, Cornelia R.
  127
Morton, Eugene E. 78
  Julia L. 85
Mosley, Mary A. 103
  Nancy 51
  V.C. Mrs. 45
  Virginia 7
Muldrow, Agnes C. 38
Mullender, Mary E. 52,53
Murphy, Emeline 63
  Louisa 121
  M.J. 121
  Mary Mrs. 95
  Mary E. 107
  Sarah S. 74
Murray, Caroline A. 95
  Caroline E. Mrs. 60
  Rebecca Ann 25
  Susan 95
Musgrove, Louisa 21
Myer, Hannah 80
Myers, Frederika 80
  Julia Ann 54
Myrick, Elizabeth 110
  Frances 123
  Jane 106
  Mary 123
Nall, Nancy A. 124
Nettles, Ailsey 12
  Anna Mrs. 99
  C.R. 75
  Caroline 47
  Eleanor 47
  Eliza 55
  Elizabeth 30
  Elizabeth J. 63
  Elizabeth M. 14
  Henrietta 16
  Isabella R.N. 109
  Jane 87
  Jenett 36
  Josiland E. 88
  June W. 12
  L.A. 38
  Liza 30
  Lydia B. 38
  Martha 3
  Martha A. 55
  Martha O. 12
  Mary 30
  Mary Jane 56
  Nancy J. 13
  Sarah 115
Nevells, Missouri A. 122
Neville, Ella 67

Newberry, Elizabeth 64
  Ellen 19
  Frances J. 117
  Georgia L. 29
  Jane 116
  M.A. 100
  Martha A. 36
  Margaret Mrs. 96
  M.E. 114
  Sarah 42
  S.E. 107
  Susan 54
Newby, James Y. 40
  Lucy 64
Newell, Eliza 106
  Elizabeth 92
  Fanny L. 24
  Susan B. 92
Nichols, Susan C. 37
Nolan, Mary E. 106
Norris, Effy 92
  J.P. 124
  Mary A. 4
  Nancy 117
Northcut, Mary E. 54
  Susannah 103
  Virginia 12
Northcutt, C. 99
  Hettie 60
  M.E. 31
Norwood, Jane 82
  Martha E. 41
  Mary J. 31
  Mary Jane 64
  Rebeca 125
Nowlin, Rebecca 7
Nutt, Milly A. 55
Odom, Celia 19
  Margaret 60
  Martha 39
  Mary Mrs. 67
  Vivian 98
Ogbourne, Emma J. 87
O'Gwynn, E.S. 113
Oliver, Catherine 1
  Polly Mrs. 66
Omen, Louisa 39
O'Neall, H.L. 91
O'Neil, Angelina D. 34
  Mary A. 69
Ousley, Elizabeth 28
Owen, Mary 18
  Mary Ann 38
  Mary Jane 45
  Nancy 90
  Permelia J. 84
Owens, Annie E. 62
  Elizabeth 3,9
  Emily E. 43
  Harriett P. 127
  Lucy 18
  Martha Jane 35
  M.F. 66
  Nancy M. 62
  Rachel L. 80
  Sarah Ann 7
Pace, Ann E. 31
  Mary Mrs. 4
  Rhoda 12
Packer, L.C. 51
Parish, Felitha 78
Parker, Elizabeth 17
  Elizabeth G. 62
  Henrietta M. Mrs. 48
  M.A. 41
  Margaret J. 46
  Martha 28
  Mary A. 4
  Matilda 54
Parrish, Eliza 80
Parsons, Martha A. 47
Partin, Elinda 72

Partin, Phebe 8
Patrick, Aggy 123
  Caroline V. 122
  Jane 48
  Mary 72
  Nancy 123
  Nancy S. 22
  Rebecca 10
Partridge, Charlsey 27
Patterson, Sarah V. 13
Paul, Lucy 96
Paulk, Mrs. Jane 66
Pearce, Elizabeth 100
  Nancy E. 83
  Tabitha Ann 42
Pearson, Mrs. Maria 88
Peebles, Amelia 33
  Elizabeth 106
  Flora 83
  Leah R. 28
  Manah L. 90
  Mary M. 121
Peoples, Ann 58
Perkins, Winneyford 128
Perrin, Fannie 14
  Mattie J. 91
Perry, Elizabeth H. 67
  Frances 24
Perryman, Annie H. 10
  Evie Mrs. 23
  Sallie 26
Pettibone, Adelide A. 16
  Allin 35
Phillips, A.C. 39
  Louisa 71
  Mary F. 62
Pierce, Jane 85
  M.E. 85
  Mosouri 20
Piner, Martha 16
Pipkins, Martha 66
Pitman, Elizabeth 1
  Elizabeth M.D. 61
  Susanna M. 44
Pitts, Frances 1
Pleasant, G.E. 71
Pollard, Frances F. 97
  Nancy P. 71
Poltson, Matilda 49
Porter, Frances H.A. 30
  L.A. 123
  Missouri E. 52
Portis, C.G. 123
  Martha R. Mrs. 91
Posey, J.C. 57
Powell, A.E. Mrs. 38
  Allice 18
  Cherry 92
  Clarissa 104
  Elizabeth 62,122
  Ella 107
  Elmira 61
  Harriett 116
  Jane 89
  Laura T. 61
  Louisa 61
  Martha 42
  Mary 62
  Mary Frances 85
  Mary J. Mrs. 21
  Mary Jane 26
  Masoney E. 30
  Melinda 127
  Nora 45
  Rebecca 105
  Susan 26
Prescoate, Martha 88
Presnall, Rebecca 94
  Rhoda 84
Preston, Margaret 24
  Margaret E. 100
  Martha E. 101

Prewett, Martha 70
Price, Mary E. 10
Pricket, Mrs. Nancy 6
Pridgeon, Georgiana 51
  Isabella 104
Priner, Sarah F. 38
Pritchett, Mary Ann 92
  Nancy 124
  Rutha 37
  W.F. 78
Pruett, Sallie 56
Pugh, Caroline Mrs. 45
  Caroline E. 73
  Laura A. 83
Pullen, June A. 103
  Willie 41
Purvis, Nancy 41
Pyrkin, Susannah J. 19
Qualls, Nancy 10
Rabb, Sarah 121
Rachels, Elizabeth 119
  Lurana 126
  Mary Ann 57,114
Raines, Almeda S. 27
  Sallie V. 123
  Sarah 95
  Sarah E. 102
Rains, Mary M. 120
Rall, M. Catherine 36
  Mary Jane 51
Rankin, Bettie 72
  Clarissa J. 27
  Elizabeth A. 43
  Flora A. 92
  Mattie 73
  N.I. 110
  Sarah Jane 104
Rauls, Mary F. 71
Rawles, J.A. 37
  Mary Mrs. 40
Rawls, Catherine 20
  Henrietta 69
  Julia 36
  Lanorah E. 9
  Lenora 58
  Mary J. 126
  Rebecca C. 120
Ray, E.V. 58
  Sarah 58
Reaves, Ann Eliza 6
  Elizabeth 104
  J.A. 79
  Julia A. 99
  Nancy 43
  R.J. 97
  Susannah 98
  Victoria 101
Reed, Florence 86
  Mary Ann 127
Reinds, Mary Ann 69
Renfro, Matilda 22
Reynolds, Margaret A. 26
  Martha J. 57
Rhoad, Elizabeth J. 46
  Martha F. 35
  M.C. 65
  N.J. 45
  Lucretia 21
Rhoades, Eliza 119
  Sarah C. 81
Rhodes, Caroline 11
  Margaret 50
Richardson, M.L.D. 50
  Martha 122
  S.J. 41
Richie, Mary F. 59
Ridd, Margaret L. 69
Riels, Mary E. 91
Rigby, Nancy A. 47
  Sarah A. 125
Rikard, Amanda 62
  Annie 55

www.ingramcontent.com/pod-product-compliance
Lightning Source LLC
Chambersburg PA
CBHW021828020426
42334CB00014B/539